SETTING
NATIONAL
PRIORITIES
The 1984 Budget

JOSEPH A. PECHMAN *Editor*

SETTING NATIONAL PRIORITIES
The 1984 Budget

Henry J. Aaron
Harvey Galper
William W. Kaufmann
Alicia H. Munnell
Joseph A. Pechman
Elisabeth H. Rhyne
Louise B. Russell
Daniel H. Saks
John Karl Scholz

THE BROOKINGS INSTITUTION
Washington, D.C.

THE BROOKINGS INSTITUTION is an independent organization devoted to nonpartisan research, education, and publication in economics, government, foreign policy, and the social sciences generally. Its principal purposes are to aid in the development of sound public policies and to promote public understanding of issues of national importance.

The Institution was founded on December 8, 1927, to merge the activities of the Institute for Government Research, founded in 1916, the Institute of Economics, founded in 1922, and the Robert Brookings Graduate School of Economics and Government, founded in 1924.

The Board of Trustees is responsible for the general administration of the Institution, while the immediate direction of the policies, program, and staff is vested in the President, assisted by an advisory committee of the officers and staff. The by-laws of the Institution state: "It is the function of the Trustees to make possible the conduct of scientific research, and publication, under the most favorable conditions, and to safeguard the independence of the research staff in the pursuit of their studies and in the publication of the results of such studies. It is not a part of their function to determine, control, or influence the conduct of particular investigations or the conclusions reached."

The President bears final responsibility for the decision to publish a manuscript as a Brookings book. In reaching his judgment on the competence, accuracy, and objectivity of each study, the President is advised by the director of the appropriate research program and weighs the views of a panel of expert outside readers who report to him in confidence on the quality of the work. Publication of a work signifies that it is deemed a competent treatment worthy of public consideration but does not imply endorsement of conclusions or recommendations.

The Institution maintains its position of neutrality on issues of public policy in order to safeguard the intellectual freedom of the staff. Hence interpretations or conclusions in Brookings publications should be understood to be solely those of the authors and should not be attributed to the Institution, to its trustees, officers, or other staff members, or to the organizations that support its research.

Foreword

THE BUDGET for fiscal 1984 is not encouraging reading. It projects deficits for the next five years that would be unprecedented in the fiscal history of the United States. Unless these deficits are cut sharply, investment will be severely reduced, foreign trade deficits will persist, and economic growth will be sluggish. The budget debate presumes that the deficits must be cut; the major issues concern how the deficits are to be reduced. This volume, the fourteenth in an annual series, explains the fiscal choices made by President Reagan and examines alternatives and their budgetary and economic implications.

The contributors to this volume first review the president's 1984 budget and the outlook under the policies he proposes. They then analyze the defense budget, increases in which more than offset requested cuts in nondefense spending. Separate chapters are devoted to the problems of social security, health policy, and employment and training for the structurally unemployed. A chapter on tax policy suggests how federal revenues can be raised without increasing tax rates. The final chapter shows what policies led to the present fiscal difficulties and presents various spending and tax options to get the deficits under control. Three appendixes set forth estimates of the structural deficit under present policies and under those proposed by the administration, the loans and guarantees that are included in the budget as well as those that remain outside, and the growing list of tax expenditures which erode the federal tax base and are in many ways equivalent to federal outlays.

This volume is a collaborative effort of the Brookings Economic Studies and Foreign Policy Studies programs. Joseph A. Pechman is director, Henry J. Aaron, Harvey Galper, and Louise B. Russell are senior fellows, and Elisabeth H. Rhyne and John Karl Scholz are research analysts, in the Economic Studies program. William W. Kaufmann, a consultant to the Foreign Policy Studies program, is a member of the faculty of the Massachusetts Institute of Technology. Alicia H. Munnell and Daniel H. Saks, associated staff members of the Economic Studies program, are vice-president of the Federal Reserve Bank of Boston and professor of economics at Vanderbilt University, respectively.

The authors are grateful to Judith Cameron, Penelope Harpold, and Alan G. Hoden, who helped to verify the factual content of the volume; to Elizabeth H. Cross, Nancy D. Davidson, Caroline Lalire, Carol Cole Rosen, and Karen J. Wirt, who edited the manuscript; to Nancy Snyder, who did the proofreading; and to Vickie L. Corey and Dorothy M. Poole, who applied computer-assisted word processing and typesetting technology to the conversion of the manuscript into a book.

The views expressed here are solely those of the authors and should not be attributed to the trustees, officers, or other staff members of the Brookings Institution.

BRUCE K. MACLAURY
President

April 1983
Washington, D.C.

Contents

Text Tables

Appendix Tables

CHAPTER ONE

Introduction and Summary

JOSEPH A. PECHMAN

FEDERAL deficits exceeding $200 billion a year are now in prospect for the immediate future. Under present budget policies—including the defense program planned by the Reagan administration—the deficit will rise from $208 billion in fiscal 1983 to $300 billion in 1988, assuming the economy grows at the rate the administration has projected. Unless real progress is made in reducing the future deficits, fiscal and monetary policies will clash once again, interest rates will rise, and economic recovery will be aborted.

The budget problem Congress now faces is the result of decisions made over the past two years to increase defense spending and reduce taxes. Nondefense spending has been cut sharply, but these cuts have not offset the increases in defense outlays and in interest payments on the rapidly rising national debt. To reduce the deficit, it will be necessary to reduce federal spending and raise taxes. President Reagan's budget for 1984 embodies his priorities. That program, and alternatives to it, are examined in this volume.

The 1984 Budget

Budget planning begins with a set of estimates of outlays and receipts on the assumption that current policy remains unchanged. These estimates—which include the administration's planned de-

THE AUTHOR thanks Henry J. Aaron, Harvey Galper, William W. Kaufmann, Alicia H. Munnell, Louise B. Russell, and Daniel H. Saks, who assisted in the preparation of this chapter. Evelyn M. E. Taylor and Valerie J. Harris typed the manuscript.

Table 1-1. Summary of President Reagan's 1984 Budget Program, Fiscal Years 1983–88
Billions of dollars

Deficits and proposed reductions	1983	1984	1985	1986	1987	1988
Current services deficit[a]	208.5	231.5	253.1	270.8	291.7	300.4
Reductions in current services deficit, excluding standby tax increases	0.8	42.7	58.9	77.1	100.6	132.3
Deficit without standby tax increases	207.7	188.8	194.2	193.7	191.1	168.1
Standby tax increases	...	...	...	46.0	49.0	51.4
Deficit with standby tax increases	207.7	188.8	194.2	147.7	142.1	116.7

Source: *Special Analyses, Budget of the United States Government, Fiscal Year 1984*, pp. A-13, A-14.
a. Includes the administration's planned defense program.

fense buildup—project outlays of $880.3 billion and receipts of $648.8 billion in fiscal 1984, leaving a deficit of $231.5 billion, or 6.6 percent of gross national product. Thereafter, the deficit will continue to rise until it reaches $300.4 billion in 1988, still 6.1 percent of gross national product (table 1-1). The budget outlook remains gloomy despite the expectation of a sustained economic recovery and declining unemployment during the next five years.

The recession explains part of the impending deficits. But even if the cyclical component of the deficit is removed, the remainder—called the structural deficit—will continue to rise. Unless current tax and spending policies are drastically altered, the structural deficit will increase from 2.6 percent of GNP in fiscal 1984 to an unprecedented 4.2 percent in 1988. Such a deficit is unacceptable. If the Federal Reserve Board were to increase the money supply enough to hold down interest rates, the deficit would generate inflation. If, as seems more likely, the Federal Reserve refused to accommodate that much fiscal stimulus, interest rates would rise sharply and economic recovery would be retarded.

To bring the structural deficit down, President Reagan has presented a program with four main components.

First, the president proposes major reforms to eliminate deficits in the social security retirement and disability programs and to restrain outlays of federal health programs and the federal civil service retirement system. For social security, he accepted the recommendations of the National Commission on Social Security Reform, comprising a six-month freeze on the cost-of-living adjustment for benefits, an acceleration of payroll tax increases already scheduled, coverage of new federal workers under social security, and many other changes.

Second, the president proposes that in keeping with the freeze on social security benefits, cost-of-living increases for all other indexed programs be delayed for six months. He would also defer for one year increases in pay and benefits of current and retired federal civilian and military employees. $\left(2\right)$

Third, the president proposes modest reductions in defense outlays in current dollars, but no change from last year's planned defense buildup in real terms. $\left(3\right)$

Fourth, the president insisted on retaining the July 1983 tax cut and the indexation of the personal income tax scheduled to begin in January 1985. But acknowledging the unacceptable size of future deficits, he recommended adopting standby taxes for a three-year period if the fiscal 1986 deficit is not brought below 2.5 percent of GNP. The standby taxes include a 5 percent surtax on individuals and an excise tax of $5 a barrel on domestically produced and imported oil.

In total, the president's program would reduce the deficit by $43 billion in 1984 and by almost $185 billion in 1988, still leaving a deficit of $117 billion in that year. Assuming these budget proposals or their equivalent were accepted by Congress, the structural deficit would fall to 0.7 percent of GNP in 1988—a tolerable level by post–World War II standards.

Defense Policy

For fiscal 1984 the president is requesting a defense budget of $274 billion in total obligational authority and $239 billion in outlays. The new five-year plan for defense, running from fiscal 1984 through 1988, would provide $1,768 billion in total obligational authority and $1,554 billion in outlays. More than half these amounts would go to the investment accounts of the Department of Defense (procurement; research, development, test, and evaluation; and military construction). The rest would be allocated to the manning, operating, and support of the forces.

The administration proposes to use most of these resources for long-standing objectives. The strategic nuclear forces will be modernized; theater nuclear forces will receive newer nuclear shells and will be supplemented by the deployment of Pershing II and ground-launched cruise missiles in Europe and Tomahawk cruise missiles in submarines; ground and tactical air forces assigned to Europe, as well as the rapid deployment force, will continue to be modernized; older surface warships, submarines, and support vessels of the Navy will be replaced; and intercontinental transport capabilities will be increased, primarily by the acquisition of additional wide-bodied aircraft and modification of eight container ships previously acquired.

In several respects, however, the defense objectives of the Reagan administration differ from those of its predecessors. It has decided to acquire at least some of the weapons systems said to be necessary to conduct—and hence to deter—a protracted nuclear war. It also hopes to have the option, primarily through naval expansion, of horizontal escalation—that is, the ability, if an enemy attacks in one area, to take the initiative and attack in another area of importance to the enemy. Since it places great emphasis on the need to be able to fight a prolonged conventional war, the administration is investing heavily in stocks of costly modern nonnuclear munitions. Finally, the pace at which all these capabilities are to be acquired is being accelerated.

There are alternatives to the administration's five-year defense plan that could provide equal security at less cost. Attempts to prepare for protracted nuclear war, horizontal escalation, *and* prolonged conventional conflict are not realistic. Furthermore, the pace of weapons acquisition may be producing both an unnecessary redundancy of systems and excessive turbulence within the armed forces as they strive to adapt to and operate the new equipment. The administration may also have overestimated the nuclear threat from the Soviet Union and underestimated the ability of its leaders to generate strong nonnuclear challenges in the late 1980s.

Scaling back these unnecessarily ambitious objectives alone would permit a five-year saving in total obligational authority of $80.6 billion: $8.6 billion from the strategic nuclear forces; $40.6 billion from naval forces (including the two nuclear-powered carriers authorized in fiscal 1983); and $31.4 billion from the program to stockpile modern conventional munitions. An additional $17.7 billion in military pay could be saved by freezing manning at 1983 levels, even after allowing for a 4 percent pay raise rather than the pay cap proposed for fiscal 1984. Another $90.9 billion could be saved by canceling redundant missiles and aircraft—specifically, the MX missile, the B-1 bomber, the F-14 and F-15 fighters, and the AV-8B close air support jump jet—while leaving all MX research and development funds available for a new missile. At least $33.9 billion could be saved by canceling the production of new chemical weapons and more wide-bodied aircraft for airlift and by stretching out the completion of several Army programs. All told, between fiscal 1984 and 1988, $223 billion in total obligational authority and $155 billion in outlays could be cut from the five-year defense plan by these measures, with little or no reduction in defense capabilities. Savings in outlays under this plan would amount to $35 billion by 1986 and $47 billion by 1988.

Even if some additional defense capabilities were considered desirable, the cost of an upgraded program would still remain well below the cost of the administration's 1984 request. Such an enhanced program would substitute fast sealift for the airlift proposed by the administration, at a five-year cost of $6.4 billion in total obligational authority. Another $28.2 billion would be devoted to modernizing the ground and tactical air components of the National Guard and Reserve and to speeding their availability in time of international crisis. Even with these extra hedges, the modified defense program would save $189 billion in total obligational authority and $136 billion in outlays during the five-year period. By fiscal 1986 savings in outlays would come to $31 billion; by 1988, they would rise to $40 billion.

Social Security

President Reagan and Congress have embraced the recommendations of the National Commission on Social Security Reform, which completed its report just before the 1984 budget was scheduled to be submitted to Congress. The commission was charged with finding a way to close the short-run deficit in social security between 1984 and 1989 and the long-run deficit estimated over the seventy-five-year planning horizon. The commission's recommendations increase the system's revenues and reduce its expenditures by $165 billion between 1983 and 1990 and eliminate two-thirds of the long-run deficit. For fiscal 1988 the reduction in the budget deficit would amount to $28 billion. Although the members failed to agree on the best way to solve the long-run problem, both Republican and Democratic appointees supported the proposition that the seventy-five-year deficit should be eliminated and each side made specific proposals to accomplish this goal.

In addition to proposals that would raise the needed revenues, the commission recommended a change in the cost-of-living adjustments to benefits that would reduce the likelihood of future deficits. If trust fund assets fall below 20 percent of the following year's planned outlays, the cost-of-living adjustment would equal the increase in consumer prices or in wages, whichever was less. Once the fund ratio was restored to 32 percent, beneficiaries would be awarded the cost-of-living adjustment previously withheld.

The principal remaining problem was to ensure the solvency of the system for the next seventy-five years. From 1983 to 1989 the old-age, survivors, and disability insurance program is projected to run a deficit of $117 billion under the intermediate assumptions of the social security trustees. With the slow growth and high unemployment encompassed in the most pessimistic assumptions, the deficit may run as high as $198 billion for the same period. The economic conditions in private forecasts generally fall between those assumed in the trustees' intermediate and pessimistic projections. Hence the $165 billion in short-term revenues produced by the commission's recommendations should be enough to cover benefit outlays over the next seven years.

Between 1990 and 2014 conditions will be favorable for social security. The number of retirees will decline, reflecting the low fertility of the 1920s and 1930s. At the same time, the baby boom generation will swell the labor force. As a result, the ratio of workers to beneficiaries will remain stable for the next twenty to thirty years. With a stable worker-beneficiary ratio, productivity gains can reduce the cost of social security as a percent of payrolls. If wages rise by 1.5 percent more a year than prices, revenues will exceed outlays for the entire period and the social security trust funds will accumulate surpluses. But if real wage growth is 1.0 percent a year or less, the system will remain in deficit and additional funds will be required.

Beginning in 2015 costs will rise significantly as the baby boom generation of the 1950s and 1960s retires. At the same time, the growth in the labor force will slow, reflecting the decline in the fertility rate that began in the mid-1960s. Without the commission's recommendations, the cost of the retirement and disability portion of the social security program is projected to rise from 11 percent of taxable payrolls to about 17 percent in the year 2030 and remain at that level through 2060.

For the entire seventy-five-year period (1983–2057), the average cost of the system, expressed as a percent of payrolls, is 14.38 under the intermediate assumptions, while scheduled payroll tax revenues average 12.29 percent, leaving a long-run deficit of 2.09 percent of payrolls. The commission's recommendations contribute 1.41 percent toward reducing long-run costs and lower the long-run deficit from 2.09 to 0.68 percent. The remaining deficit has been eliminated in the 1983 social security legislation by a gradual increase in the retirement age to sixty-seven after the turn of the century.

Future trends in fertility and economic performance will determine whether the long-run solution is adequate. The intermediate projections assume that the fertility rate will rise steadily from its current level of 1.8 to a long-run rate of 2.0. The fertility rate has increased in four of the past five years, and the data on expected births indicate that young women continue to have more than two children over their lifetimes.

The more uncertain assumption is that productivity growth will return to the historical rate of 1.5 percent a year. Without such an increase in real wages, the long-run costs of social security will be higher than those projected under the intermediate assumptions. But if the intermediate assumptions were borne out and productivity increased at an average rate of 1.5 percent over the long run, the commission's proposals and the extension of the retirement age would finance the system for the next seventy-five years.

Health

In 1981 Congress enacted legislation that broke sharply with past federal health policy. As part of the Omnibus Budget Reconciliation Act of 1981, Congress placed limits on the matching funds available to the states for their medicaid programs; in effect, many states found their matching rates reduced. To help the states live within the new constraints, the law loosened many of the requirements for medicaid. Congress followed this action with another unprecedented move in 1982. As part of the 1982 tax bill, it temporarily limited increases in hospital payments per admission under medicare to the inflation rate plus 1 percent, well below the historical rate of growth. The temporary program was to continue for three years, and the secretary of health and human services was directed to submit a permanent plan by the end of 1982.

The recent legislated changes are important because they abandon the principle pursued for many years, through medicare, medicaid, and other, smaller programs, that medical care should be provided whenever needed, whatever the cost. These programs have greatly improved the access to medical care of the elderly and the poor. The life expectancy of the elderly has risen much faster since 1965 than it rose in the preceding fifteen years. Similarly, infant mortality rates have fallen dramatically since 1965, especially among blacks. But the gains have been costly—federal and national expenditures have increased rapidly year after year, despite efforts to slow their growth without sacrificing the basic principle. Medical care now absorbs 10 percent of the nation's output, up from 6 percent in 1965, and public programs for health take up 10 percent of the federal budget.

The only way to bring costs under control is to forgo some medical benefits in the future; to insist on having them all will mean that expenditures will continue to rise rapidly. Either more cost sharing for individuals or budget limits on providers can accomplish the necessary rationing. Many variations of these approaches are possible, and evidence of their effectiveness has been growing in recent years. A reluctance to accept the consequences, rather than a lack of evidence, has prevented their adoption. Because expenditures have continued to rise and the federal deficit has become alarming, Congress has been forced to act.

In the 1984 budget the administration proposes further cuts and plans to make permanent the temporary changes already made. More cost sharing is proposed for hospital care under medicare, to be partly offset by an upper limit on cost sharing for very long stays. Premiums for the part of the program that covers physicians' services are to be raised more rapidly, so that they will supply 35 percent of the necessary revenues by 1988, and the deductible for physicians' services, now $75, is to be indexed to inflation. A new plan to pay hospitals flat rates based on the doctor's diagnosis—the permanent replacement for the temporary limits passed in 1982—has already been approved by Congress as part of the 1983 social security legislation. To cut expenses still further in 1984, the administration would freeze physicians' fees under medicare for the year. Under medicaid, the administration proposes to require the states to charge recipients small amounts for care and to extend the reductions in matching funds legislated in 1981.

In an initiative of considerable importance for the private sector, the administration proposes that employer contributions for health insurance in excess of $175 a month for a family and $70 a month for an individual be subject to tax as part of the employee's income. Besides raising additional revenues, the new tax would encourage employers and employees to restrain the growth of health insurance, which, in turn, would help to slow the growth in medical expenditures. In total, the administration's health proposals would reduce the deficit by $4 billion in fiscal 1984, $11 billion in 1986, and $20 billion in 1988.

The administration has not followed any particular model, either market-oriented or regulatory, for changing the medical care system. Instead, it continues the tradition of tackling problems one at a time, with a strong focus on the public sector. The proposals will intensify what has become a struggle among those involved in federal and state programs and private insurance to shift the problem to someone else. In the end, all the parties may conclude that some sort of joint solution will more fairly serve them. The 1984 budget proposals are a realistic step in this transitional process.

Jobs and Training

More than 10 percent of the work force is unemployed, and the administration is forecasting that the unemployment rate will not fall below 9 percent, its previous post-depression peak (in 1975), for three more years. The situation is especially serious for those who work in interest-sensitive or declining industries.

The president has said that finding jobs for the unemployed is the most crucial domestic challenge. Four strategies are available to help the unemployed: (1) general economic recovery, (2) income support for the unemployed, (3) direct job creation, and (4) training for those whose unemployment problems will outlast the recovery.

An economic recovery is the best jobs program because it puts people to work in places where they are most valuable, without the administrative problems of direct job creation. The administration is counting on a recovery to solve most of the unemployment problem. But it is projecting the recovery to be slower than after previous recessions, and unemployment will remain at a relatively high level for several years.

No matter how fast the recovery, there will be an unprecedented number of long-term unemployed workers in the next few years. They are bearing the brunt of the recession, and many of them need help. Although the 1981–82 recession was the most severe in the postwar period, the government has provided less jobless aid than in previous recessions. In 1976 approximately two-thirds of the unemployed were recipients of unemployment benefits, and coverage extended to sixty-five weeks everywhere. By the end of 1982 the unemployment insurance system was providing benefits to only a little more than half the unemployed, for anywhere from thirty-two to fifty-five weeks, depending on the state in which they live. The administration proposes keeping the fifty-five-week maximum only through September 1983 and then cutting that back to thirty-nine weeks. This will be accomplished by phasing out the federal supplemental compensation program, which extends eight to sixteen weeks of additional benefits to those exhausting regular benefits, depending on the level and history of insured unemployment in a state. The current program, which links the duration of benefits to the difficulty of finding jobs in the states where the workers reside, should be kept in place as long as the rate of unemployment is excessive.

For the one-half of the unemployed not covered by unemployment insurance, some help can be given by a well-designed job creation program that would terminate when unemployment falls to more normal levels. Such a program would subsidize jobs in the private or public sector for those who most need assistance—the long-term unemployed. The administration is supporting an accelerated government construction program, but it is trying to keep expenditures for direct job creation to a minimum. It is opposed to public service jobs in government and nonprofit agencies. Instead, it is proposing a modest tax credit for employers who hire long-term unemployment insurance beneficiaries. The idea is to get such people to the head of the reemployment line in the private sector. Unfortunately, similar tax credits have not been effective in the past, and the proposed credit is too small to have much impact.

Despite the administration's objections, public service employment can be cost-effective in helping the long-term unemployed if it is targeted to the right groups and is not used to subsidize regular state-local employment. Local public works provide fewer jobs per dollar spent than public service employment. Since big construction projects usually hire high-wage workers, they provide even fewer jobs. Only if the value of the projects is high are they more desirable than public service employment during periods of high joblessness.

Finally, long-term unemployed and poor workers need help in getting basic training and access to on-the-job experience. Total outlays for employment and training have been reduced from $9.8 billion in fiscal 1981 to $5.8 billion in 1983 and a proposed $5.4 billion in 1984. Job Corps, a successful federal residential training program for disadvantaged youths, is being continued, but it will provide only 40,000 training positions in 1984, the same as in 1983. The administration also requested funds to continue the 1983 level of 718,000 summer jobs for youths. For adult workers, only training programs run by local industry councils under the oversight of the state governments remain. Such programs are not likely to generate jobs for long-term unemployed workers unless the training is combined with wage subsidies, which would add greatly to cost. Under the circumstances, income support will be the only hope for the structurally unemployed until the labor market improves.

Taxation

In the 1984 budget, barely two years after endorsing large-scale tax cuts to reduce the role of the federal government in the national economy, President Reagan has recommended tax increases of $61 billion in fiscal 1986 and $84 billion in 1988. Of these amounts, $15 billion in 1986 and $33 billion in 1988 would come from the tax increases in the social security program and the limit on tax-free health insurance premiums for employees. The remaining $46 billion in 1986 and $51 billion in 1988 would be raised by the proposed standby tax increase on individuals and the excise tax on petroleum. This considerable change in policy has set the stage for an examination of the current tax structure and of the appropriate ways to raise revenues to reduce future deficits.

Two important principles should guide this search for more revenues. First, revenue increases should be achieved whenever possible by broadening the tax base rather than by increasing tax rates. Raising rates increases the tax-related distortions between economic activities subject to tax and those that are exempt; broadening the base reduces those distortions. Second, the tax base should be broadened in a way that leads to a sound tax structure.

The current tax system is deficient in important respects. Many deductions, exclusions, and tax credits erode the tax base and require higher tax rates to raise the needed revenues. Effective tax rates on corporate profits differ greatly among different industries because of the depreciation provisions enacted in 1981. Moreover, full deduction is allowed for interest expenses, and the gross return to capital may be taxed at zero or preferential rates. These preferences make it profitable for taxpayers to invest in projects yielding negative rates of return, whereas far more productive investments are not undertaken because they are fully taxed.

The structural deficiencies of the current tax system can be corrected either by widening the base of the income tax or moving toward a broad-based consumption expenditure tax. Under either approach tax preferences would be removed and the return to capital would be treated uniformly. If the return from assets was fully taxed under the income tax, deductibility of interest expenses would be appropriate. A comprehensive consumption tax would provide a full deduction for saving, but all sources of consumption expenditures—including borrowing—would be included in the tax base. A consumption tax would exempt capital income from tax and not allow a deduction for interest expense. As a complement to a comprehensive consumption tax, estate and gift taxes would need to be strengthened to prevent increases in the concentration of wealth resulting from the exemption for saving.

Broadening the tax base under either a comprehensive income tax or a comprehensive consumption tax could easily raise as much revenue as the standby income tax increases proposed by the president for fiscal years 1986–88 (table 7-4). It would also improve the efficiency and equity of the tax system. Efficiency would be improved by treating consistently the interest cost of borrowed funds and the gross return to capital and by not discriminating among firms, industries, or forms of compensation. Equity would be improved by taxing individuals in the same circumstances more nearly the same. Tax reform along these lines is preferable both to the tax-rate increases proposed by the president and to the repeal of indexation that has been proposed by others as an alternative.

The proposed excise tax on domestically produced and imported oil raises different issues. With the recent decline in oil prices, a tax on oil would encourage businesses and households to continue to conserve energy. Moreover, by reducing the demand for oil, an oil tax would make it more difficult for producing countries to continue to cartelize their production. Even if the cartel holds, the price it can maintain would probably be lower with such a tax than without it. In either case, part of the tax burden would be shifted abroad, to the overall benefit of the U.S. economy. These considerations argue for the imposition of the oil tax even sooner than the October 1985 date requested by the president, and not for a temporary period as the president proposed.

Budget Options

Because of tax cuts enacted in 1981 and the large buildup in national defense planned for future years, deficits will continue to grow even if the economy recovers. The administration proposes to deal with this problem through tax increases and further cuts in nondefense spending. Changes in the political composition of Congress and in the state of the economy make it unlikely, however, that the president will be as successful in securing acceptance of his program as he was during his first two years in office.

Reducing the deficit can be achieved in a variety of ways, some of which are outlined in chapter 8. For example, if the full defense buildup sought by President Reagan were enacted, but none of his nondefense cuts other than the social security reforms, a tax increase of $153 billion in 1988 would be needed to eliminate the structural deficit. If Congress enacted the modified defense budget described earlier and accepted the president's proposed nondefense cuts, no tax increase at all would be necessary to reduce the structural deficit to 1 percent of GNP. Under more plausible assumptions—that defense spending continues to grow more rapidly than under the modified plan but less rapidly than the president wishes, and that Congress accepts only a few of the president's proposed cuts in nondefense spending—it would be necessary to increase taxes by about $100 billion in fiscal 1988 to eliminate the structural deficit and by about $55 billion to reduce it to 1 percent of gross national product.

The 1984 budget and the budget options examined here place more emphasis than usual on reducing the deficit. Unless the structural deficit is reduced, it will distort output and endanger economic recovery. When the economy is weak, as it is projected to be in the immediate future, demand generated by a federal deficit can be a source of strength. But as the economy moves toward high employment, government deficits present a serious problem. Government borrowing is a drain on private saving, diverting credit otherwise available for investment in plant and equipment, housing, consumer durables, and inventories. The deficits projected for the late 1980s will absorb most of the net private saving the economy is projected to generate; the exact proportion depends on economic and budget projections. But the drain on saving will be large, and the urgency for a change in policy beyond dispute.

Deficits of such a size are unprecedented since the Second World War and will cause serious, painful side effects. The heavy demand on credit will keep real interest rates high. (Real interest rates are the excess of actual interest rates over the current rate of inflation.) High interest rates will reduce housing and automobile sales and will choke off investment by private businesses and state and local governments. The result will be a slowdown in the growth of productive capacity. Furthermore, high real interest rates will cause the price of the U.S. dollar in foreign markets to remain relatively high; as a result, foreigners will find U.S. goods dear and U.S. residents will find imports cheap. In short, the direct result of large federal budget deficits would be a high consumption–low investment economy that would tend to grow slowly, run persistent deficits in trade with other nations, and encounter industrial bottlenecks (because of low investment) before full employment of the labor force is reached.

For these reasons, the way in which Congress deals with the 1984 budget is unusually important. Not only must it resolve the ever present trade-offs among outlays for various purposes, but it must also come to grips with the serious imbalance between total federal spending and total receipts created by policies adopted in 1981 and 1982. Failure to correct this imbalance will produce slow growth and undermine prospects for recovery from the most serious economic slowdown since the Second World War.

CHAPTER TWO

The Budget and the Economy

JOSEPH A. PECHMAN

THE FISCAL 1984 budget reflects the continuing problems of the Reagan administration and Congress in reconciling their fiscal objectives. The budget deficit has risen sharply since President Reagan took office, partly as a result of decisions to accelerate the rate of defense spending and to phase in large tax cuts over three years and partly as a result of depressed economic conditions. In preparing his 1984 budget, the president was faced for the second year in a row with large and growing deficits, even assuming that the economy will recover from the 1981–82 recession. This chapter explains the origins of the budget problem, the president's proposals to cope with it, and the impact of his budget plans on the economy.

Recent Budget Developments

President Reagan had unusual success in persuading Congress to accept his spending and tax proposals during his first year in office but met considerable resistance to the budget he proposed a year later for fiscal 1983. The president's 1983 proposals did little to reduce the mismatch between outlays and receipts, and Congress substituted its own budget for the president's in an effort to stem the tide of rising debt.

THE AUTHOR is grateful to Henry J. Aaron, Barry P. Bosworth, Ralph C. Bryant, and George L. Perry for helpful comments and suggestions. Evelyn M. E. Taylor typed the manuscript.

15

The 1982 Budget

To implement the promises he made during the 1980 campaign, President Reagan completely overhauled the budget initially planned by President Carter. Congress approved most of the proposed increases in defense spending and four-fifths of the recommended cuts in nondefense outlays. Individual income tax rates were cut by an average of 23 percent in three steps (on October 1, 1981, July 1, 1982, and July 1, 1983); new tax deductions were added to stimulate saving; personal exemptions and rate brackets under the individual income tax were indexed beginning in 1985; estate and gift taxes were reduced; and tax allowances for depreciation of business investment were greatly liberalized.[1] As a result of these actions, fiscal 1982 outlays were reduced by an estimated $24.3 billion,[2] and 1982 receipts were cut by an estimated $38.3 billion. The tax reduction was expected to rise to $139.0 billion in 1984 and $286.5 billion in 1987.

The economy took a turn for the worse even as Congress was completing action on the Reagan budget during the summer of 1981. With support from the administration, the Federal Reserve Board continued to restrain the growth of money and credit. Financial markets reacted to the prospect of increasing budget deficits in a period of monetary restraint by bidding up interest rates, and the stock market continued a slide begun early in 1981. Real gross national product, which had risen at an annual rate of 5.2 percent in the six months ending March 30, 1981, remained virtually at a standstill in the spring and summer months and then plunged at an annual rate of 5.3 percent in the last quarter of the year. Unemployment rose sharply from 7.2 percent of the civilian labor force in July to 8.8 percent in December.[3] As a result of deepening recession and reductions in oil and other commodity prices, the rate of inflation began to decline in the last few months of the year.

1. Numerous other changes were made in the tax laws. For a detailed description of these changes, see Joseph A. Pechman, ed., *Setting National Priorities: The 1983 Budget* (Brookings Institution, 1982), pp. 26–29, 251–62.

2. This is a net figure. Defense spending was increased by $2.8 billion and nondefense spending was reduced by $27.1 billion. Because of long lead times, the planned acceleration of defense outlays was expected to affect spending primarily in later years.

3. Beginning in January 1983, the Bureau of Labor Statistics included members of the armed forces in the labor force, which is the base it uses in calculating unemployment. This adjustment reduced the unemployment rate by about 0.2 percentage points. Unless otherwise noted, unemployment rates in this book are based on the civilian labor force.

Table 2-1. The Federal Budget, Fiscal Years 1980–83

Billions of dollars

Item	1980[a] January 1979 estimate	Actual	1981[a] January 1980 estimate	Actual	1982[a] February 1981 estimate	Actual	1983 January 1982 estimate	January 1983 estimate
Outlays	528.7	576.7	612.4	657.2	688.0	728.4	757.6	805.2
Receipts	499.7	517.1	596.7	599.3	646.6	617.8	666.1	597.5
Deficit	29.0	59.6	15.8	57.9	41.5	110.6	91.5	207.7

Sources: *Budget of the United States Government, Fiscal Year 1980*, p. 579; *Fiscal Year 1981*, p. 614; *Fiscal Year 1982*, p. 613; *Fiscal Year 1983*, p. M-5; *Fiscal Year 1984*, pp. M-11, 6-33; and The White House, "America's New Beginning: A Program for Economic Recovery," February 18, 1981, p. 12. Figures are rounded.

a. Beginning in 1983, noncompulsory medicare premium items formerly classified as budget receipts are classified as offsets to outlays. To be consistent with the 1983 figures, the original estimates of receipts and outlays have been reduced by $2.9 billion in 1980, $3.3 billion in 1981, and $3.9 billion in 1982, but the deficit figures were not affected. In addition, Public Law 97-35 classified purchases of petroleum for the strategic petroleum reserve as off-budget; this reduced outlays and the deficit for 1982 by $3.5 billion.

The deteriorating economic situation greatly altered the fiscal picture. President Reagan estimated the deficit for fiscal 1982 at $41.5 billion in February 1981[4] and $38.5 billion in July 1981. By early 1982, when it was clear that the economy was in recession, the estimate was raised to $95.1 billion, and ultimately the fiscal year ended with a deficit of $110.6 billion (table 2-1).

These developments repeated a pattern—going back to the 1980 budget—of successive upward revisions of the deficit, reflecting mainly the great instability of the economy. In 1980 and 1981 higher than expected inflation and interest rates, which raised outlays, were major causes of the ballooning deficit; in 1982 the major cause was the decline in business activity, which reduced receipts sharply (table 2-2).

The 1983 Budget

In preparing the budget for fiscal 1983, President Reagan was faced with disagreeable choices. The deficit under the nondefense programs then authorized and the administration's accelerated defense plans—what he called "current services with an adequate defense"—was projected to amount to $146 billion in 1983. Even this deficit was based on the assumptions that the recession would end by

4. If it were adjusted to reflect definitions in the 1983 budget (see table 2-1, note a), the Carter budget would have projected a 1982 deficit of $24.0 billion. The increase to $41.5 billion was the result mainly of President Reagan's decision to cut taxes by more than he proposed to cut spending.

Table 2-2. Changes in the Actual Budget from Original Estimates, Fiscal Years 1980–83

Billions of dollars

Item	1980	1981	1982	1983 (projected)
Outlays				
Change in economic conditions	27.1	32.3	22.4	8.1
Inflation	12.0	14.8	−1.1	−1.2
Unemployment	6.5	. . .	6.2	11.2
Interest rates and increased borrowing	6.8	14.5	15.5	−1.9
Support for financial institutions	1.8	3.0	1.8	. . .
Policy and other changes[a]	20.9	12.5	18.0	39.5
Total change from original estimate	48.0	44.8	40.4	47.6
Receipts				
Change in economic conditions	13.5	4.6	−48.0	−70.1
Policy and other changes[a]	3.9	−2.0	19.2	1.5
Total change from original estimate	17.4	2.6	−28.8	−68.6
Deficit				
Change in economic conditions	13.6	27.7	70.4	78.2
Policy and other changes[a]	17.0	14.5	−1.2	38.0
Total change from original estimate	30.6	42.2	69.1	116.2

Sources: *Budget of the United States Government, Fiscal Year 1980*, p. 25; *Fiscal Year 1981*, p. 71; *Fiscal Year 1982*, p. 83; *Fiscal Year 1983*, pp. 2-14, 6-27; *Fiscal Year 1984*, pp. 2-11, 2-19, 6-33; White House, "America's New Beginning"; and author's estimates. Figures are rounded.

a. Includes changes resulting from congressional action.

mid-1982 and that strong economic growth would be resumed in the last half of 1982. If no further action were taken to curtail spending or increase tax receipts, the deficits would continue to rise indefinitely.

Despite these projected deficits, the president refused to moderate the buildup in defense spending, reverse or delay the income tax cuts, or recommend any other major tax increases. Instead he proposed further large cuts in nondefense spending, modest reforms in income taxes and tax collection and enforcement procedures, and improvements in the management of the federal government. All told, these proposals would reduce the deficits—on the president's optimistic economic assumptions—to $92 billion in 1983, $83 billion in 1984, and $72 billion in 1985.

The public and congressional reaction to the 1983 budget was one of dismay. For the first time in recent memory, a president had submitted a budget that did not propose closing the gap between outlays and receipts in the foreseeable future. Moreover, on closer examination it became clear that the planned deficits were grossly underestimated, even if the economy improved and all the president's spending and tax proposals were enacted without change. The Congressional Budget Office, for example, estimated that the deficits under the president's program would rise from $137 billion in 1983 to $152 billion in 1985. Stock and bond prices continued to decline and the economic recession deepened as high interest rates reduced business and consumer spending. By mid-1982 the unemployment rate reached 9.5 percent and was continuing to rise rapidly.

Under the circumstances, the congressional budget and tax committees struck out on their own. The first congressional budget resolution, passed on June 18, 1982, virtually discarded the president's budget (similar action was taken on the Carter budget two years earlier) and substituted a plan that included cuts in defense spending, larger cuts than those proposed by the president in nondefense spending, a freeze on federal pay and pensions for one year and a 4 percent limit on cost-of-living pay adjustments for two more years, an increase in taxes of close to $100 billion over three years, and higher user fees for federal programs that provide benefits to identifiable groups. The net result of these changes, if enacted, would have been to reduce the prospective deficits by much more than the president had proposed. The deficit reductions in the congressional budget resolution exceeded the reductions in the president's budget by $28 billion in 1983, $52 billion in 1984, and $76 billion in 1985 (table 2-3), when priced out on the economic assumptions of the resolution. But the estimates of the remaining deficits continued to be high: $104 billion in 1983, $84 billion in 1984, and $60 billion in 1985.

During the spring and summer of 1982, Congress concentrated mainly on the implementation of the three-year $100 billion tax increase required by the budget resolution. Since the Democrats in the House did not relish the idea of originating a tax increase, the chairman of the Senate Finance Committee, Robert Dole of Kansas, took the lead in designing a bill that Congress would approve and the president would sign. The bill he proposed, entitled the Tax Equity and Fiscal Responsibility Act of 1982, reversed some of the business tax cuts adopted just a year earlier, removed numerous special provisions in the tax code (many of which had been considered inviolate), expanded the income tax withholding system to include inter-

**Table 2-3. Comparison of President Reagan's 1983 Budget Program and the 1982
Congressional Budget Resolution, Fiscal Years 1983–85**

Billions of dollars

	1983		1984		1985	
Item	Reagan program	Congres- sional resolution	Reagan program	Congres- sional resolution	Reagan program	Congres- sional resolution
Current services deficit	180.7	180.7	214.6	214.6	231.0	231.0
Reduction in current services deficit	48.3	76.8	78.7	130.7	94.6	171.0
Revenue increases	6.8[a]	20.9	6.9[a]	36.0	−3.3[a]	41.4
Defense[b]	0.4	7.8	0.4	8.3	0.4	10.3
Federal pay raises	1.6	5.1	3.4	8.9	5.2	12.1
Nondefense discretionary programs	10.2	5.7	17.1	10.2	26.0	18.8
Entitlement programs	10.7	6.9	16.6	10.7	23.1	13.6
User fees and other program changes	3.4	2.2	5.4	2.7	5.6	2.9
Management savings	8.9	13.7	12.1	17.1	12.8	15.8
Net interest	6.2	14.5	16.6	36.8	24.7	56.4
Remaining deficit	132.4	103.9	135.9	83.9	136.4	60.0

Sources: House and Senate budget committees. Estimates assume growth of real gross national product of 4.4 percent in calendar year 1983, 3.6 percent in 1984, and 3.5 percent in 1985. Figures are rounded.

a. Represents the difference between the Treasury's current services revenue estimates and the Congressional Budget Office's estimates for the president's reestimated request. The president's proposed revenue increases were $10.7 billion, $16.8 billion, and $16.9 billion for fiscal 1983, 1984, and 1985, respectively.

b. Excludes military pay and entitlements.

est and dividends, and increased the cigarette and telephone excise taxes. Although still reluctant to agree to tax increases of these magnitudes, the president was persuaded to approve the bill, which he signed on September 3, 1982. The bill increased revenues by $15.9 billion in fiscal 1983, $35.3 billion in 1984, and $40.3 billion in 1985.

Congress was not nearly as successful in implementing the outlay targets stipulated in the congressional budget resolution. Only three appropriations bills were passed before Congress adjourned for the 1982 election on October 2,[5] and President Reagan called it back into session after the election to complete action on the budget. During this lame-duck session, the main issue was whether the administration and Congress could agree on a jobs program to moderate unemployment, then approaching 11 percent. The administra-

5. The three bills were for the Department of Housing and Urban Development, the legislative branch, and military construction.

tion proposed a program to improve the nation's highways, with the higher outlays to be financed by an increase in the gasoline tax. Congressional Democrats also supported a separate jobs program, without additional financing. The president refused to accept the jobs program, and in the end Congress approved the highway program and a gasoline tax increase of five cents a gallon, effective April 1, 1983.

The lame-duck session completed action on the appropriations for the Departments of Agriculture and Transportation and for the District of Columbia, but most of the appropriations bills—which authorize well over half of total federal spending—were still pending by the time the session was scheduled to end. To keep the government operating through the remainder of the fiscal year, Congress passed a continuing budget resolution that included specific appropriations for the Departments of Defense, Labor, Health and Human Services, and Education (the bills for these agencies were already far along in the legislative process). Congress also provided that the remaining agencies—which account for about 20 percent of total outlays—would be allowed to spend at the rate of the previous fiscal year or at a rate stipulated in an appropriations bill passed by either house, if lower.[6]

Congress did not meet the goals of its own budget resolution. Spending cuts called for in the budget resolution for a number of nondefense programs were not implemented. The higher user fees proposed in the resolution were not enacted. The savings expected from improved management and tax collection procedures proved to be ephemeral. Interest payments rose in the face of unforeseen deficits and continuing monetary restraint. And in the meantime, outlays for farm price supports, unemployment compensation, and other federal programs continued to rise as the economy sagged. All told, actual spending for fiscal 1983 is expected to exceed the administration's original budget estimate by $48 billion (table 2-2).

As a result of these developments, the estimates of the deficit for fiscal 1983 continued to soar. Instead of the $92 billion in the original budget and the $104 billion in the congressional budget resolu-

6. If both houses had passed an appropriations bill for a particular agency but had not yet agreed to a compromise, spending was authorized at the lesser of the two appropriated amounts. The spending authorized by such continuing resolution formulas was for energy and water resources, foreign operations, the Department of State and the judiciary, the Department of the Interior, and the Department of the Treasury and the Postal Service.

tion, the 1983 deficit was reestimated by the administration in January 1983 to be $208 billion (table 2-1), and for future years the estimates were even higher. Much of the increase in the deficit was the result of the recession, which reduced revenues and increased outlays for unemployment benefits. The failure to keep spending within the limits originally proposed by the president, let alone the stricter limits in the first congressional budget resolution, also accounted for a significant portion of the rise in the projected 1983 deficit (table 2-2).

A major issue not specifically addressed either by the administration or Congress in 1982 was the condition of the social security trust funds. The reserve balance of the largest fund—for retirement and survivors' benefits—was declining rapidly and was expected to be depleted before the end of the year. The two other trust funds—for disability benefits and medical hospital insurance—were still in surplus, but the projections for health insurance were not reassuring. In 1981 Congress authorized the trustees to permit the funds to borrow from one another temporarily. This borrowing authority was used for the first time in October 1982 to continue payment of retirement and survivors' benefits.

As the economic situation worsened, it became clear that even the pooled resources of all three social security funds would not be sufficient to meet all benefits beyond 1983. In December 1981 President Reagan had created a bipartisan National Commission on Social Security Reform to recommend changes that would put the social security system on a sound financial basis. But because of the political sensitivity of the issues, the commission members were unable to reach agreement among themselves and with the White House by the end of 1982, when the commission was originally scheduled to report its findings. However, under the pressure to submit the fiscal 1984 budget on time, an agreement was reached on January 15, 1983, and the commission filed a report that recommended changes in benefits and taxes amounting to $168 billion to finance the system through the remainder of the decade.

The 1984 Budget

President Reagan's fiscal 1984 budget reflects the same priorities he established two years earlier. He rejected proposals to slow defense spending significantly and refused to modify the third installment of the 1981 personal income tax cut, effective on July 1, 1983, or the indexing of the individual income tax, which becomes effective on January 1, 1985. He accepted the eleventh-hour compromise on social security worked out by the National Commission on Social Security Reform and recommended further cuts in other nondefense programs. He also recommended a standby tax increase for 1986 and later years.

Current Services

Budget planning begins with estimates of current services, which show outlays and receipts on the assumption that policy remains unchanged. The outlay estimates reflect the expected cost of continuing ongoing federal programs at 1983 levels in real terms. Changes that can be anticipated in current programs (such as increases in the number of federal retirees) are included, but new initiatives either by the president or Congress are excluded. Programs that are temporary are assumed to expire. For national defense outlays, the estimates are those planned by the administration in February 1982, which the president clearly regards as his basic policy.[7] Estimates of receipts are based on current law, including any changes already scheduled for the future, under the economic assumptions made by the administration.

In January 1983 the estimate of outlays for current services in fiscal 1983 was $806.1 billion. To continue federal nondefense programs at the levels authorized for 1983 and to finance the proposed defense program, total outlays would reach $880.3 billion in 1984—$74.2 billion more than in 1983. More than half of this increase—$39.1 billion—is accounted for by the defense program. Only $10.7 billion of this amount would be required to maintain the program at real 1983 levels; $28.4 billion would pay for the buildup proposed by the administration. Most of the remainder is accounted for by increases in outlays for social security, medicare and medicaid, and interest on the national debt (table 2-4).

Current services receipts rise from $597.5 billion in fiscal 1983 to $648.8 billion in 1984, an increase of $51.3 billion. The 1981 tax act reduces receipts by $47.7 billion, but the expected economic recovery would raise receipts by $71.8 billion; the 1982 tax act adds

---

7. This is a departure from previous practice. In earlier years the national defense estimates in the current services budget reflected only the authorizations approved by Congress.

Table 2-4. Changes in the Current Services Budget, Fiscal Years 1983–84

Billions of dollars

Item	Amount
Outlays	
1983 current services	806.1
1983–84 change	74.2
Defense	39.1
Social security	12.1
Medicare and medicaid	10.3
Net interest	16.2
All other	−3.5
1984 current services	880.3
Receipts	
1983 current services	597.5
1983–84 change	51.3
Effect of economic recovery	71.8
Economic Recovery Tax Act of 1981	−47.7
Tax Equity and Fiscal Responsibility Act of 1982	21.0
Payroll taxes	3.9
Highway Revenue Act of 1982	2.1
Other	0.2
1984 current services	648.8
Deficit	
1983 current services	208.5
1983–84 change	23.0
Outlay increases	74.2
Revenue increases	51.3
1984 current services	231.5

Sources: *Budget of the United States Government, Fiscal Year 1984*, p. 4-19; and *Special Analyses, Budget of the United States Government, Fiscal Year 1984*, pp. A-9, A-14. Figures are rounded.

another $21 billion and the highway act $2.1 billion; and scheduled increases in the payroll tax for social security raise receipts by $3.9 billion.

With outlays increasing by $74.2 billion and receipts rising by $51.3 billion, the current services deficit would increase from $208.5 billion in fiscal 1983 to $231.5 billion in 1984. Thereafter, the current services deficit continues to rise every year until it reaches $300.4 billion in 1988 (table 2-5). It is important to realize that this projected increase in the deficit occurs despite the assumption of sustained economic recovery and declining unemployment, which tend to reduce the deficit.[8] This was the background against which the president planned the 1984 budget.

8. For estimates of the effect of the business cycle on the budget, see appendix A.

Table 2-5. Current Services and Changes Proposed in President Reagan's 1984 Budget Program, Fiscal Years 1984-88

Billions of dollars

Item	1984	1985	1986	1987	1988
Outlays					
Current services[a]	880.3	966.4	1,051.7	1,140.8	1,227.0
Proposed reductions	31.8	47.9	62.1	82.4	100.1
Proposed outlays	848.5	918.5	989.6	1,058.4	1,126.9
Receipts					
Current services[a]	648.8	713.3	780.9	849.1	926.7
Proposed increases	10.9	11.0	61.0	67.3	83.6
Proposed receipts	659.7	724.3	841.9	916.3	1,010.3
Deficit					
Current services[a]	231.5	253.1	270.8	291.7	300.4
Proposed reductions	42.7	58.9	123.2	149.6	183.7
Proposed deficit	188.8	194.2	147.7	142.1	116.7

Source: *Special Analyses, Fiscal 1984*, p. A-13. Figures are rounded.
a. Includes the Reagan defense program.

The Reagan Budget

The budget plan for fiscal 1984 contains four major features: (1) a freeze on all federal pay, cost-of-living adjustments, and reimbursement formulas and on aggregate discretionary spending; (2) structural reforms of the social security system, health programs, federal retirement programs, and means-tested benefits; (3) modest reductions in the defense buildup, including a freeze on pay for military personnel; and (4) contingency tax increases in the event that the deficit remains above 2.5 percent of GNP in 1986-88. The budgetary effects of these proposals are summarized in table 2-6.[9]

The social security agreement was perhaps the key element in the budget planning for fiscal 1984. Without it, the other decisions would have been hard to justify, and it would have been even more difficult to persuade Congress to accept them. The agreement called for freezing benefits from July 1, 1983, to January 1, 1984, extending social security coverage to new federal employees and employees of all nonprofit agencies,[10] taxing half of the social security benefits received by single persons with other income of more than

9. The discussion in this chapter is confined to the proposals for the regular or "unified" budget. For an analysis of the fiscal activities of "off-budget" and federal credit agencies, see appendix B.

10. In addition, state and local governments now under social security would not be permitted to withdraw.

Table 2-6. President Reagan's 1984 Budget Program, Fiscal Years 1984–88

Billions of dollars

Item	1984	1985	1986	1987	1988
Current services deficit	231.5	253.1	270.8	291.7	300.4
Reduction in current services deficit	42.7	58.9	77.1	100.6	132.3
Social security[a]	12.2	10.0	13.6	15.8	27.7
Federal pay and COLA freeze[b]	7.4	10.0	10.8	11.5	12.3
Health care[c]	4.2	8.1	11.1	15.0	19.9
Federal retirement	1.4	2.8	3.2	4.0	4.8
Means-tested entitlements	1.4	2.1	2.3	2.4	2.4
Discretionary nondefense programs	6.2	10.0	12.8	16.5	20.8
Farm price supports	3.1	6.0	6.8	7.6	5.3
Defense[d]	4.1	2.8	3.7	4.5	4.8
Other tax changes[e]	−0.8	−1.5	−2.2	−2.5	−2.6
Net interest	2.0	6.1	12.5	22.1	32.9
Other	1.5	2.5	2.5	2.7	4.0
Budget deficit without standby tax increases	188.8	194.2	193.7	191.1	168.1
Standby tax increases	...	...	46.0	49.0	51.4
Budget deficit with standby tax increases	188.8	194.2	147.7	142.1	116.7

Sources: *Budget of the United States Government, Fiscal Year 1984*, pp. 4-19, 3-32 to 3-39; and *Special Analyses, Fiscal 1984*, pp. A-13, A-14.

a. Includes tax changes and freeze in cost-of-living adjustments.

b. Excludes freeze in cost-of-living adjustments for social security. Includes military pay and retirement.

c. Includes cap on tax deductibility of private health insurance premiums.

d. Excludes military pay and retirement.

e. Includes tax incentives for enterprise zones, higher education, and Caribbean economic development; also includes tax credits for tuition and job creation.

$20,000 and married couples with other income of more than $25,000, increasing taxes paid by the self-employed to match the rate of the combined employer-employee tax, and advancing currently scheduled payroll tax increases to 1984 and 1988–89 (with an income tax credit for the 1984 increase).[11] By accepting the package, the president was able to reduce the deficit by $12.2 billion in fiscal 1984 and $27.7 billion in 1988.

Following the precedent of social security, the president recommended that cost-of-living adjustments for benefits paid by other transfer programs (mainly supplementary security income for the aged, food stamps and other nutrition programs, and veterans' benefits) be deferred for six months and that adjustments in pay and benefits for current and retired federal workers be deferred for one year. If accepted, these recommendations would reduce outlays by amounts ranging from $7.4 billion in fiscal 1984 to $12.3 billion in 1988.

11. These proposals are analyzed in detail in chapter 4.

The health care reform initiative is intended to restrain the explosive growth of medical care costs in recent years. The proposals include higher copayments by patients for the first sixty days of medicare hospitalization and full coverage after sixty days, increases in supplementary medical insurance premiums and deductibles, a permanent system for limiting payments to hospitals under medicare to replace the temporary system created by the Tax Equity and Fiscal Responsibility Act of 1982, a stricter limit on reimbursement under that temporary system in 1984 while the new system is being debated, and a one-year freeze on physicians' reimbursements. Furthermore, monthly health insurance premiums paid by employers in excess of $175 for families and $70 for individuals would be included in the taxable income of the employees. These proposals are intended to make patients, hospitals, and physicians more conscious of costs.[12] The budgetary savings from the health care proposals are projected to rise from an estimated $4.2 billion in fiscal 1984 to $19.9 billion in 1988.

The long-run cost of the federal retirement system is estimated to be about 35 percent of the federal payroll, of which employees contribute one-fifth, or 7 percent of their pay.[13] The administration proposes to reduce the cost of the system to 22 percent of the payroll and to raise the employee contribution to half that amount. The savings would be achieved by raising the retirement age from fifty-five to sixty-five (with a reduction of 5 percent a year for earlier retirement), by calculating benefits on the basis of the highest five years of earnings instead of the highest three currently used, and by reducing the benefit rate credited for each year of service. Employee contributions for retirement would rise to 9 percent in 1984 and 11 percent in 1985.[14] These modifications would reduce the deficit by $1.4 billion in fiscal 1984 and $4.8 billion in 1988.

Substantial modifications have already been made in the last two years to restrain the growth of costs in the means-tested entitlement programs. The president proposes further changes in the adminis-

12. The health care proposals are discussed in chapter 5.
13. By contrast, the cost of social security retirement and disability benefits over the next seventy-five years is 13–19 percent of the payroll of covered employees. The exact percentage depends on the economic and demographic assumptions made. Employees share the cost equally with their employers.
14. For an analysis of the federal pay and retirement system, see Robert W. Hartman, *Pay and Pensions for Federal Employees* (Brookings Institution, 1983).

tration of these programs to cut spending. Able-bodied recipients of food stamps or of aid to families with dependent children (AFDC) would be required to participate in work-related activities as a condition of eligibility (workfare). State governments would be held liable for overpayments of food stamps that exceed 3 percent of their total benefit payments, a condition that is already being applied to AFDC and medicaid.[15] The administration will also seek legislation to increase the responsibility of absent parents to support their families. Spending on these programs would be reduced by $1.4 billion in fiscal 1984 and $2.4 billion in 1988 if these proposals were implemented.

For the discretionary nondefense programs in the budget, the president proposes to freeze budget authority at the 1983 level for three years, thus eliminating any inflation adjustment for these programs in the aggregate. This policy corresponds to a reduction of about 5 percent a year in real terms as inflation erodes the spending power of appropriations. Funds for some programs—such as law enforcement, Head Start, and the National Science Foundation— would be raised, but these increases would be offset by reductions in other programs—for example, education, social services, and mass transit. Because of the interest of Congress in new jobs programs, the proposed budget emphasizes improving federal training and employment programs, but total spending for these programs would be cut in 1984.[16] The limit on aggregate spending for the discretionary programs reduces projected outlays by $6.2 billion in 1984 and $20.8 billion in 1988 because current services are calculated at the same real level as in 1983.

Outlays for farm price support programs increased from $4.1 billion in fiscal 1981 to $11.7 billion in 1982 and are expected to reach $18.9 billion in 1983 under current law. To reverse this sharp increase in budget costs, the administration has announced a new program called PIK—payments in kind—under which farmers would be given commodities rather than cash for reducing production. In addition, legislation is being requested to freeze target prices on wheat, corn, and other commodities rather than to increase them

15. However, no penalty is imposed for denying legitimate payments.

16. After the budget was submitted in late January, President Reagan agreed to a special jobs program that would cost $4.3 billion, most of which was already in the budget. See chapter 6 for an analysis of these programs.

annually as the law now requires. The budgetary savings from these and other minor changes in the farm program would rise from $3.1 billion in 1984 to $7.6 billion in 1987 and then decline to $5.3 billion in 1988.[17]

Although he resisted cuts in his defense plans, the president reduced his own outlay estimates by an average of $9.4 billion a year in fiscal years 1984–88, including $4.6 billion from the proposed freeze on military pay and retirement benefits. Within the defense budget, more money would be allocated to military equipment and supplies and less to pay and retirement than originally planned.[18] The reductions are roughly equal to the effect of the lower inflation rate assumed in the new budget, so that total defense outlays in real terms would be about the same as those projected a year earlier.

Several new tax proposals—in addition to the cap on employers' deductions of health insurance premiums—are included in the 1984 budget program. The administration repeated last year's proposals to introduce tax incentives for the redevelopment of economically distressed areas designated as enterprise zones and to provide a tax credit for tuition payments to private elementary and secondary schools. A new exclusion was proposed for interest on savings deposited by taxpayers in accounts to pay future expenses of higher education for their children. A jobs tax credit to encourage employers to hire long-term unemployed workers was also proposed.[19] These changes would reduce receipts by $0.8 billion in fiscal 1984 and $2.6 billion in 1988.

The president stated that he would not agree to a delay or modification of either the individual income tax rate cuts scheduled for July 1, 1983, or the indexation of personal exemptions and tax brackets now scheduled to begin on January 1, 1985.[20] However, he proposed a contingency tax plan consisting of a 5 percent surtax on individuals and an excise tax of five dollars a barrel on domestically

17. The commodities to be given to farmers under the PIK program would come from the reserves of the Commodity Credit Corporation or from the farmer-owned reserves. In the latter case, the reserve loan is in effect forgiven. If these reserves were later replenished, the budgetary savings would not be permanent.

18. The defense budget is analyzed in chapter 3.

19. The budget also endorsed a tax proposal included in the Caribbean Basin initiative passed by the House of Representatives in 1982 to permit a deduction for expenses incurred in attending a business convention in the area.

20. The rate cuts reduce receipts by $30 billion in fiscal 1984 and $40 billion in 1988. Indexation reduces receipts by $17 billion in 1986 and then cumulates to $40 billion in 1988.

produced and imported oil, both to remain for a period of up to thirty-six months.[21] These taxes would become effective if Congress adopts the administration's deficit reduction measures, if the unified budget deficit for fiscal 1986 forecast on July 1, 1985, is more than 2.5 percent of GNP, and if the economy is growing on July 1, 1985. The standby tax increases are estimated to raise receipts by $46.0 billion in fiscal 1986, $49.0 billion in 1987, and $51.4 billion in 1988.

The proposed budget would greatly reduce the growth of the national debt and thus reduce interest costs. Interest costs would also be held down, the budget assumes, by a steady decline in interest rates. For example, the interest rate on ten-year Treasury notes is expected to decline from an average of 10.2 percent in calendar 1983 to 6.7 percent in 1988. If the proposed budgetary savings are realized, interest payments on the national debt would be reduced from the current services estimates by only $2.0 billion in fiscal 1984, but by sharply increasing amounts thereafter.[22] The deficit reduction would reach $32.9 billion in 1988.

The long list of proposals made in the budget would cut the projected deficits by significant amounts but would not eliminate them. The current services deficit for fiscal 1984 would be reduced from $231.5 billion to $188.8 billion, or by $42.7 billion. In the following four years, the cuts would be even larger, but the remaining deficits would still be large. Without the standby tax increases, the deficits would remain at about $190 billion through fiscal 1987 and would decline to $168 billion in 1988. If the standby tax increases were enacted, the deficits would be cut to between $140 billion and $150 billion in 1986 and 1987 and then would drop to $117 billion in 1988 (table 2-6).

Policies for Economic Expansion

In contrast to the excessive optimism of previous years, the fiscal 1984 budget is based on a set of cautious economic assumptions for the period 1983–88 (table 2-7). Growth of real output is expected to

21. The budget states that the surtax would apply to individuals and corporations. However, according to the Congressional Budget Office, the revenue projections include a 5 percent surtax only on individual income taxes. The CBO also points out that the revenue estimates in the budget are based on a seven dollar, not five dollar, a barrel tax on oil. For an analysis of the president's tax proposals, see chapter 7.

22. These are reductions in interest payments to the public, after allowing for interest paid to federal agencies.

Table 2-7. **Economic Assumptions of the Reagan Budget, Calendar Years 1982–88**
Percent

		Projected					
Economic indicator	1982	1983	1984	1985	1986	1987	1988
			Year-to-year change				
GNP in current dollars							
Reagan administration	4.1	6.7	9.3	9.1	8.8	8.7	8.6
Congressional Budget Office	4.1	6.8	9.6	9.0	8.1	7.6	7.4
GNP in constant dollars							
Reagan administration	−1.8	1.4	3.9	4.0	4.0	4.0	4.0
Congressional Budget Office	−1.8	2.1	4.7	4.1	3.7	3.5	3.5
GNP deflator							
Reagan administration	6.0	5.2	5.2	4.9	4.6	4.5	4.4
Congressional Budget Office	6.0	4.6	4.7	4.7	4.3	3.9	3.7
Consumer price index							
Reagan administration	6.0	4.9	4.6	4.6	4.6	4.5	4.4
Congressional Budget Office	6.0	4.5	5.0	4.7	4.1	3.9	3.7
			Annual average				
Unemployment rate[a]							
Reagan administration	9.5	10.7	9.9	8.9	8.1	7.3	6.5
Congressional Budget Office	9.5	10.6	9.8	9.0	8.4	8.0	7.5
Treasury bill rate							
Reagan administration	10.7	8.0	7.9	7.4	6.8	6.5	6.1
Congressional Budget Office	10.7	6.8	7.4	7.2	6.6	6.1	5.9

Sources: *Budget of the United States Government, Fiscal Year 1984*, pp. 2-9, 2-10; and Congressional Budget Office, *The Outlook for Economic Recovery* (Government Printing Office, 1983), p. 7.
a. Percentage of the labor force, including armed forces stationed in the United States.

resume in early 1983, but at a modest rate compared with previous recoveries. Real gross national product is projected to rise 3 percent from the fourth quarter of 1982 to the fourth quarter of 1983 and to increase at a 4 percent rate annually thereafter.[23] These modest growth rates reduce unemployment by somewhat less than one percentage point a year, which is still respectable by historical standards. Unemployment in the budget projection averages 10.7 percent of the labor force in 1983 and then declines gradually to 6.5 percent in 1988.[24] Inflation remains between 4 and 5 percent throughout the period, while interest rates decline moderately from early 1983 levels.

23. Because the year started out close to the low point of the recession, real GNP increased only 1.4 percent from the 1982 average to the 1983 average.
24. Rates are percentages of the total labor force, including armed forces stationed in the United States.

The Congressional Budget Office expects a somewhat faster recovery in 1983–84, about the same rate of growth in 1985, and slower growth in 1986–88 (table 2-7). The CBO also expects the inflation and interest rates to decline more rapidly. Productivity growth is somewhat higher in the CBO projection than in the administration's; as a consequence, the CBO foresees a slower decline in the unemployment rate. By 1988 unemployment averages 7.5 percent of the labor force in the CBO projection and 6.5 percent in the administration's projection, with virtually identical estimates of real output. As a result of these and other technical differences, the CBO estimates that the deficit in the current services budget is $17 billion less than the administration's projection for fiscal 1984 but will be $12 billion more than its projection for fiscal 1988.[25]

President Reagan's budget reflects his response to the large deficits that would remain even after five years of recovery. The problem of dealing with the long-run deficits is complicated by the conflict between the short- and long-run objectives. In periods of economic recession or early expansion, tax increases and spending cuts retard recovery. But when the economy is operating at a high level and the growth of money and credit is restrained by monetary policy, the competition by the federal government in the capital markets for funds to finance large deficits drives up interest rates and chokes off the expansion. This happened in 1980 and 1981 and could happen again in 1984 or 1985, if the long-run deficits are not drastically reduced.

The Structural Deficit

Budget deficits reflect both the basic tax and spending policies of the federal government and the fluctuations of economic activity. Since tax receipts fall off and government spending rises as income and employment decline, deficits rise sharply during a recession.[26] As income and employment increase during an expansion, receipts rise automatically and spending on unemployment benefits and other entitlement programs declines. The deficit that would remain if the economy were operating at a high level is called the *structural*

25. See Congressional Budget Office, *An Analysis of the President's Budgetary Proposals for Fiscal 1984* (GPO, 1983), p. 2.

26. The increase in spending during recessions is mainly for unemployment benefits. Social security and welfare benefits also increase but by much smaller amounts.

Table 2-8. Actual and High-Employment Deficits in the Current Services Budget and President Reagan's 1984 Budget Program, Fiscal Years 1979 and 1982-88[a]

Percent of gross national product

| | Current services budget[b] | | | Reagan budget | | | |
| | | | | Actual deficit | | High-employment deficit | |
Year	Actual deficit	Cyclical component	High-employment deficit	Without standby taxes	With standby taxes	Without standby taxes	With standby taxes
1979	1.2	...	1.2	1.2	1.2	1.2	1.2
1982	3.6	2.8	0.8	3.6	3.6	0.8	0.8
1983	6.5	4.3	2.2	6.5	6.5	2.1	2.1
1984	6.6	4.0	2.6	5.4	5.4	1.5	1.5
1985	6.6	3.5	3.1	5.1	5.1	1.7	1.7
1986	6.5	3.0	3.5	4.7	3.6	1.8	0.7
1987	6.5	2.6	3.9	4.2	3.2	1.9	0.8
1988	6.1	1.9	4.2	3.4	2.4	1.7	0.7

Source: Appendix tables A-1 and A-3.

a. High-employment deficits are calculated at a constant 6 percent unemployment rate and a 2.9 percent annual rate of growth of real GNP beginning in fiscal 1979.

b. Includes the Reagan defense program.

or *high-employment* deficit, two terms that are used interchangeably (see table 2-8).[27] Since the cyclical component of the deficit automatically disappears as the economy recovers, the structural deficit is a measure of the fiscal stimulus provided by the budget. Reduction or elimination of this deficit as the economy recovers would increase national saving and permit a larger increase in investment, which would in turn help to stimulate productivity.

The smallest federal deficit in the last half of the 1970s was in fiscal 1979, when it reached a low of $28 billion, or 1.2 percent of the gross national product. In that year unemployment averaged 5.9 percent of the labor force. The unemployment rate then climbed to almost 11 percent, and the deficit exploded. It reached $111 billion in 1982 and is projected at $208 billion in the current services budget for 1983. The structural deficit, which remained about the same between 1979 and 1982, is expected to increase $51 billion between 1982 and 1983, or by over half of the increase in the actual deficit.

The rise in the structural deficit in 1983 is not out of line with

27. The high-employment deficit is calculated assuming a 6 percent unemployment rate and a 2.9 percent annual rate of growth of real GNP. Appendix A explains the methods used to calculate the high-employment deficits more fully.

actions taken in prior recessions—such as the one in 1975—to restore high employment. The disturbing element in the budget outlook is that, even as a percentage of GNP, the structural deficit
continues to grow every year thereafter to 1988, if current budget
policies continue unchanged. This state of affairs is brought about
by several factors: the defense buildup greatly outpaces the growth
of the economy; large future deficits add to the annual interest bill
despite projections of declining interest rates; and the new tax laws
keep federal revenues rising only in proportion to the rise in GNP
rather than more than proportionately, as they have in the past.
Furthermore, the slowdown in the inflation rate reduces the growth
of tax receipts more than it does the growth of outlays. As a result,
the structural deficit in the current services budget increases from
2.2 percent of GNP in 1983 to 4.2 percent in 1988.

A high-employment deficit of 4.2 percent of GNP is unprecedented since the Second World War. It would absorb over a quarter
of gross private saving and almost two-thirds of net private saving.
The Federal Reserve Board would be reluctant to accommodate that
much fiscal stimulus in a period of economic expansion; if it did not
accommodate it, there would be continued upward pressure on interest rates. The higher interest rates would, in turn, retard the
growth of the economy.

Monetary Policy

Monetary policy has played a major role in recent economic developments and will continue to do so. Since the mid-1970s, the
Federal Reserve has established target ranges for the growth of
monetary aggregates, and it restated its commitment to the use of
money targets in October 1979, when it changed its operating procedures in a way that permitted much greater short-run fluctuations in
interest rates. The October 1979 policy change was intended to
strengthen the Federal Reserve's effort to restrain inflation.

Following his inauguration in early 1981, President Reagan emphasized his support for the Federal Reserve's policy of specifying
money targets and gradually reducing the target growth rates for
1981 to 1986. However, he adopted a highly stimulative program of
tax cuts and defense spending increases, which put fiscal policy on a
collision course with monetary policy. The basic emphasis of fiscal

policy was on economic expansion, whereas monetary policy emphasized restraint.

The conflict between fiscal and monetary policies has been evident in the behavior of interest rates. During 1981 and the first half
of 1982, the actual growth of the most widely used measure of
money, M1, was broadly consistent with the Federal Reserve's
targets.[28] As the deficit kept rising and monetary policy remained
unchanged, interest rates reached extraordinarily high levels and
were a major cause of the protracted recession of 1981–82.

The most important financial development of 1982 was the sharp
decline in interest rates that began about midyear. This was in part
the result of the declining demand for credit by households and
businesses as the recession continued, but it was also attributable to
an easing of monetary policy by the Federal Reserve. In March 1982
the Federal Reserve announced that it would accept a more rapid
growth of the money supply, if such growth appeared to be associated with continued sluggish demand for credit and unusual demands for liquidity by the private sector of the economy. In October
it stated that it would temporarily disregard the figures for the narrow M1 measure of money because those figures would be distorted
by reactions to tax and regulatory developments in the financial
sector. (One development was the maturing of the tax-exempt all-
savers certificates created in the 1981 tax bill, and another was the
introduction of new money market deposit accounts by banks and
thrift institutions.)[29] The Federal Reserve insisted, however, that its
reduced emphasis on changes in the money supply did not represent
a weakening of its commitment to fight inflation.

As is usual during a period of declining credit demands in the
private sector of the economy, the reduction in interest rates was
much sharper for short-term than for long-term securities. Between
June and December 1982, the yield on short-term Treasury bills
declined from 13 percent to 8 percent, while the yield on twenty-year
federal bonds declined from 14 percent to about 11 percent. These

---

28. The measure M1 is defined as the sum of currency, demand deposits, and other
checkable deposits. A broader measure, M2, includes M1 plus a variety of savings and time
deposits at banks and thrift institutions and certain other types of liquid assets (including
balances in money market mutual funds).

29. Although the Federal Reserve said it would temporarily disregard above-target
figures for M1, it stated that it would continue to monitor the behavior of the broader monetary aggregates in relation to their target ranges.

reductions occurred despite rising estimates of the federal deficit, which serves as a reminder that the level of interest rates depends as much on monetary policy and private credit demands as on the size of the federal deficit. The lower interest rates have already reversed the decline in residential construction and automobile output, the sectors most dependent on credit to finance sales.

Coordinating Fiscal and Monetary Policies

Under the current services budget (including the administration's defense plans), fiscal policy would have an extremely stimulative impact on the economy in future years. The deficit would remain above 6 percent of GNP despite the steady decline in unemployment anticipated by the administration, and the structural deficit would rise steadily between 1983 and 1988. The deficits for the next year or two would help to sustain economic recovery, but the deficits in later years when the economy would be approaching full capacity would be unacceptable.

With the budget changes proposed by the administration, the structural deficit goes from an average of 1.7 percent of GNP in 1983–85 to 0.7 percent in 1988 if the standby taxes are enacted. With these taxes, the projected 1988 deficit is not high by postwar standards for periods of high employment. But achieving this result requires approval by Congress of all the administration's proposed deficit reductions or their equivalent. This would mean cutting outlays or raising taxes by about $185 billion in 1988, or more than 3.5 percent of GNP. Options to reduce the deficit to 1 percent of GNP or less are presented in chapter 8.

Resumption of economic growth in 1983 depends heavily on the coordinated use of fiscal and monetary policies. Although nominal interest rates have declined, real interest rates are still high. Fiscal policy will clearly stimulate private demand in the short run. If the Federal Reserve accommodates the credit demands of the government as well as those of the private sector in 1983, interest rates might continue to decline and further stimulate consumer and business spending. With so much slack in the economy, there is little danger that such a policy would reignite inflation.

However, the uncertainty about the long-run budget outlook is having an adverse impact on prospects for continued growth in future years. Because the impending structural deficits for current services are so large, few people believe they will be brought down to manageable proportions. This has kept long-term interest rates high and has led the Federal Reserve to adopt a policy of cautious support for the recovery. Congress and the administration must agree on a package of spending cuts and tax increases that will sharply and believably reduce future deficits. Otherwise, the nation will not be able to avoid still another clash between monetary and fiscal policies that would keep interest rates high and interfere with the investment needed for improving growth in the years ahead.

CHAPTER THREE

The Defense Budget

WILLIAM W. KAUFMANN

THE GERMAN philosopher Hegel once wrote that "amid the pressure of great events, a general principle gives no help." He may have had something like the present situation in mind. President Reagan, at the midpoint in his term of office, certainly faces a number of powerful and competing pressures as he seeks passage of his defense budget for fiscal year 1984 and approval of his five-year defense plan. The deepest recession in the postwar era has brought strong demands for a priming of the economic pump at the same time that the recovery expected in 1983 and subsequent years makes it equally imperative that the trend of growing budgetary deficits be brought under control and reversed. The continued increases in Soviet defense spending have emphasized the need for an expansion in the U.S. defense effort just as public enthusiasm for the administration's proposed pace of expansion has begun to wane, dampened not only by the recession but also by the signals from the new leadership in Russia that its appetite for at least the appearance of arms control remains keen. Whether the general principle of rearming America can muster public support for further large increases in defense spending remains to be seen. For the moment, it seems to have lost its power to protect the defense budget from close scrutiny.

THE AUTHOR is grateful to Henry J. Aaron and John D. Steinbruner for their wise comments, Susan E. Nichols for her impeccable secretarial assistance, and Patricia A. O'Brien for her administrative skills.

Requirements and Equity

What might replace rearming America as a guide to action is not yet clear. The Department of Defense naturally continues to insist that its "requirements" for weapons, research, and military construction are essential to national security and must be met. But the dominant voice now belongs to those who insist that if future federal budgets must be cut, defense must bear its "fair share" of the reductions. As a gesture to that sentiment, Secretary of Defense Caspar Weinberger agrees to accept a freeze, not on nuclear weapons, but on the pay of departmental personnel, military and civilian. At the same time, he implies that he will get all the money back in future years, even though budgetary deficits will be more troublesome and pressure to reduce the defense budget even greater.

Catchwords are not entirely unfamiliar in American political life. It is disconcerting, nonetheless, to see the debate on national priorities polarized between requirements and equity when neither principle provides a particularly good test of the adequacy of the defense budget or the wisdom of its allocation. In an era of commitment to such instant panaceas as supply-side economics, constitutional amendments to balance the federal budget, or verified nuclear freezes, it may be too much to ask for a more serious approach to the issue of national security and international stability. But no harm can come from asking what it might take in the way of resources to acquire a balanced defense posture capable of maintaining the conditions of U.S. security, and doing so with reasonably assured success.

The Reagan Plan

The answer of the administration, not surprisingly, is that the resources will have to be extremely large: on the order of $1,768.1 billion between fiscal years 1984 and 1988. Table 3-1 summarizes how this most recent five-year plan compares with the final proposal of the Carter administration and the last two plans submitted by Reagan.

When President Reagan came into office, not only did he revise the Carter defense plan; he proposed that the 1981 budget, already enacted, be increased by $7 billion as well. Table 3-2 indicates how Congress has reacted thus far to these proposals. As the secretary of

Table 3-1. Successive Five-Year Defense Plans, Fiscal Years 1982–88
Billions of dollars

Administration and date of projection	1982	1983	1984	1985	1986	1987	1988	Total
Total obligational authority								
Carter (January 1981)	196.4	224.0	253.1	284.3	318.3	...	...	1,276.1
Reagan (March 1981)	222.2	254.8	289.2	326.5	367.5	...	...	1,460.2
Reagan (February 1982)	...	258.0	285.5	331.7	367.6	400.8	...	1,643.6
Reagan (January 1983)	...	...	274.1	322.4	357.2	389.2	425.2	1,768.1
Outlays								
Carter (January 1981)	180.0	205.3	232.3	261.8	293.3	...	...	1,172.7
Reagan (March 1981)	184.8	221.1	249.8	297.3	336.0	...	...	1,289.0
Reagan (February 1982)	...	215.9	247.0	285.5	324.0	356.0	...	1,428.4
Reagan (January 1983)	...	...	238.6	277.5	314.9	345.6	377.0	1,553.6

Sources: *Department of Defense Annual Report, Fiscal Year 1982; Department of Defense Annual Report to the Congress, Fiscal Year 1983* and *Fiscal Year 1984;* Joseph A. Pechman, ed., *Setting National Priorities: The 1983 Budget* (Brookings Institution, 1982), p. 52; *Budget of the United States Government, Fiscal Year 1984,* p. 9-54; and author's estimates.

defense is quick to point out, more than $30 billion in total obligational authority has been cut from the original requests. Even so, the department now carries large balances of budget authority from prior years: $108 billion obligated but not spent and another $35 billion not yet obligated. These balances, and the commitments they imply, help explain why defense outlays will continue their rapid increase in the years ahead.

The latest five-year defense plan will accelerate the momentum. Roughly half of the nearly $1.8 trillion will go to what are considered the investment accounts: procurement; military construction; and research, development, test, and evaluation. The remainder will be allocated to the operating accounts—military personnel, operation and maintenance, and family housing—and to retired military pay. These accounts are scheduled to grow on the average by about 5 percent a year in real terms. By contrast, the investment accounts will increase an average of 10 percent a year even after the effects of inflation have been removed. Because outlays for capital goods lag behind the appropriations for them, the bills will be coming due for some years after these commitments have been made.

This heavy emphasis on investment is said to have three main purposes. The first is to acquire increased stocks of spare parts and modern munitions, which will improve the readiness of existing forces. The second is to raise the effectiveness of the nuclear and

Table 3-2. Congressional Action on the Defense Budget, Fiscal Years 1981–83
Billions of dollars

	1981		1982		1983		Total reduc- tion
Item	Re- quested	Ap- proved	Re- quested	Ap- proved	Re- quested	Ap- proved	
Total obligational authority	178.0	176.1	222.2	211.4	258.0	240.5	. . .
Outlays	158.6	156.1	184.8	182.9	215.9	208.9	. . .
Reductions							
Total obligational authority	. . .	1.9	. . .	10.8	. . .	17.5	30.2
Outlays	. . .	2.5	. . .	1.9	. . .	7.0	11.4

Sources: *Department of Defense Annual Report, Fiscal Year 1982, Fiscal Year 1983,* and *Fiscal Year 1984.*

nonnuclear forces by means of a rapid modernization of their weapons and equipment. The third is to add new units to the naval, tactical air, and intercontinental mobility forces, presumably to increase the flexibility of the U.S. conventional posture. The expected expansion of the active-duty forces is shown in table 3-3. This growth could lead to the addition of approximately 200,000 civilian and military personnel to the current departmental total of 3.1 million.

In justification of these programs, the administration continues to cite the window of vulnerability and the desirability of discarding outworn strategies in favor of preparations for protracted nuclear war, horizontal escalation, and conventional conflict of indefinite length—all in the cause of deterrence. For the most part, however, the programs themselves are familiar and fit into the traditional mold of U.S. defense policy. To the extent that they do differ, it is in the degree to which the secretary of defense appears to have been influenced by the individual preferences of the three military services and the pace at which particular investment programs are being implemented.

As in preceding administrations, all three legs of the strategic nuclear triad (consisting for many years of about 2,000 delivery vehicles) are being modernized. Only this time the strategic forces will acquire not only the MX intercontinental ballistic missile (ICBM), Trident submarines, and air-launched cruise missiles, but also the B-1 bomber, a second submarine-launched ballistic missile (SLBM), and new F-15 fighters and airborne warning and control aircraft for U.S. continental antibomber defenses—defenses that, with the advent of Soviet ICBMs and SLBMs, four previous admin-

Table 3-3. Expected Changes in the U.S. Force Structure, Fiscal Years 1982 and 1988

	1982		1988	
Item	Active	Reserve	Active	Reserve
Strategic missiles	1,056	. . .	1,000	. . .
Strategic submarines	32	. . .	40	. . .
Strategic bombers	376	. . .	389	. . .
Army divisions	16	8	16	10
Marine Corps divisions	3	1	3	1
Air Force tactical fighter wings	24	12	28	15
Navy attack carriers	13	. . .	14	. . .
Intercontinental lift aircraft	304	. . .	312	. . .
Intratheater lift aircraft	218	336	218	302

Source: *Armed Forces Journal International*, vol. 119 (August 1982), p. 38.

istrations have regarded as of too low priority to warrant a major modernization. In keeping with the decisions of the Carter administration, Pershing II ballistic missiles and ground-launched cruise missiles will be produced for possible deployment in Western Europe, and more modern nuclear bombs, shells, and enhanced radiation weapons will be provided for tactical aircraft and a variety of shorter-range delivery vehicles.

The Army and the Air Force will continue to strive, as they have been doing for nearly a decade, to replace the weapons and equipment they inherited from the war in Vietnam. The Navy, having invented a goal of 600 ships led by 15 large-deck attack carriers, will try once again (as it did in 1976) to persuade Congress to add new and expensive combatants at the same time that ships in the fleet that are reaching the end of their useful service life are being replaced. Even the objective of expanded intercontinental airlift, primarily in the form of wide-bodied aircraft, has a familiar ring. It has been put forward for the last ten years, along with proposals for an augmented aerial tanker force more readily available to support conventional deployments than the KC-135s of the Strategic Air Command. The costs of these programs over the coming five fiscal years are estimated in table 3-4.

With so much modernization being undertaken simultaneously and at such a rapid pace, there can be no mystery about why the outlays for defense are scheduled to continue their growth in the coming years, especially if the funds to operate the equipment are also made available. What is much less clear is whether the proposed

Table 3-4. Major Modernization Programs, Fiscal Years 1984–88[a]
Billions of dollars

Program	Estimated cost
Strategic nuclear forces	
Offense	109.6
Defense	15.6
Theater nuclear forces	
Ballistic and cruise missiles	7.0
Artillery	0.2
Land forces	
Close air support helicopters	16.7
Missiles	14.8
Tanks and tracked vehicles	31.1
Chemical weapons	8.0
Tactical air forces	
Close air support aircraft	7.0
Fighter and attack aircraft	63.8
Naval forces	
Carrier task forces	42.6
Attack submarines	16.8
Other ships	38.0
Mobility forces	
Airlift aircraft	6.4
Tanker aircraft	3.4
Total	381.0

Source: Congressional Budget Office, *Baseline Budget Projections for Fiscal Years 1984–1988*, pt. 2 (Government Printing Office, 1983), pp. 100–06.
a. On the average, half the procurement budget each year is allocated to major programs.

size and allocation of the planned resources are adequately related to the dangers that may lie ahead for the United States and its allies. Not surprisingly, the administration claims that they are. Nevertheless, there are still a number of reasons for questioning the claims and considering alternatives to the Reagan plan.

The Basis for Alternatives

The administration has made a great deal of its forthrightness about the costs of its defense programs, and there is no reason to believe that it has deliberately understated those costs. Furthermore, its estimates of prices should be less plagued by increases in inflation than the estimates of its predecessors, and those prices may prove more stable than in the past because of the institution of multiyear contracting. Still, the real increase in the cost of defense goods has probably been underestimated, largely because improvements in the weapons will be introduced during their production, driving up their prices, and because expensive modifications will be needed to make them reliable and effective. This continuing process, which is rarely allowed for in cost estimates, means that the procurement account has probably been underfunded by nearly $28 billion, in current dollars, for the next five years.

But that is not the only possible source of underestimating. The rapid introduction of more sophisticated weapons into service inventories is bound to mean increased maintenance and operating costs if the weapons are to be kept in high states of readiness. The trend is well documented: to date, complex systems incorporating new technologies have suffered more frequent breakdowns and require more spare parts and hours of repair than their predecessors. Yet the evidence is at best slim that the five-year defense plan has allowed sufficiently for this trend in its budgeting of the operating accounts. These accounts are programmed to grow at an average rate of about 5 percent a year in real terms over the next five years, whereas they should probably grow at an average rate of nearly 8 percent if high readiness is to be maintained. To fund the faster rate of growth would require an additional $230 billion over the five-year period. All told, full funding of the procurement and operating accounts could take $258 billion more than the administration has budgeted in its plan.

This is not to say that an unbalanced defense posture is necessarily unacceptable. In fact, if forced to choose, the services would probably be willing to sacrifice increased readiness for new weapons, on the premise that full readiness can be restored in a shorter time than weapons that take so many years to produce. But the administration has given first priority to defense readiness and has pledged itself to a posture that is both modern and fully prepared to fight. If the logic of its case is compelling, it should actually be advocating even higher defense budgets. Defense, after all, is the foundation necessary to the conduct of the rest of the nation's business. Moreover, the country can certainly afford $2 trillion as readily as $1.8 trillion, even though spending on some other programs may have to be forgone. The United States does not have to choose between more defense and less welfare, lower pensions, or poorer medical care. But it does have to choose between more defense and less of something else. However, despite the desirability of and consensus for an increased defense effort, the administration has not persuaded the nation or its representatives that the proposed rate of growth in defense spending, much less a higher rate, is truly justified.

Although this could prove regrettable, it is not surprising, for the Department of Defense has not yet forged a strong link between what it cites as the dangers of the future and the programs it advocates. At the heart of its case for those programs is the general proposition that the Soviet Union has moved ahead of the United States in the arms competition, particularly because of its sustained investment in large numbers of modern weapons. The United States, having failed to meet the competition in the 1970s, thus has a great deal of catching up to do. Furthermore, if the challenge is not met, and met soon, the USSR—already playing an aggressive role in Afghanistan, Poland, Africa, Central America, and Southeast Asia —will be in a position to expand its empire around the world.

As evidence of this emerging danger and in support of its own programs, the administration points to a number of diverging trends that are allegedly unfavorable to the United States. Not only is the Soviet Union estimated to have increased its defense budget an average of about 4 percent a year in real terms for nearly two decades, and to have kept that budget at 12 to 14 percent of its gross national product; it has also managed to invest a large percentage of the total in research and development and defense capital goods. The United States, by contrast, allowed its defense budget to decline in real terms during the 1970s, permitted the totals to slide as a percentage of the gross national product and the federal budget, and failed to undertake a major program of investment in weapons and equipment. These trends are shown in table 3-5.

To emphasize the consequences of such contrasting patterns of behavior, the administration cites the dramatic differences between the United States and the USSR in their inventories of selected weapons and forces. As can be seen from table 3-6, the Soviet Union is now ahead of the United States in almost all of these categories, and has held the lead in most of them for many years. Moreover, because of the investment lag in the United States, most Soviet weapons are considered more modern (and implicitly more effective) than their American counterparts. When allied capabilities are included in these comparisons, the results look somewhat less favor-

Table 3-5. Trends in Outlays for National Defense, Selected Fiscal Years, 1964-84[a]
Billions of dollars unless otherwise specified

Fiscal year	Outlays			Percent of GNP	Federal budget	Percent of federal budget
	Current dollars	1984 prices	GNP			
1964	51.5	199.1	618.2	8.3	118.6	43.4
1966	54.9	196.6	724.1	7.6	134.7	40.8
1968	78.8	261.5	831.3	9.5	178.1	44.2
1970	78.6	232.2	968.8	8.1	195.7	40.2
1972	76.6	196.9	1,128.8	6.8	230.7	33.2
1974	77.8	175.0	1,379.4	5.6	267.9	29.0
1976	89.4	172.1	1,640.1	5.5	364.5	24.5
1978	105.2	174.4	2,091.3	5.0	448.4	23.5
1980	135.9	187.8	2,573.9	5.3	576.7	23.6
1982	187.4	212.6	3,033.0	6.2	728.4	25.7
1984[b]	245.3	245.3	3,488.7	7.0	848.5	28.9

Source: *Budget of the United States Government, Fiscal Year 1984*, pp. 9-53, 9-54.

a. National defense outlays include atomic energy defense activities as well as the military functions of the Defense Department.

b. Estimated.

able to the USSR. But Soviet military superiority is seen as a clear and growing fact of life.

If these comparisons were taken seriously as measuring the relative capabilities of the two powers, the course of action to be followed by the administration would be straightforward. It would seek, at a minimum, to match the USSR in every one of the major weapon categories. As should be evident, however, there is no intention whatsoever of adding hundreds of ICBMs, thousands of interceptors, 160 divisions, or 30,000 tanks to the U.S. defense inventory. The president, in fact, proposes to deploy 100 fewer MX missiles than were programmed by the Carter administration. In sum, as the Defense Department implicitly recognizes, these measures of comparative strength are virtually worthless as a basis for evaluating or designing U.S. forces.

They can also be misleading as indicators of trends. It is certainly true that with the withdrawal of U.S. forces from Southeast Asia, the defense budget declined as a percent of GNP and the federal budget. But both GNP and the federal budget have been growing in real as well as in nominal terms; consequently, the burden of proof for holding its share of them constant must rest with the Defense Department. It is not automatically entitled to such a share.

Claims about what it would cost the U.S. economy to acquire a

Table 3-6. Selected U.S. and Soviet Military Capabilities, 1982

Item	United States	Soviet Union
Military personnel (thousands)	2,117	4,265
ICBM launchers	1,052	1,398
SLBM launchers	520	989
Long-range bombers	316	150
Intermediate- and medium-range ballistic missiles	. . .	606
Medium-range bombers	60	535
Air defense aircraft	258	2,250
Surface-to-air missile launchers	. . .	10,000
Army and Marine Corps divisions	19	180
Tanks	12,130	50,000
Armored fighting vehicles	20,000	62,000
Artillery tubes	5,459	27,200
Multiple rocket launchers	68	4,000
Armed helicopters	1,000	2,300
Oceangoing ships and submarines	467	563
Tactical aircraft	2,534[a]	4,480

Source: International Institute for Strategic Studies, *The Military Balance, 1982–1983* (London: IISS, 1982), pp. 4–10, 13–17.

a. This total does not include aircraft of the Navy, the National Guard, or the Reserve.

defense establishment like that of the Soviet Union, or about adverse trends in the investment "balance," hardly constitute such proof. It may be true that the cumulative Soviet investment during the last decade exceeded that of the United States by more than 50 percent. But such a comparison says little about the ability of the United States to defend its interests. Not only has the USSR been building up its strategic nuclear forces from a very low base and strengthening with more up-to-date weapons the ground and tactical air forces that Khrushchev did so much to eviscerate in the 1950s and early 1960s; it has also felt impelled to invest heavily in forces deployed to its far eastern frontier. When these factors are taken into account and when the allies of the two sides are included in the comparison, the investment trends look different. Furthermore, what tends to be overlooked in these crude comparisons is the differing procurement strategies the two sides follow. While the United States may be slow to invest in a new generation of weapons and equipment, it spends a substantial portion of its annual procurement budget on upgrading the matériel it already has. Thus the public is frequently reminded that the last B-52 bomber came off the production line in 1962. It is not reminded that in the ensuing twenty years more than the original cost of the bomber has been spent on rebuilding it. The issue, therefore, is not its calendar age but whether it can continue to have a high probability of getting through Soviet antibomber defenses.

There are still further problems with using the investment "balance" as a guide to defense planning. If individual Soviet weapons have now risen to a level of effectiveness comparable or even superior to that of their American counterparts, observers are bound to wonder how (largely) U.S.-equipped Israelis achieved such stunning results in Lebanon against Soviet-equipped Syrians during their clashes in 1982. Were the outcomes simply a function of superior Israeli training, planning, and tactics, or did U.S. equipment make a contribution? If it did not, why is the administration so concerned about the transfer of U.S. military technology to the USSR? Surely, if the Russians possess a better military technology and immense superiority in the number of forces that can be brought to bear against the West, the United States should be worried less about the theft of its ideas and products than about the acquisition of Russian technology.

The alleged state of the investment balance is not the only argument advanced for the administration's programs. The Defense Department has also made it clear that, despite the feared weaknesses and vulnerabilities of existing U.S. forces, the defense objectives of the past twenty years must be changed and made more ambitious. In particular, the United States—for purposes of deterrence and regaining the initiative in the military competition with the USSR—must be prepared to fight a protracted nuclear war and, with its conventional forces, engage in the process of horizontal escalation: that is, expand the nonnuclear conflict by attacking the enemy's vulnerable points. Furthermore, the conventional forces must have the stocks of modern munitions and war reserve matériel to conduct an unspecified number of simultaneous nonnuclear operations for an indefinite period.

In principle, these are unexceptionable goals. If the Soviet Union has discovered how to conduct, and gain an exploitable advantage in, a protracted nuclear war, the United States would be ill advised not to take countermeasures. Similarly, if the Soviet Union has vulnerabilities that can be efficiently exploited, there is nothing reprehensible about acquiring the capability to take advantage of them.

But whether these are realistic defense goals for the United States is another matter. A number of demanding conditions would have to be met before it could be said that either the USSR or the United States had obtained the capability to conduct and successfully conclude a protracted nuclear war. Leaders, weapons, and communications would have to be made survivable for more than a few hours or days. Postattack damage assessment and retargeting facilities would have to be available. Major economic and population targets would have to be saved from destruction. Not only would the belligerents have to be able to communicate with one another somehow and with timeliness; they would also have to arrive at an agreement on the course and probable outcome of the conflict. And having reached that understanding, they would have to agree on the terms under which the exchange would come to an end. The process of meeting these conditions in the fog of traditional warfare has proved prolonged and painful despite clear lines of battle, well-defined advances and retreats, a tempo of action involving months and even years, the ability to communicate in detail either directly or through neutral parties, and damage that, while vast, has been gradual in its cumulative effect. To pretend that the technical and other means of satisfying such conditions would exist during the almost-certain chaos of a nuclear war is at best wishful thinking. To invest resources in the attempt to meet one or two of these conditions while the means to satisfy the others are lacking has to be counted as ill advised. It is one thing for the United States to require a certain degree of flexibility in its nuclear plans and forces so as to halt a conflict before the advent of mutual annihilation; it is another matter entirely to pursue an illusory capability for protracted nuclear war.

On the surface the idea of exploiting Soviet vulnerabilities appears considerably more practical and promising. But here, too, certain conditions would have to be met to make practical sense out of the notion. First, the United States and its allies would have to be confident of their ability to protect regions they consider vital. Second, they would have to identify the specific Soviet vulnerabilities that they proposed to exploit. Third, they would have to demonstrate that it would cost the enemy more to protect the particular points of vulnerability than it would the allies to attack them. Fourth, they would need to show that widening the war would have fewer negative effects and prove more efficient than concentrating scarce military resources at the point of attack.

To state these conditions indicates why horizontal escalation may not always be the preferred strategy. Much of the strategic debate during World War II focused on this issue, with Generals George C. Marshall and Dwight D. Eisenhower having to fend off two formidable advocates—Winston Churchill and the U.S. Navy—in order to concentrate allied resources on the invasion of northern Europe. Whether the same arguments that won the case for Overlord in 1944 would hold true in the 1980s cannot be stated with confidence. What does seem unrealistic, however, is to attempt to acquire forces—and naval forces in the bargain—for the purpose of horizontal escalation (particularly to Murmansk or Vladivostok) when the protection of U.S. and allied vital interests is not assured.

Despite all the hand wringing about the great advances in Soviet military technology, current programs are also being justified on the ground that the United States, by the rapid deployment of new and sophisticated hardware, can take the initiative in the continuing and inevitable competition with the Soviet Union and make major portions of the Soviet military inventory obsolete. But Congress may well resist a still greater emphasis on high technology when the current products of that technology are already so costly and prone to breakdowns. And there are bound to be serious reservations about focusing on how to outstrip the Soviet Union in a technological race (with an open invitation to technical gimcrackery, especially in space) when there is still a need to concentrate on the acquisition of the capabilities necessary to deter attacks on U.S. and allied interests.

Another argument is that perceptions of the military balance, whatever their merit, justify the U.S. buildup. No doubt Samuel Johnson was too harsh when he described patriotism as the last refuge of scoundrels. And it would be equally unfair to suggest that perceptions have become the last refuge of planners who can think of no other excuse for their programs. Yet perceptions are no better as a basis for determining the size and composition of U.S. forces than crude comparisons of the investment balance.

This is not to say that perceptions are unimportant. The issue is whether it makes sense to correct mistaken perceptions by an expensive deployment of weapons and forces and, if so, how to determine the scale of the deployment. It is conceivable, for example, that the USSR has more nuclear launchers aimed at targets in Western Europe than NATO deploys against Eastern Europe and the Soviet Union. It is also conceivable that after Western and Eastern Europe had suffered the effects of a nuclear exchange, the USSR could still claim a numerical superiority in surviving launchers. But how meaningful would that superiority be? How could it be exploited to achieve any rational objectives? If Soviet planners have been foolish enough to buy more of these launchers than makes military sense, does that mean that NATO, at great expense, must follow suit? Is it beyond the wit of U.S. policymakers to find cheaper ways to reassure nervous allies and correct their misperceptions about the significance of the regional nuclear "balance of forces"?

Substitutes for the deployment of further weapons are obviously feasible. Presidents and secretaries of defense do not have to subscribe to questionable notions about windows of vulnerability. Nor do they have to respond with expensive military Band-Aids whenever a new misperception arises. Instead, they can set realistic defense objectives, engage in serious assessments of U.S. and allied capabilities, and relate their programs to these assessments in a systematic way. The results of this kind of planning (developed largely within the military community) are likely to be much more persuasive to friends and enemies alike than ill-founded slogans or sudden military lurches designed to correct faulty conceptions of U.S. and allied vulnerabilities.

Defense Objectives

What constitutes realistic defense objectives for the United States and its allies is not often but surely should be the subject of periodic review. Assessments, after all, are bound to change regarding the responsibilities of the United States in the world and the ability of the Soviet Union, along with other potentially hostile powers, to challenge them. Yet the United States continues to shoulder a number of overseas commitments in addition to the basic duty of providing for its own defense. It is frequently argued, in fact, that these commitments substantially exceed the ability of this country to honor them.

Such arguments, however, overlook two realities. The first is that the United States has strong allies that, while they can and should contribute more to their own defense, already play a significant role in the postwar system of collective security. The second is that the

Soviet Union, as the main challenger to that system, not only has a number of policing problems within its empire, but also suffers from serious limits on its ability to operate simultaneously with conventional forces in two or more theaters and to support sustained engagements at any great distance from its home bases.

Similarly, the USSR shows no significant signs of being able, in a nuclear war, either to exercise much selectivity in its attacks under the stress of countermeasures or to control the allocation of its forces for an extended period of time. Nor is there any evidence to suggest that, even if greater flexibility, control, and sustainability were to be built into Soviet strategic capabilities, this could prevent the United States from destroying targets vital to the achievement of Soviet objectives.

For the foreseeable future, then, the critical question for the United States is not whether it must adjust its commitments to suit its military capabilities, or vice versa. The question is what forces would be required to deter if possible, and deal with if necessary, a realistic number of nuclear and conventional contingencies. Another issue is what specific objectives these forces should be prepared to achieve in what period of time.

Strategic Nuclear Forces

For more than twenty years the primary planning objective for the strategic nuclear forces has been the survival of sufficient delivery vehicles and warheads, even after an enemy surprise attack, to be able to destroy a large number of targets in the Soviet Union. These targets now include missile silos, bomber bases, naval facilities, headquarters, ground and tactical air forces, transportation networks, energy supplies, and urban-industrial centers (that is, cities). They add up to thousands of individual aiming points.

A second objective has been to develop the plans and communications necessary to permit the president either to launch the entire surviving force or to withhold attacks on certain classes of targets in the hope of being able to end the exchange before the damage has become apocalyptic. Still a third objective has been to minimize the risk of failure in these second-strike operations by maintaining a triad of offensive forces—ICBMs, SLBMs, and bombers—each having a different mode of surviving an attack and each a somewhat different way of attacking enemy targets.

Less ambitious objectives such as minimum deterrence, which requires only the ability to attack a small number of enemy cities, have been considered and consistently rejected on two grounds. They give the president little or no choice in the event of a nuclear crisis, and they do not provide a credible deterrent to the full range of nuclear contingencies that could arise, including threats to allies. More ambitious objectives such as limiting damage, which requires not only diversified offensive forces, but also a variety of active and passive defenses, have also been examined in some detail and, until recently, abandoned, largely for two reasons. First, the initial cost of such damage-limiting measures would be high and could be quite cheaply negated by enemy countermeasures. And second, active and passive defenses would only exacerbate the strategic nuclear competition by raising fears about strategic stability in a crisis, and make even more difficult the already difficult process of arms control and reduction. After seeking some meaningful form of nuclear superiority in the face of evolving Soviet strategic capabilities and finding the search fruitless, the United States has adopted the role of the counterpuncher and spoiler, with the goal of making certain that the Soviet Union cannot develop any plausible route to exploitable superiority for itself. Despite the rhetoric about protracted nuclear war and achieving a favorable outcome for the United States in such a war, second-strike, countervailing capabilities still seem to be the most reasonable and plausible planning objective for the U.S. strategic nuclear forces.

Theater Nuclear Forces

Exactly what the planning objectives for the so-called theater nuclear forces should be has always been clouded by a delusion of extraordinary proportions: that it would be possible to conduct a tactical nuclear campaign along conventional lines, with armies advancing and retreating and tactical air forces attacking their traditional targets—all in a choreographed fashion—but with the enhanced firepower of nuclear mines, shells, warheads, and bombs. Serious planners, however, have been forced to recognize two facts: that nuclear weapons differ in effects from their conventional counterparts, whatever their similarities in shapes and methods of delivery; and that an exchange of nuclear fire by both sides is likely to produce chaos and destruction in a very short time. Furthermore, because of their high costs and effectiveness in destroying targets, it would be absurd to stockpile nuclear weapons like conventional ordnance. As with the strategic forces, specific targets must be identified and decisions made on how many of the targets are to be attacked and with what probability of success.

Presumably, the purpose of having these capabilities is to halt conventional or nuclear attacks such as might occur in Europe and deny the enemy any hope of conquering the area. The targets that would have to be destroyed to produce this effect would probably consist of enemy nuclear capabilities, troop concentrations, airfields, headquarters, transportation networks, and other facilities necessary to the conduct of an offensive. In a theater such as central Europe, the number of these targets could run to several thousand, even though the probability that all of them could be attacked before confusion and collapse set in is very low.

Whatever the contingency plans, the United States and its allies could not count on mounting the first strike with these weapons. One would therefore expect the capabilities to be designed for second-strike operations. Indeed, it seems only reasonable to insist that, since the theater-based systems have many of the same types of targets as the strategic forces, though more at the tactical level of conflict, they should be deployed and controlled on the same principles rather than sprinkled about and made organic to regular ground and tactical air units.

Nonnuclear Forces

The planning objectives for the U.S. conventional forces are substantially affected by the number of more or less simultaneous contingencies for which they are to be prepared. Thus in the 1960s, when it was felt that the Soviet Union and its clients might be able to launch coordinated attacks in Europe, Korea (or Southeast Asia), and one lesser theater, the U.S. objective was to be able, in conjunction with allies, to conduct a forward defense in these theaters for at least ninety days. During this time mobilization would begin, reserves would be deployed, and further decisions would be taken about objectives and forces. This came to be known as the two-and-a-half-war strategy.

When in the 1970s the split between the Soviet Union and China became public, one of the large contingencies was dropped for planning purposes, leaving a one-and-a-half-war strategy. However, the initial objectives and goals for forces for the other two theaters remained essentially unchanged, except that the forces were to be able to sustain combat for at least as long as their opponents, which was believed to be no more than several weeks. Supporting naval capabilities were to be sufficient to maintain the sea lines of communication in the Atlantic, Mediterranean, and western Pacific, primarily by holding the Soviet fleet based on Murmansk north of the line formed by Greenland, Iceland, and the United Kingdom, and by bottling up the other three Soviet fleets in the Baltic and Black Seas and the Sea of Japan. Despite controversies about the future utility of the Marine Corps, it was also decided to maintain the amphibious capability for slightly more than one division-sized landing operation.

The Reagan administration has been highly critical of this approach to planning for the conventional forces. Supposedly, linking decisions about force structure to a limited number of contingencies is too rigid and defensive and prevents the United States from preparing to gain the initiative against prospective enemies. For all practical purposes, however, objectives for the ground and tactical air forces remain about as they were under previous administrations, with planners focusing primarily on the defense of central Europe and the area of the Persian Gulf. And although the goal for naval forces has been raised to 600 ships, the justification for it is, if possible, even less rigorous than the earlier case for a 500-ship navy.

Once contingency planning became the basis for determining the need for conventional forces, the issue of where forces should be deployed in peacetime and how threatened theaters should be reinforced arose. To gain flexibility and agility, that issue has been resolved by minimizing overseas deployments and relying heavily on a combination of pre-positioned equipment in the most sensitive theaters and airlift to move men and matériel rapidly to wherever they might be needed as reinforcements. To illustrate what is involved, it might be necessary on relatively short notice to deliver 500,000 tons of equipment and supplies to Europe and another 300,000 tons to the area of the Persian Gulf. How many days would be available to deploy these large tonnages would depend critically on the size of the expected attacks and the speed with which they could be organized, and the timeliness with which American policymakers reacted to warning of the preparations. The standard assumption for nearly a decade has been that the Soviet Union could mobilize and deploy with such efficiency that U.S. reinforcements moving by sealift would arrive too late to counter the enemy offensive. Consequently, the demand for wide-bodied aircraft for airlift tends to be very large.

Assessments

It has become increasingly characteristic of arms control negotiations that equality of forces is seen as a primary goal, regardless of whether it offers military stability (or mutual deterrence), and that equality is defined by numbers of delivery vehicles, warheads, men, tanks, and the like. Unfortunately, equality in this sense has also been applied with growing frequency to test the adequacy of U.S. forces outside the context of arms control. By that test, at least in its raw form, not only is the United States bound to be inferior to the Soviet Union in most categories of military capability, as President Reagan has asserted, but it is also difficult to see how, even after the completion of his defense program, U.S. forces will look anything but inferior in the future.

This anomaly suggests, as does common sense, that a much more satisfactory way to determine the adequacy of U.S. forces, and of the programs to improve them, is to estimate the extent to which they are capable of reaching realistic objectives. When that test is applied, U.S. capabilities come much closer to adequacy than is suggested by the current wisdom, and the improvements required to increase their effectiveness tend to be somewhat different from and less demanding than the programs proposed by the administration.

Strategic Nuclear Capabilities

The capabilities of the U.S. strategic nuclear forces make it particularly evident why raw numerical comparisons have little utility for defense planning purposes. As table 3-7 shows, even after a Soviet surprise attack on the U.S. forces in their regular peacetime posture (a day-to-day alert), and even assuming that Soviet ICBMs have high probabilities of destroying U.S. missile silos, the surviving forces should be able to deliver more than 3,300 warheads on targets in the USSR in an all-out retaliatory strike. To give only one example, such a retaliation could cause the destruction of 200 cities and

Table 3-7. U.S. Second-Strike Strategic Nuclear Capability, 1983 and 1988

Launchers	Total warheads	Day-to-day alert		Generated alert	
		Alert warheads	Deliverable warheads	Alert warheads	Deliverable warheads
1983					
Minuteman II	450	405	18	405	18
Minuteman III	1,650	1,485	67	1,485	67
Poseidon	4,960	2,728	2,455	3,968	3,571
Trident	480	288	259	384	346
B-52G	1,208	362	290	966	773
B-52H	720	216	172	576	461
FB-111	240	72	58	192	154
Total	9,708	5,556	3,319	7,976	5,390
1988					
Minuteman II	400	360	16	360	16
Minuteman III	1,800	1,620	73	1,620	73
Poseidon	4,960	2,728	2,455	3,968	3,571
Trident	2,400	1,440	1,296	1,920	1,728
B-52G	2,420	726	581	1,936	1,549
B-52H	720	216	173	576	461
FB-111	240	72	58	192	154
Total	12,940	7,162	4,652	10,572	7,552

Sources: IISS, *The Military Balance, 1982–1983*, pp. 4–5; and author's estimates.

1,500 other targets, including airfields, army bases, naval installa-
tions, transportation centers, and a variety of economic facilities. If
the Soviet attack were to come during a major crisis or a conventional conflict, with U.S. forces fully alerted, the expected number of
weapons delivered in a full-scale retaliation could run to as many as
5,400, and the number of targets destroyed to 200 cities and 3,600
other assets of military and economic value. How many weapons
would actually be launched and against which targets would depend
on the retaliatory option selected by the president. For example, he
could order attacks on selected military targets, hold the countercity
capability in reserve, and attempt to bring the exchange to the
speediest possible end.

The lower half of table 3-7 suggests that, even without the B-1
bomber and the MX missile, the strategic forces of the future should
still be able to cover a wide range of targets in a retaliatory strike. In
part, this is because two legs of the nuclear triad have been undergo-
ing a major modernization with the deployment of the Trident sub-
marine and C-4 missile and with the introduction of 2,400 air-

launched cruise missiles (ALCMs) on at least 120 B-52G bombers, which could be put on a higher alert than is now customary in peacetime, thus ensuring even greater target coverage.

It is difficult to see how Soviet leaders, in the face of this kind of retaliatory power from the two surviving legs of the triad, could expect to profit from an attack. The argument nonetheless can be made that Soviet planners, having put the U.S. ICBM force at risk, will have the resources and the incentives to undermine the survivability of the U.S. SLBMs and bombers unless American planners are allowed to take still further actions. The administration currently sees these actions as, first, deployment of B-1 bombers so as to maintain the ability of the Air Force to penetrate with a manned system Soviet active defenses (supposedly to be upgraded by a look-down shoot-down capability against low-altitude aircraft); second, deployment of 100 MX missiles in a survivable basing mode so as to improve current hard-target kill capabilities and force Soviet planners to look to the survivability and future costs of their own ICBMs; third, deployment of some unknown number of D-5 Trident missiles, also with a hard-target kill capability and the potential for a faster time to such targets than the MX has; fourth, deployment of at least 100 Stealth bombers, also to provide for the manned penetration of still more sophisticated defenses; fifth, development of a ballistic missile defense to assure the survivability of a significant fraction of the MX force in the event that Soviet planners produce even more accurate ICBMs than the SS-18 and SS-19; sixth, development of what promises to be an expensive and unworkable civil defense system (funded in the budget of the Federal Emergency Management Agency) as a counterpart to an equally ineffective Soviet civil defense system; seventh, modernization of the continental air defense system, even though it could be knocked out by early-arriving ballistic missiles; and finally, acquisition of communication networks intended to survive and function throughout a protracted nuclear war, regardless of whether there are any leaders left to use them or any ability to communicate with the enemy.

This is hardly lean cuisine. It is, in fact, about as rich and costly a menu as even the hungriest planner could imagine. What is more, it contains a good deal of fat. To the extent that it seems desirable to continue with a manned penetrating bomber and to put the Soviet ICBM force at risk, a more measured and less redundant program would be in order. This would consist of completing the ALCM deployment and the upgrading of the B-52H bombers, both of which will continue to pose a severe challenge to the Soviet air defense system; canceling the B-1 bomber and the MX missile; proceeding with the development of the D-5 Trident missile as the main hard-target killer of the future while backfitting improved guidance to the C-4 Trident missile; maintaining the investment in the Stealth aircraft as the manned penetrating bomber of the 1990s; reducing the ballistic missile defense program to the level of exploratory development and making civil defense primarily an agency for peacetime disaster relief; canceling the modernization of the continental air defense system; and designing systems that would permit reliable communication with Soviet leaders even after the onset of a nuclear exchange.

The Reagan administration plans to allocate approximately $331.1 billion in total obligational authority to the strategic nuclear forces between fiscal years 1984 and 1988.[1] A more gradual and less redundant approach to the improvement of U.S. countervailing capabilities would reduce that total by $68.9 billion over the same period of time. Table 3-8 indicates what the changes in the Reagan program would be in fiscal 1983 and between 1984 and 1988. Because of these changes, the modified program for the strategic nuclear forces would increase, on the average, at a real rate of 7.1 percent a year, only slightly lower than the 7.9 percent proposed in the Reagan five-year plan but from a lower base in fiscal 1983. Even so, the resulting forces would be able, in a second strike, to deliver substantially more warheads against Soviet targets than the current capability. The Reagan strategic posture would give a somewhat higher performance. But the case has still to be made that the increase would be worth the large additional cost.

Theater Nuclear Capabilities

For some years the theater nuclear capabilities (principally but not exclusively deployed in Europe) have escaped review as policymakers have concentrated on the strategic nuclear and conventional deterrents. However, with the Soviet deployment of the SS-20, an intermediate-range movable missile, and the Backfire bomber, the

---

1. The total of $331.1 billion includes a prorated share of defense support costs.

Table 3-8. Alternative to the Reagan Defense Plan for the Strategic Nuclear Forces, Fiscal Years 1983 and 1984–88

Billions of dollars unless otherwise specified

	Total obligational authority			
Item	1983	1984–88	Annual rate of real growth, 1983–88 (percent)	Outlays, 1984–88
Reagan plan	38.3	331.1	7.9	290.9
Alternative				
Cancel MX missile	1.6	19.1	. . .	15.9
Cancel B-1B bomber	4.8	38.6	. . .	31.9
Reduce ballistic missile defense program	. . .	3.9	. . .	3.5
Cancel continental air defense program	. . .	2.8	. . .	1.9
Reduce command-control-communications program	. . .	1.9	. . .	1.6
Freeze personnel at 1983 levels	. . .	2.6	. . .	2.6
Total reduction	6.4	68.9	. . .	57.4
Modified program	31.9	262.2	7.1	233.5

Sources: CBO, *Baseline Budget Projections for Fiscal Years 1984–1988*, pt. 2, p. 106; Pechman, ed., *Setting National Priorities: The 1983 Budget*, p. 60; and author's estimates.

accepted wisdom is that theater nuclear deterrence has been undermined.

The fact is that these deployments and the Soviet modernization of its shorter-range, nuclear-capable delivery vehicles have not changed what has been and remains a bizarre situation. Without British and French nuclear capabilities (which apparently are of such low utility that they are not to be considered counterweights to any Soviet medium-range systems), the United States and its other allies continue to be able to cover all significant targets in Eastern Europe and the western military districts of the USSR with existing strategic and theater-based delivery vehicles. NATO also has at its disposal enough nuclear warheads to wreak havoc on any attempt at an invasion of Western Europe.

Thus one difficulty in planning the defense of central Europe arises, not from an inequality in theater nuclear weapons, but from a basic contradiction in policy. Whatever their declaratory statements, neither the United States nor its allies have the slightest intention of releasing nuclear weapons for a first strike in Europe or elsewhere, and they would spend days or even weeks debating the decision in the event of a conventional attack. Yet military authorities in NATO plan their deployments and operations on the premise that they will be given the authority for an early first use against such an attack. The upshot of this misunderstanding is doubly unfortunate. Theater-based nuclear capabilities tend to be excessively vulnerable to surprise attack, even to one with conventional ordnance. Admittedly, these capabilities would be dispersed once NATO's alerting system was put into effect. But the process would almost certainly divert personnel and dual-purpose delivery vehicles from their conventional missions at precisely the time when the need for nonnuclear capabilities was greatest.

It may be necessary to deploy Pershing II missiles and ground-launched cruise missiles (GLCMs) to Europe if the negotiations with the Soviet Union on intermediate-range nuclear forces produce no agreement by the end of 1983. It may also be desirable at some point to modernize the nuclear stockpile in Europe with more efficient shells and bombs. But from the standpoint of deterrence and military operations, it is much more important to put existing nuclear weapons and specialized delivery vehicles (such as the Lance and Pershing I missiles) under a separate and specialized command with its own alerting system, move them out of areas where the main conventional forces are deployed, and, where battlefield targets are concerned, provide a capability with the mobility both to disperse in peacetime and to deploy rapidly forward should a release of nuclear weapons eventually be authorized. As an illustration of the kind of mobility that would be desirable for nuclear weapons designated for use against enemy troop concentrations, a fleet of helicopters could be acquired as a substitute for the dual-purpose artillery now burdened with this mission. Such a fleet, consisting of about 220 helicopters, would cost in the neighborhood of $2.2 billion.

The Reagan administration has already programmed $13.7 billion in total obligational authority for the theater nuclear capabilities between fiscal 1984 and 1988. Of this total, more than $5 billion will go for the deployment of the Pershing II and the GLCM in Europe. Another $2.2 billion is allocated to the nuclear land-attack Tomahawk submarine-launched cruise missile, which duplicates the functions of the Pershing II and the GLCM and also creates serious arms control problems. And at least another $200 million is for the production of nuclear artillery projectiles; this excludes the cost of the nuclear cores, which is borne by the Department of Energy.

In a modified program, cancellation of the nuclear Tomahawk and these projectiles would more than cover the costs of the 220 helicopters, the establishment of a separate nuclear command in Europe, and the redeployment of atomic demolition weapons and other excess warheads to the United States. The net effect of such a modified program would be to require about the same obligational authority as the Reagan plan. The average annual increase in the program would amount to 7.3 percent in real terms between fiscal 1983 and 1988.

Ground and Tactical Air Capabilities

When assessments are made of the capability of U.S. and allied ground and tactical air forces to achieve such initial military objectives as the forward defense of a theater, the results tend to be much less discouraging than are suggested by crude comparisons of manpower and weapons. That is because military assessments dealing with results take account of more factors bearing on the outcome of a campaign than rough comparisons can do. The assessments also permit inferences about appropriate programs; the comparisons do not.

What do these assessments show? They indicate that, on the average, U.S. and allied ground and tactical air forces have better than a 50 percent probability of conducting a successful forward defense in any one theater—whether central Europe, South Korea, or on the borders of Iran—provided certain conditions are satisfied. These conditions are: (1) the enemy attacks with the expected number of forces; (2) the United States and its allies respond promptly and efficiently to the warning they would almost certainly receive of preparations for the attack; (3) allies have sufficient stocks of ammunition and other combat consumables to fight for roughly thirty days; (4) the allied commander makes efficient use of his scarce reserves in responding to enemy feints and concentrations; and (5) no other conflict or crisis is pinning down unexpectedly large U.S. forces or virtually monopolizing its long-range airlift and sealift.

These are not, for the most part, unreasonable conditions to anticipate at the present time. Defense planners should also be expected to look at "worst cases"—cases that cannot be excluded because they violate physical laws or basic rules of plausibility. Indeed, much of current planning deals with cases of this kind. But under current conditions it seems much more likely than not that any conflict involving the United States and the Soviet Union would be preceded by a major crisis and a gradual mobilization by both sides as tension rose. And certainly a conflict between the two in any given theater would bring high alerts and rapid preparations in all the other areas of potential contact.

It is quite probable, however, that if the Soviet Union continues to pump additional resources into its conventional forces, it will obtain greater readiness, flexibility, and effectiveness from these forces despite the patent inefficiencies of its economic and political systems. Consequently, planners are bound to face considerable uncertainty about whether the conditions that currently permit modest confidence in the adequacy of the collective security system for conventional defense will continue in the future.

Several ugly possibilities exist. Most calculations about the defense of central Europe assume that the Warsaw Pact countries could attack NATO with a force of around ninety divisions. Many of these units would have had to be filled out with reservists and equipped with older weapons; a third of them would have come from East Germany, Czechoslovakia, and Poland. If they attacked after only two weeks of mobilization and deployment, they might catch NATO less than fully prepared. But they would not themselves be a fully effective force. A more dangerous possibility is that the USSR would sacrifice the uncertain advantages of surprise in favor of a longer period of mobilization and deployment. This would afford Soviet planners the time to bring all units to a higher state of effectiveness and to reinforce the attack with as many as twenty more divisions from the general staff reserve. An attack of this magnitude by fully trained and coordinated units would have a strong probability of stretching even a well-deployed and reinforced allied force too thin.

There is the further danger that the United States and its allies would not respond promptly or adequately to a warning of Soviet preparations for an attack, whether in Europe or elsewhere. Largely because of this, NATO in most cases is thought to be unable to conduct a successful forward defense in central Europe. Of perhaps equal danger is the future possibility that while the United States was preparing to deal with a threat in the Persian Gulf or Korea the Warsaw Pact would strike with its full conventional weight in Europe. Although U.S. planners have tried to design American capabilities with this contingency in mind, there are several reasons for believing that the current posture would fail this kind of extreme test. First, there would be a shortage of the long-range, fast lift needed to conduct two nearly simultaneous reinforcements over intercontinental distances, even with the proposed expansion of airlift. Second, if U.S. forces were to become tied down by a third threat (in Korea, for example) and heavily committed in response to a second (possibly near the Persian Gulf), U.S. reinforcements for the European theater would almost certainly be late and small.

Such future dangers may seem remote. Moreover, they can always be swept under the rug with the more or less comforting thought that the United States could resort to its nuclear weapons in the unlikely event of their occurrence. But while Soviet capabilities have developed more gradually than is generally advertised, it is quite possible that by the late 1980s they will reach a sufficient degree of sophistication, flexibility, and agility to permit adventurous Russian leaders the luxury of stirring up large troubles in several areas relatively close to their borders.

The low probability that the United States would make a first use of nuclear weapons in these circumstances is unlikely to increase with the passage of time. The practical question is thus what kind of conventional insurance could be acquired against the danger of multiple contingencies, and what such insurance might cost during the period of the five-year defense plan.

Essentially three main programs, undertaken by the United States and its allies in collaboration, should suffice to provide the necessary insurance. The first and most critical would concentrate on developing major obstacles (possibly field fortifications) to an attack across the border of West Germany. Not only would this hedge against surprise and delays in NATO's mobilization and deployment; it would also allow NATO military authorities to man their forward defenses somewhat more lightly and thereby increase the reserves available to deal with heavy enemy concentrations. Germans, admittedly, are likely to see fortifications as a barrier to reunification rather than an obstacle to aggression. But a fortified zone has contributed to peace and stability in Korea for thirty years, and it could serve equally well in a divided Europe. Such zones have the further advantage that they are relatively cheap. A substantial belt of obstacles along the border between East and West Germany would probably cost no more than $1.1 billion in 1984 dollars, of which the U.S. share might amount to $400 million.

The second major measure would consist of acquiring modern fast sealift well beyond the eight roll-on–roll-off ships the Navy has purchased from commercial sources. Such a program is desirable for several reasons. If two serious contingencies were to occur simultaneously, the United States would have the task of delivering some 800,000 tons of men and matériel to the threatened theaters. How soon this delivery would have to be made is uncertain. The Defense Department assumes that no more than two weeks would be available for completion of the deployment; consequently, it emphasizes airlift as the prime mover and requests more C-5 aircraft. Even with its modernization programs, however, the USSR is unlikely to be able to organize several simultaneous attacks in less than three months.

Suppose the Soviet offensives are directed at central Europe and the Persian Gulf, and that the United States and its allies spend two months wondering what to do and thirty days responding to the Russian mobilization and deployments. Depending on the allocation, the current airlift force could deliver no more than 200,000 tons to the two theaters during that thirty days. With the addition of the fifty C-5B aircraft proposed by the administration at a cost of $6.4 billion, airlift capability would increase by about 35 percent. But the two theaters would still be short of 530,000 tons after thirty days.

For about the same investment, thirty-two fast sealift ships could be acquired. If seven days out of the thirty are allowed for loading and unloading time, these ships, together with the eight others already available, could deliver 800,000 tons to the two theaters in the remaining twenty-three days. Airlift, it is true, can deliver relatively small amounts of tonnage to a distant theater on short notice, and this no doubt has some deterrent value. But that is hardly an argument for expanding the current airlift force. The same effect can be achieved by forces deployed in Europe and the Arabian Sea and prepositioned equipment in the two theaters—both of which already exist—combined with current airlift. For large-scale reinforcement, the additional thirty-two fast roll-on–roll-off ships are more efficient.

Table 3-9. Estimated Need for U.S. Conventional Forces, Greater-than-Expected Threat

Mission	Divisions	Land-based tactical air squadrons	Aircraft carriers	Amphibious ships	Convoy escorts	Attack submarines
Atlantic sea lanes	...	...	2	...	60	40
Norway	1	...	2	...	...	...
Central Europe	20	90	...	...	...	...
Mediterranean sea lanes	...	...	2	...	...	...
Persian Gulf	9	36	2	60	50	...
Korea	3	15	...	...	...	...
Pacific sea lanes	...	...	2	...	20	40
Alaska, Panama, Cuba	2	6	...	...	...	...
Overhaul and training	...	...	2	5	23	14
Total	35	147	12	65	153	94

Source: Author's estimates based on standard planning factors.

The third program would modernize existing U.S. Reserve ground and tactical air units, increase their training, and provide them with war reserve stocks. The European allies would be expected to make a comparable effort. Table 3-9 estimates the forces that would be needed by the United States, assuming appropriate contributions from allies, in the event of simultaneous contingencies in Europe (involving a greater-than-expected threat), the Persian Gulf area, and Korea.[2]

Such an emergency may seem extreme, even allowing for the expected improvements in Soviet conventional capabilities and the expansion that has taken place in the forces of North Korea. But the costs of hedging against an international breakdown on this scale, immense though it would be, are not excessive. Both the United States and its European allies maintain reserve units that, as currently constituted, would be deployed to combat only after a matter of months. Yet in the case of the United States, $11.6 billion is provided in the 1984 budget for National Guard and Reserve forces, most of it going for the equivalent of about sixteen divisions and fifteen tactical air wings, together with the units required to round out and support active-duty divisions. An additional $28.2 billion, programmed over five years, would give these reserve units the equipment and training needed to make their readiness and effectiveness more nearly comparable to those of the active-duty forces.

2. At the same time, U.S. units would be withheld for duty in Alaska and Panama and for possible troubles with Cuba. These units are counted as part of the requirement.

The addition by the allies of another eight divisions and seven interceptor wings would bring the strength of the collective security system to the seventy-five divisions and seventy-five fighter wings necessary to deal with the most severe conventional emergency that can be plausibly anticipated during the late 1980s.

These three programs seem more likely to give U.S. (and allied) forces the appropriate strength and agility for the future than what has been undertaken and proposed by the administration. This is not to deny that the plans of the Defense Department will improve the performance of existing ground and tactical air forces and even add slightly to their active-duty components. But they will do so at the cost of future block obsolescence and severe limits on the number of units that could be combat-ready and deployed quickly in a worldwide emergency. That seems a poor trade when designing for conventional deterrence, despite all the multiplier effects that are supposed to result from applying high technology to numerically inferior U.S. forces. But at least it is a more defensible approach than attempts to rectify an alleged weapons imbalance between the Soviet Union and the United States.

A less demanding (and less costly) approach to modernization makes four assumptions about the U.S. ground and tactical air forces. The first is that the United States does not need six different aircraft for the performance of two tactical missions. The second is that the combat performance of the ground and tactical air forces is already high relative to their Soviet counterparts, as shown by their much greater cost per unit and by the effectiveness of their weapons in Lebanon. The third is that it makes no sense to program stocks of modern munitions (many of which are still in the experimental stage) for more than forty-five days of intense combat when the allies certainly have and the Warsaw Pact probably has supplies for even fewer days. The fourth is that an expansion of expensive active-duty forces is not necessary to deal with the expected threat in the late 1980s, nor is it the most efficient way to meet the challenge of a greater-than-expected threat.

Thus a modified program for the ground and tactical air forces would entail canceling production of three aircraft—the AV-8B close air support aircraft and the F-14 and F-15 fighters—together with a stretch-out of other plans for modernization, at a five-year saving of $60.7 billion;[3] a reduction in the pace at which modern munitions are acquired, at a further five-year saving of $31.4 billion; and a freeze on military and civilian personnel numbers at 1983 levels, which, even after the restoration of a 4 percent pay increase for military personnel in fiscal 1984, would save another $10.1 billion over five years. To the extent that it seems desirable to hedge against the greater-than-expected threat, the necessary insurance can be added to this modified program by improving the combat readiness and equipment of the National Guard and Reserve, at a five-year increase in obligational authority of $28.2 billion, and by substituting fast sealift for the planned increment of C-5 aircraft, at equal cost.

The Reagan administration plans to commit approximately $805.1 billion to the ground, tactical air, and mobility forces between fiscal 1984 and 1988. The modified program would reduce that total by $108.6 billion, and the modified program with insurance would decrease it by $74 billion. These changes are shown in table 3-10. For the Reagan plan, the average annual real increase in costs would amount to 7.1 percent. The modified program would reduce that rate of growth to 3.8 percent, and the modified program with insurance to 4.9 percent.

Naval Capabilities

That leaves the issue of whether, as its proponents might put it, the U.S. Navy is losing its edge of superiority to the Soviet Union. More relevant is whether it is still capable of performing its essential wartime missions. In this connection the stress is on wartime missions, although it is frequently argued that peacetime activities such as maintaining a naval presence overseas, or showing the flag, are what should determine the size and composition of the fleet. The difficulty with this argument, however, is that the demands of showing the flag give no real clues to how many carriers, destroyers, amphibious ships, or submarines (which are not supposed to show anything) should be included in the force. Furthermore, if wartime missions can be successfully completed, the result is likely to be a fleet that has all the capability necessary to maintain a peacetime presence overseas. By contrast, design based on peacetime criteria,

3. Of these savings, $8 billion results from outright cancellation of the binary chemical program.

Table 3-10. Alternatives to the Reagan Defense Plan for the Land, Tactical Air, and Mobility Forces, Fiscal Years 1983 and 1984–88

Billions of dollars unless otherwise specified

	Total obligational authority			
Item	1983	1984–88	Annual rate of real growth, 1983–88 (percent)	Outlays, 1984–88
Reagan plan	108.4	805.1	7.1	707.4
Alternative				
Land forces				
Reduce M-1 tank program	...	5.0	...	3.2
Reduce M-2 armored fighting vehicle program	...	2.2	...	1.3
Reduce AH-64 attack helicopter program	...	7.2	...	4.7
Reduce Patriot air defense program	...	2.9	...	2.2
Reduce truck program	...	2.2	...	2.2
Cancel binary chemical munitions program	...	8.0	...	4.7
Tactical air forces				
Cancel F-14 aircraft program	...	8.2	...	5.5
Cancel F-15 fighter program	...	18.0	...	10.7
Cancel AV-8B close air support aircraft	1.0	7.0	...	5.9
Mobility forces				
Cancel C-5B airlift aircraft	...	6.4	...	4.2
Munitions				
Reduce modern munitions program	...	31.4	...	21.7
Pay				
Freeze personnel at 1983 levels	...	10.1	...	10.1
Total reduction	1.0	108.6	...	76.4
Modified program	107.4	696.5	3.8	631.0
Increases				
Add 32 fast sealift ships	...	6.4	...	1.9
Modernize 16 reserve divisions	...	14.1	...	8.8
Modernize 51 reserve fighter squadrons	...	14.1	...	9.2
Total increase	...	34.6	...	19.9
Modified program with insurance	107.4	731.1	4.9	650.9

Sources: CBO, *Baseline Budget Projections for Fiscal Years 1984–1988*, pt. 2, p. 106; Pechman, ed., *Setting National Priorities: The 1983 Budget*, p. 60; and author's estimates.

assuming it can be done at all systematically, does not ensure that the fleet will be adequate by wartime standards.

There are a number of different rules by which to count naval vessels and compare general-purpose fleets. At the present time, as table 3-11 indicates, the U.S. Navy (excluding ballistic missile sub-

Table 3-11. Deployable Naval Battle Forces, End of Fiscal Years 1980–83

Type of ship	1980	1981	1982	1983
Aircraft carriers	13	12	13	13
Battleships	. . .	. . .	. . .	1
Cruisers and destroyers	106	110	112	97
Frigates	72	78	86	95
Nuclear attack submarines	76	82	91	91
Diesel attack submarines	5	5	5	5
Amphibious warfare ships	66	65	65	60
Patrol combatants	3	1	4	6
Mine warfare ships	3	3	3	3
Mobile logistic ships	68	72	72	73
Combat support ships	26	22	23	22
Total[a]	438	450	474	466
Additional naval reserve and fleet auxiliary ships	58	56	56	56
Total[b]	496	506	530	522

Sources: *Department of Defense Annual Report, Fiscal Year 1981*, p. 170; *Fiscal Year 1982*, p. 154; and *Fiscal Year 1984*, p. 140.

a. Current counting rules.

b. Old counting rules.

marines and their tenders) consists of either 474 or 530 ships, depending on how many fleet auxiliary and naval reserve vessels are included. Not counted in these totals are the 333 land-based patrol aircraft of the Navy, the older bombers of the Air Force that can be used for long-range surveillance, mining, and attacks on enemy surface combatants, and the mine-laying capability of the Navy; or, of course, substantial allied fleets, consisting of more than 220 ocean-going surface combatants and attack submarines. Nor is it customary in discussing the so-called naval balance to include the great geographical advantages that U.S. and allied navies have over the four Russian fleets.

Because of these advantages, the allies could with existing naval forces institute long-range blockades of all the Soviet fleets with attack submarines, mines, and patrol aircraft. Such blockades would make it extremely difficult for enemy surface combatants and submarines to sustain operations south of the Norwegian Sea or outside the Seas of Japan and Okhotsk. Long-range allied aircraft could fly over these waters, and attack submarines—at a minimum —could go hunting in them. If necessary, six U.S. attack carriers could be deployed, along with land-based interceptors, to defend against Soviet long-range bombers, leaving three more (out of a total of twelve) for the support of amphibious operations in an area such as the Persian Gulf. At the same time current allied destroyers and frigates could supply protection for at least eight large convoys a month, with perhaps six in the Atlantic and two in the Pacific.

If the Soviet naval forces chose to leave the relative security of their home waters and attack these deployments, they could undoubtedly inflict serious damage on allied convoys and perhaps on allied capital ships, primarily with their submarines. But they would pay a terrible price for these excursions: in all probability the decimation of their surface combatants and attack submarines, and the subsequent vulnerability of their home waters to allied offensive operations.

Whether the outcome of such a campaign could be characterized as reflecting U.S. and allied naval superiority over the Soviet Union is not particularly important. Of much greater importance would be the high probability of keeping open the main sea lines of communication, the primary naval objective. Moreover, even though losses of supplies for the land-based fighting forces could be severe, the combination of stocks pre-positioned in overseas theaters and the surviving cargoes should suffice to keep these forces operating. The larger fleet sought by the administration would not significantly increase the probability that the U.S. Navy could successfully take the offensive against the main Soviet fleets in their home waters at the outset of a war. But it would undoubtedly give the Navy a slightly higher probability of keeping allied shipping losses at a tolerable level.

That this higher probability is worth the very large incremental cost of roughly thirty-three more ships and submarines is questionable, especially since the Navy—already beset by manning problems with the current fleet—would have to find another 80,000 people for the additional capacity. The Reagan administration nonetheless proposes to commit $395.6 billion to the U.S. general-purpose naval forces (exclusive of their tactical aviation) between fiscal 1984 and 1988. The modified program, by contrast, would eliminate from the planned shipbuilding and conversion budget at least three new nuclear-powered attack carriers (two of them already authorized in fiscal 1983), two battleships, nine Aegis air defense cruisers, nine new and very costly guided missile destroyers (the DDG-51 class), and eleven nuclear-powered attack submarines. Total savings in obligational authority, as shown in table 3-12, would amount to $45.6 billion during the five-year period, including

Table 3-12. An Alternative to the Reagan Defense Plan for the General-Purpose Naval Forces, Fiscal Years 1983 and 1984–88

Billions of dollars unless otherwise specified

	Total obligational authority			
Item	1983	1984–88	Annual rate of real growth, 1983–88 (percent)	Outlays, 1984–88
Reagan plan	53.0	395.6	7.2	347.6
Alternative				
Cancel 3 new attack carriers	7.2	5.4	...	6.3
Cancel 9 new Aegis air defense cruisers	...	12.6	...	5.0
Cancel 11 new nuclear attack submarines	...	8.8	...	2.9
Cancel 2 battleships	...	1.2	...	0.5
Cancel 9 new guided missile destroyers	...	12.6	...	1.9
Freeze personnel at 1983 levels	...	5.0	...	5.0
Total reduction	7.2	45.6	...	21.6
Modified program	45.8	350.0	6.4	326.0

Sources: CBO, *Baseline Budget Projections for Fiscal Years 1984–1988*, pt. 2, p. 106; Pechman, ed., *Setting National Priorities: The 1983 Budget*, p. 60; and author's estimates.

$5 billion in military pay. Real growth in the Reagan plan is estimated at an average annual rate of 7.2 percent, whereas the modified program grows in real terms at an average annual rate of 6.4 percent from a lower base in fiscal 1983.

The modified program would hold the fleet at 474 general-purpose ships (by current counting rules), including 12 attack carriers available for deployment. Before that total is increased with additional carrier battle groups and battleships in surface action groups, the Navy should be required to justify its requests more plausibly than by a simple listing of current treaty commitments, the demands of a peacetime presence overseas, the overall size of the Soviet navy (including riverine craft and destroyers in the Caspian Sea), or the requirements of war plans largely designed by naval planners in search of a rationale for building more ships.

The Nonnuclear Budget

Summarized in table 3-13 are the Reagan plan for the conventional general-purpose forces from fiscal 1983 to 1988, the modified program for the same period, and the modified program with insurance. Adoption of the modified program for the conventional forces would result in a saving of $154.2 billion in total obligational au-

Table 3-13. Alternatives to the Reagan Defense Plan for the Conventional Forces, Fiscal Years 1983 and 1984–88

Billions of dollars unless otherwise specified

	Total obligational authority			
Item	1983	1984–88	Annual rate of real growth, 1983–88 (percent)	Outlays, 1984–88
Reagan plan	161.4	1,200.7	7.1	1,055.0
Possible reductions	8.2	154.2	. . .	98.0
Modified program	153.2	1,046.5	4.6	957.0
Possible additions	. . .	34.6	. . .	19.9
Modified program with insurance	153.2	1,081.1	5.4	976.9

Sources: Tables 3-10 and 3-12; and author's estimates.

thority during the period of the five-year plan. The modified program with insurance would naturally save a lesser amount—$119.6 billion—between fiscal 1984 and 1988.

The Reagan plan for the conventional forces has built into it an average annual growth rate of 7.1 percent, measured in real terms. The modified program grows at a rate of only 4.6 percent, and the modified program with insurance at a rate of 5.4 percent.

Five-Year Options

When general principles such as the need to rearm America become entangled with other priorities and the political process, rationality and coherence are likely to be the losers. Winston Churchill, recalling a debate about the battleship program that took place in the British cabinet before World War I, wrote: "In the end a curious and characteristic solution was reached. The Admiralty had demanded six ships: the economists offered four: and we finally compromised on eight."

Whatever the compromises of the future, three more or less plausible models on which to base the five-year defense plan can be constructed. The first is reflected in the underfunded Reagan program. It rests primarily on the assumption that during the past decade the Soviet Union has outstripped the United States in the acquisition of modern weapons and is thus developing the capability for across-the-board military superiority, if not now, in the relatively near future. The appropriate response of the United States to this is to invest heavily in the modernization of existing U.S. capabilities, nuclear and nonnuclear, to increase research and development for the next generation of weapons, and eventually to begin the expansion of its forces. By the late 1980s this strategy will provide higher performance per unit of capability rather than any major growth in the number of somewhat less effective but combat-ready units. As summarized in table 3-14, it will also provide a five-year budget plan that commits essentially half of the programmed resources to the three main investment accounts: procurement; research, development, test, and evaluation; and military construction.

The second model, which leads to a more gradual and less redundant modernization of existing forces, makes two assumptions, one about the past and the other about the future. The first is that the Soviet investment effort, while perhaps larger than that of the United States during the past decade (though not during the last twenty-five years), has not produced any exploitable Russian superiority in those areas of the world where East and West might come into conflict. The second assumption is that the ability and willingness of the Soviet Union and its clients to engage simultaneously in a number of overt conflicts will continue to be severely limited. In these circumstances, the resumption of normal peacetime modernization on the part of the United States and its allies will prevent the development of any such superiority in the future. Specifically, the appropriate strategy for the United States is to press its allies for larger defense efforts, to increase the readiness of existing forces, and to concentrate its investments on the gradual and selective upgrading of existing forces as losses of equipment occur from peacetime attrition and as older weapons come due for retirement. In effect, the existing posture would be maintained, but its performance would be improved at a pace deemed commensurate with future increases in Soviet effectiveness. The five-year budget plan for this modified program is shown in the middle section of table 3-14. The allocation between investment and operating accounts reflects both a lesser emphasis on weapons modernization than the Reagan plan and a greater effort to keep the operating accounts in balance with the pace of modernization.

The third model, which requires an expansion of the conventional forces along with gradual and selective modernization, acknowledges greater uncertainty about the future. It is still assumed that,

William W. Kaufmann

Table 3-14. The Reagan Defense Plan and the Two Alternative Plans, Fiscal Years 1983–88
Billions of dollars

Item	1983	1984	1985	1986	1987	1988	1984–88
THE REAGAN DEFENSE PLAN							
Total obligational authority	**240.5**	**274.1**	**322.4**	**357.2**	**389.2**	**425.2**	**1,768.1**
Investment	110.0	132.6	163.5	183.0	199.5	221.3	899.9
Procurement	81.2	94.9	120.4	137.1	150.4	170.3	673.1
Research, development, test, and evaluation	22.8	29.6	32.2	34.1	37.2	39.9	173.0
Military construction	4.5	5.8	9.9	10.3	10.7	11.1	47.8
Revolving and management funds	1.5	2.3	1.0	1.5	1.2	. . .	6.0
Operating and support	114.3	124.7	141.5	155.7	170.4	183.7	776.0
Military personnel	45.5	47.9	54.2	58.1	61.8	65.4	287.4
Operation and maintenance	66.3	74.0	83.8	93.7	104.3	113.5	469.3
Family housing and homeowners' assistance	2.5	2.8	3.5	3.9	4.3	4.8	19.3
Retired military pay	16.2	16.8	17.4	18.5	19.3	20.2	92.2
Outlays	**208.9**	**238.6**	**277.5**	**314.9**	**345.6**	**377.0**	**1,553.6**
THE MODIFIED DEFENSE PROGRAM							
Total obligational authority	**225.9**	**245.5**	**282.9**	**311.7**	**337.4**	**367.5**	**1,545.0**
Investment	95.4	103.3	127.0	141.7	152.9	169.6	694.5
Procurement	66.6	66.0	84.3	96.2	104.2	119.0	469.7
Research, development, test, and evaluation	22.8	29.6	32.2	34.1	37.2	39.9	173.0
Military construction	4.5	5.4	9.5	9.9	10.3	10.7	45.8
Revolving and management funds	1.5	2.3	1.0	1.5	1.2	. . .	6.0
Operating and support	114.3	125.4	138.5	151.5	165.2	177.7	758.3
Military personnel	45.5	48.6	51.2	53.9	56.6	59.4	269.7
Operation and maintenance	66.3	74.0	83.8	93.7	104.3	113.5	469.3
Family housing and homeowners' assistance	2.5	2.8	3.5	3.9	4.3	4.8	19.3
Retired military pay	16.2	16.8	17.4	18.5	19.3	20.2	92.2
Outlays	**207.9**	**231.8**	**254.0**	**279.5**	**302.9**	**330.0**	**1,398.2**
THE MODIFIED DEFENSE PROGRAM WITH INSURANCE							
Total obligational authority	**225.9**	**251.1**	**288.9**	**318.5**	**345.0**	**376.1**	**1,579.6**
Investment	95.4	108.9	133.0	148.5	160.5	178.2	729.1
Procurement	66.6	71.6	90.3	103.0	111.8	127.6	504.3
Research, development, test, and evaluation	22.8	29.6	32.2	34.1	37.2	39.9	173.0
Military construction	4.5	5.4	9.5	9.9	10.3	10.7	45.8
Revolving and management funds	1.5	2.3	1.0	1.5	1.2	. . .	6.0
Operating and support	114.3	125.4	138.5	151.5	165.2	177.7	758.3
Military personnel	45.5	48.6	51.2	53.9	56.6	59.4	269.7
Operation and maintenance	66.3	74.0	83.8	93.7	104.3	113.5	469.3
Family housing and homeowners' assistance	2.5	2.8	3.5	3.9	4.3	4.8	19.3
Retired military pay	16.2	16.8	17.4	18.5	19.3	20.2	92.2
Outlays	**207.9**	**232.2**	**256.5**	**284.1**	**308.6**	**336.7**	**1,418.1**

Sources: *Department of Defense Annual Report, Fiscal Year 1984*, p. 319; *Budget of the United States Government, Fiscal Year 1984*, p. 5-8; tables 3-8 and 3-13; and author's estimates.

despite the alleged differences in investment during the past decade, U.S. weapons and technology remain substantially superior to those of the Soviet Union, and that there is therefore no need to commit resources to the process of catching up with the USSR, however "catching up" may be measured. But in this more cautious view the possibility cannot be precluded that a greater-than-expected threat could materialize in Europe, especially in the wake of an extended crisis between the Warsaw Pact and NATO (over Berlin, Poland, a collapse of communist authority in East Germany), and that hostile forces could deploy opposite Iran and South Korea at about the same time. Accordingly, in addition to the program of modernization called for by the modified program, insurance is provided in the form of more modern and combat-ready reserve units and fast sealift to deploy forces from the United States to the threatened areas. The upshot is that, while the total inventory of active-duty and reserve forces does not change, sixteen divisions and fifteen fighter wings with modern equipment are added to the units ready for early deployment. The five-year budget plan for this modified program with insurance is shown in the bottom section of table 3-14.

All three of the programs contain virtually the same amounts of resources for the operating and support accounts, but these accounts are in better balance with the investment accounts in the last two programs than in the Reagan plan.[4] The Reagan plan would have to be increased by about $230 billion to give it a comparable balance.

By 1988 all three of the forces will have the second-strike strategic nuclear capability to deliver at least 4,600 weapons on targets in the Soviet Union. All three will also acquire an increased hard-target kill capability whether or not the MX missile is deployed. However, only the modified program with insurance will give a high probability of a successful initial defense against more than one major conventional contingency. Yet as can be seen from the comparisons of total obligational authority and outlays estimated in table 3-15, the modified program with insurance, with its slower pace of investment, costs less than the Reagan plan. Moreover, both it and the modified program, without sacrificing essential capabilities, could ease the fiscal problems of the future. The expenditures required by the Reagan plan will increase at an average annual rate of 7.3 percent in real terms between fiscal years 1983 and 1988. By contrast, the outlays resulting from the modified program would rise by only 4.5 percent a year, or by 4.9 percent if the insurance measures were added to it. By fiscal 1986 the modified program would

4. The operating and support accounts comprise military pay, operation and maintenance, and family housing.

Table 3-15. Comparison of Defense Plan Alternatives, Fiscal Years 1983–88

Billions of dollars

Item	1983	1984	1985	1986	1987	1988	1984–88
Total obligational authority							
Reagan plan	240.5	274.1	322.4	357.2	389.2	425.2	1,768.1
Modified program	225.9	245.5	282.9	311.7	337.4	367.5	1,545.0
Reduction from Reagan plan	14.6	28.6	39.5	45.5	51.8	57.7	223.1
Modified program with insurance	225.9	251.1	288.9	318.5	345.0	376.1	1,579.6
Reduction from Reagan plan	14.6	23.0	33.5	38.7	44.2	49.1	188.5
Outlays							
Reagan plan	208.9	238.6	277.5	314.9	345.6	377.0	1,553.6
Modified program	207.9	231.8	254.0	279.5	302.9	330.0	1,398.2
Reduction from Reagan plan	1.0	6.8	23.5	35.4	42.7	47.0	155.4
Modified program with insurance	207.9	232.2	256.5	284.1	308.6	336.7	1,418.1
Reduction from Reagan plan	1.0	6.4	21.0	30.8	37.0	40.3	135.5

Source: Table 3-14.

spend $35.4 billion less than the Reagan plan; by fiscal 1988 the saving would rise to $47 billion. Even the modified program with insurance would reduce outlays by $30.8 billion in 1986 and by $40.3 billion in 1988. Over the coming five years, total savings in outlays could amount to as much as $155.4 billion or as little as $135.5 billion if one of these alternatives to the Reagan plan should be chosen.

No doubt as the debate over the 1984 defense budget continues, those supporting the Reagan program to rearm America will argue that any further reductions in the five-year defense plan beyond the $55 billion already proposed by the administration will result in disaster. Allusions to the 1930s, appeasement, and Pearl Harbor will proliferate.

It remains to be seen whether such allusions will suffice to justify nearly $1.8 trillion for defense. For those who doubt their relevance, it may help to recall one of the more celebrated remarks of the Duke of Wellington. At the height of the duke's renown, a man named Jones was frequently mistaken for him. On one occasion a stranger approached the duke and said, "Good morning, Mr. Jones." The duke fixed him with a stare and replied, "Sir, if you believe that, you'll believe anything."

Under present conditions it is not enough to assert that there is a window of vulnerability or an investment imbalance and that America must be rearmed. Specific threats, objectives, and programs still must be related and justified, especially when $1.8 trillion is at stake. Without those steps, a certain doubt about the need for a program of this magnitude is bound to linger.

CHAPTER FOUR

Social Security

ALICIA H. MUNNELL

PROPOSED changes in the retirement and disability portion of the social security program, based on the recommendations of the bipartisan National Commission on Social Security Reform, were the centerpiece of President Reagan's 1984 budget. Immediate revenues are needed because the combined retirement and disability programs face a shortfall of about 6 to 11 percent of outlays in the next seven years. To cover these short-run deficits, the commission proposed tax increases, benefit reductions, and extension of coverage that will produce $165 billion between now and 1990. Because some of this money will come either directly or indirectly from general revenues, the effect of the social security proposals on the unified budget will be somewhat smaller, about $122 billion for 1983 through 1989. Thus, although the proposals greatly help to build trust fund reserves and to restore confidence in the social security program, they provide only a small fraction of funds required to eliminate the large deficits in the unified budget projected for the remainder of the decade.

The decision to tackle the social security short-run financing problems also heightened interest in dealing with the long-run deficits that will arise after the turn of the century as the baby boom generation begins to retire. Although the recommendations of the

THE AUTHOR is grateful to Henry J. Aaron and Robert M. Ball for numerous comments and suggestions. Kristine M. Keefe provided research assistance; Anna M. Estle and Kirk W. Kimmell, secretarial help.

Table 4-1. Benefits, Beneficiaries, and Assets of the Old-Age and Survivors Insurance, Disability Insurance, and Hospital Insurance Programs, Selected Calendar Years, 1950–83

	Benefits (billions of dollars)				Beneficiaries (millions)				Total assets (billions of dollars)
Year	OASI	DI	HI	Total	OASI	DI	Total	HI[a]	
1950	1.0	...	...	1.0	2.9	...	2.9	...	13.7
1960	10.7	0.6	...	11.3	13.7	0.5	14.2	...	22.6
1970	28.8	3.1	5.1	37.0	22.6	2.6	25.2	20.4	41.3
1980	105.1	15.4	25.1	145.6	30.4	4.7	35.1	27.6	40.1
1983	154.5	18.0	40.7	213.2	31.9	4.0	35.9	29.1	21.8

Sources: Department of Health and Human Services, Social Security Administration, *1982 Annual Report of the Board of Trustees of the Federal Old-Age and Survivors Insurance and Disability Insurance Trust Funds* (Government Printing Office, 1982), pp. 51, 54, 63, 65, 84 (hereafter *1982 Trustees' Report*); SSA, *1982 Annual Report of the Board of Trustees of the Federal Hospital Insurance Trust Fund* (GPO, 1982), p. 29; and SSA, *Social Security Bulletin, Annual Statistical Supplement, 1981* (GPO, 1981), pp. 79–82. The Social Security Administration, Office of the Actuary and Division of Medicare Cost Analysis, provided some additional unpublished data.

a. Includes both aged and disabled beneficiaries. Since July 1, 1973, hospital insurance protection has been extended to persons entitled to monthly benefit payments under social security because of disability.

commission eliminate about two-thirds of the long-run deficit, some further changes were needed to put the social security system in long-run actuarial balance. While the members of the commission could not agree on the best way to eliminate the remaining long-run deficit, both Republican and Democratic appointees supported the proposition that over the next seventy-five years the deficit should be eliminated, and each side made a specific proposal to accomplish this goal. These additional changes are not part of the budget proposals but have been included by Congress in its 1983 social security legislation.

This chapter summarizes the outlook for social security financing and explores the options that have been considered for eliminating both the short- and long-term deficit in social security spending.

Financing Social Security

The social security system consists of three programs financed through separate trust funds. The old-age and survivors insurance program (OASI), which pays benefits to retired workers, their dependents, and survivors, is the largest program and will dispense about $155 billion in benefits to almost thirty-two million beneficiaries in 1983 (table 4-1). The disability insurance program (DI), which awards benefits to disabled workers and their dependents, will pay $18 billion to about four million beneficiaries in 1983. The third program, hospital insurance (HI) or medicare, pays benefits to workers covered by both OASI and DI programs and to beneficiaries under the railroad retirement program. Benefit payments from this last fund will amount to almost $41 billion in 1983.

The social security system is financed on a pay-as-you-go basis. The 115 million active workers pay taxes to finance the benefits of the 36 million retired and disabled workers and their dependents and survivors, rather than to build a large reserve from which their own benefits will be paid. In 1983 the payroll tax rate for retirement, survivors, and disability insurance is 5.4 percent each for the employee and employer on the first $35,700 of wage earnings; the ceiling rises automatically with the wage level. Taxes for hospital insurance are 1.3 percent, which raises the overall payroll tax rate to 6.7 percent each for the employee and employer. Self-employed persons pay 9.35 percent of their earnings.

Because social security benefits are paid from the current flow of payroll taxes, the trust funds are designed only to provide a buffer against brief unanticipated economic fluctuations. The funds since 1970 have held substantially less than one year's benefits. But the small amount of reserves should not be a source of concern in a social insurance program. Private pension plans, on the other hand, must have sufficient assets to meet all previous and current commitments because such plans cannot be certain of receiving future premiums. The social security system, as a mandatory and permanent program, can rely on the taxing power of the government to meet its obligations and can levy taxes on successive generations of workers to pay for retirement, disability, and hospital benefits. In effect, the system as it has evolved is a compact between generations, with each generation depending on the next to finance a reasonable amount of benefits. However, pay-as-you-go financing can lead to short-run problems if economic fluctuations adversely affect receipts or outlays. Long-run financing problems can also arise if the size of the beneficiary population increases relative to the working population. The social security system has faced both these difficulties.

The trustees of the social security system each year are required under the Social Security Act to report on the condition of and prospects for the OASI, DI, and HI funds, both in the near and distant future.[1] In the case of the OASI and DI funds, costs—mea-

1. Department of Health and Human Services, Social Security Administration, *1983*

sured as a percentage of covered payrolls—are compared with the scheduled contribution rates for the employer and employee for the next seventy-five years. Because of the great uncertainty about the nature of medical care in the distant future, however, the trustees have traditionally made cost estimates for HI for only twenty-five years. The projections for all three funds are based on four alternative sets of economic and demographic assumptions: an optimistic (I), two intermediate (II-A and II-B), and a pessimistic (III) set. The more pessimistic of the intermediate sets (II-B) is the projection preferred by the social security trustees as the basis for setting contribution rates and for long-range planning, and is the intermediate set referred to throughout this chapter.

The easiest way to understand the financing of the retirement and disability portions of social security (OASDI) is to divide the future into three separate periods—1983–89, 1990–2014, and 2015–60. In the first period, under the trustees' most pessimistic economic assumptions, the OASDI portion of the system is projected to have a substantial deficit. Slow economic growth and high unemployment could result in a deficit as high as $198 billion for 1983–89. If the economy recovers moderately, with unemployment dropping gradually to 7.5 percent by 1989 and productivity growth returning gradually to 1.1 percent a year, the shortfall is projected to be $117 billion. In any event, if the borrowing among the OASI, DI, and HI funds that Congress authorized had been allowed to expire in July 1983, the OASI trust fund, the largest of the social security trust funds, would have been unable to pay all benefits on time.[2] Even with the extension of interfund borrowing, all three funds—OASI, DI, and HI—may well be exhausted by mid-1984.

In marked contrast to 1983–89, the outlook for OASDI financing is favorable in 1990–2014. The primary reason is demographic. The low fertility rates of the late 1920s and 1930s are expected to reduce

---

Annual Report of the Board of Trustees of the Federal Old-Age and Survivors Insurance and Disability Insurance Trust Funds (Government Printing Office, 1983).

2. Although the economy has continued to weaken since the trustees first sounded the initial alarm in their annual report for 1980, two legislative changes have extended until July 1983 the date on which the OASI program will be able to pay benefits on a timely basis. The Omnibus Reconciliation Act of 1981, which was signed into law on August 13, 1981, reduced benefits by about 2 percent by eliminating benefits to students, limiting benefits to families of disabled workers, and lowering the cost of medicare. Amendments to the act, passed on December 29, 1981, authorized borrowing among the OASI, DI, and HI trust funds until January 1983. A provision that permits borrowing for deficits up to six months in advance will ensure sufficient revenues to carry the OASI fund through July 1983.

the rate of increase in the population over age sixty-five during the 1990s. Although the average annual increase in the number of persons over sixty-five will be about 600,000 during the 1980s, the net increase will drop to about 400,000 a year between 1990 and 2010 under the trustees' intermediate assumptions, despite a projected improvement in the mortality rate. At the same time, the baby boom generation born after World War II will continue to swell the labor force. As a result, the ratio of workers to beneficiaries, which has declined continually since 1940, is estimated to remain stable for the next twenty to thirty years at its current level of about three to one. With this stable ratio, productivity gains can reduce the cost of social security as a percent of payrolls. If historical levels of productivity growth return so that wages rise by 1.5 percent more than prices, as assumed under the intermediate economic assumptions, revenues will exceed outlays for the entire period and the trust funds will accumulate surpluses reaching 161 percent of the annual outlays by 2013. On the other hand, with a weaker economy and real wage growth of 1.0 percent a year, as under the pessimistic assumptions, outlays will slightly exceed revenues—an average of 12.9 percent versus 12.4 percent of taxable payrolls—and the system will remain in deficit.

During the third period, 2015–60, costs will rise rapidly as the baby boom generation starts to retire. At the same time, the growth in the labor force will slow, reflecting the decline in the fertility rate that began in the mid-1960s. Under the trustees' intermediate assumptions mentioned above, these two factors will cause the ratio of workers to beneficiaries to decline from three to one to a ratio of two to one. With a pay-as-you-go system, the decline in this ratio increases costs as a percentage of payrolls. Despite the increasing gap between costs and revenues, however, the large accumulated trust funds are sufficient under the intermediate assumptions to finance OASDI through 2024.

Future health care costs are exceedingly difficult to forecast. There is no question, however, that outlays for the HI program will greatly exceed income in the next twenty-five years. The factors that led to the projected increases in the HI program differ in character from the economic and demographic factors contributing to the increase in OASDI outlays for cash benefits. The problem arises mainly from the accelerating cost of hospital care, which is causing the price of both private and public hospital insurance to skyrocket. Restoring long-run balance will require more than modest tax increases and benefit reductions. Rather, solving the financial problems of the HI program will undoubtedly involve fundamental reform in the way the United States provides medical care. For this reason the National Commission on Social Security Reform and previous commissions have focused their attention on the OASDI portion of the social security system. It is important, however, to consider the financial status of the HI program in evaluating alternative proposals for the short run, such as an extension of interfund borrowing, and proposals for the long run, such as an increase in the payroll tax contribution rate.

Short-Run Financing Problems and Options, 1983–89

The immediacy of the projected shortfall in the combined OASDI trust funds has caused many observers to characterize the short-run problems as catastrophic, and the press constantly refers to the impending "bankruptcy" of the system. In fact, the magnitude of the deficits forecasted for the next seven years is relatively manageable —as mentioned in the beginning of this chapter, roughly 6 to 11 percent of annual outlays over the period. Numerous options are available for restoring balance between expected outlays and receipts, but more important, the reasons for the current deficits are well understood and can be avoided in the future.

The Origins of the Current Deficits

The most appropriate point from which to trace the origins of the current financing problems is 1977. Legislation passed in that year dramatically revised the social security financing and benefit provisions to restore fiscal balance to the program. Payroll tax rates were set on the assumption that taxable wages would grow at the rate of increase in prices plus an additional amount for productivity growth. This reasonable assumption reflected the performance of the U.S. economy during the entire postwar period. After 1977, however, the traditional relation between prices and wages reversed and price increases exceeded wage growth (table 4-2).

The projected balance in the trust funds is extremely sensitive to the relation between these economic variables. With prices rising faster than wages, benefits, which are linked to the consumer price

Table 4-2. Prices, Wages, and Unemployment, 1950–76, and Comparison of Assumptions Underlying the Social Security Trustees' 1977 Projections with Actual Experience, Calendar Years 1977–82

Percent

Year or period	Increase in consumer price index		Real wage differential[a]		Unemployment rate	
	Trustees' assumptions	Actual	Trustees' assumptions	Actual	Trustees' assumptions	Actual
1950–76	. . .	3.4	. . .	2.0[b]	. . .	5.1
1977	6.0	6.5	2.4	0.4	7.1	7.0
1978	5.4	7.7	2.7	0.5	6.3	6.1
1979	5.3	11.3	2.5	−3.1	5.7	5.9
1980	4.7	13.5	2.4	−5.0	5.2	7.2
1981	4.1	10.4	2.3	−0.9[c]	5.0	7.6
1982	4.0	6.1	2.0	n.a.	5.0	9.7

Sources: Intermediate (II-B) assumptions from Social Security Administration, *1977 Annual Report of the Board of Trustees of the Federal Old-Age and Survivors Insurance and Disability Insurance Trust Funds* (GPO, 1977), p.45; and National Commission on Social Security Reform, *Report of the National Commission on Social Security Reform* (The Commission, 1983), app. K, p. 84.

n.a. Not available.

a. The difference between the percentage increase in average annual wages in covered employment and the percentage increase in the annual consumer price index.

b. The percentage increase of average wages for covered employment was 5.4 over 1950–76. See Social Security Administration, *Social Security Bulletin, Annual Statistical Supplement, 1981,* pp. 84–85.

c. Estimate.

index, increased faster than payroll tax revenues, which are dependent on the growth in wages. As a result, trust fund balances were rapidly depleted. The financial situation was further weakened by high unemployment, which meant that fewer people contributed revenue into the trust funds; and more people, finding themselves unemployed, retired early. The weak economy and high inflation fully explain the current deficit of the social security system.

The Short-Run Outlook

Annual net income figures for the OASI and DI trust funds without the 1983 social security legislation are presented in table 4-3 for 1983–89. The annual deficits for the OASI fund hover around $30 billion under the intermediate assumptions, but rise from $30 billion to $52 billion under the pessimistic assumptions. These deficits are offset partially by growing surpluses in the DI program. The surpluses have grown because disability claims have been substantially lower than that anticipated when increased payroll taxes were allo-

**Table 4-3. Projected Net Income or Deficit of OASI and DI Trust Funds, Intermediate
and Pessimistic Assumptions, Calendar Years 1983-89**
Billions of dollars

	Intermediate assumptions			Pessimistic assumptions		
Year	OASI	DI	Combined OASDI	OASI	DI	Combined OASDI
1983	−26.2	5.1	−21.1	−27.1	5.0	−22.1
1984	−25.4	7.3	−18.1	−30.1	6.6	−23.5
1985	−22.7	12.8	−9.9	−31.7	11.6	−20.1
1986	−26.3	14.6	−11.7	−37.3	13.3	−24.0
1987	−29.1	16.3	−12.8	−42.3	14.9	−27.4
1988	−31.8	17.9	−13.9	−47.5	16.5	−31.0
1989	−34.3	19.6	−14.7	−52.0	18.2	−33.8
Total	−195.8	93.6	−102.2	−268.0	86.1	−181.9

Source: Projected revenues based on intermediate (II-B) and pessimistic (III) assumptions in Social Security Administration, *1983 Annual Report of the Board of Trustees of the Federal Old-Age and Survivors Insurance and Disability Insurance Trust Funds* (GPO, 1983). Figures exclude interest.

cated for the DI program under the 1977 amendment.[3] Considering
the OASI and DI funds combined, the intermediate assumptions
project annual deficits averaging about $15 billion; the pessimistic
assumptions, about $26 billion.

In addition to reducing deficits, additional funds or benefit reductions are needed to restore trust fund balances to a level sufficient to
cover temporary fluctuations in revenue. The amounts required over
1983-89 to reach a target ratio of assets to outlays of 15 percent by
1988 under the intermediate and pessimistic assumptions are $117.4
and $198.5 billion, respectively.[4]

Because the current financing problems can be traced to past
experience with overly optimistic assumptions, the obvious question
is whether the deficits projected for the next seven years are realistic.
Table 4-4 compares the trustees' projections of the difference between the rate of increase in wages and in prices, that is, the real
wage differential, and the unemployment rate underlying the intermediate and pessimistic assumptions with projections by two independent forecasters, Chase Econometrics and Data Resources, Inc.

3. Legislative changes in 1977 and 1980 further lowered the costs of the DI program. See
Mordechai E. Lando, Alice V. Farley, and Mary A. Brown, "Recent Trends in the Social
Security Disability Insurance Program," *Social Security Bulletin*, vol. 45 (August 1982), pp.
3-14.
4. Based on data from the Social Security Administration, Office of the Actuary, letter
from John A. Svahn, commissioner of social security, to Daniel Rostenkowski, chairman of
the Committee on Ways and Means, February 10, 1983, table 10.

Table 4-4. Comparison of Projections of the Real Wage Differential and Unemployment Rate, Trustees and Private Forecasters, Calendar Years 1983–89

Percent

	Real wage differential[a]				Unemployment rate			
	Trustees' estimate				Trustees' estimate			
Year	Intermediate assumptions	Pessimistic assumptions	Chase estimate	DRI estimate	Intermediate assumptions	Pessimistic assumptions	Chase estimate	DRI estimate
1983	0.2	−1.0	3.2	2.1	10.7	11.0	10.3	10.2
1984	1.1	−0.7	1.4	0.3	9.7	10.8	9.6	9.2
1985	0.4	−0.7	1.0	0.1	8.8	10.1	8.8	8.2
1986	0.9	0.2	1.9	−0.1	8.4	9.3	8.4	7.6
1987	1.3	0.7	1.8	0.6	8.1	9.0	7.9	7.1
1988	1.4	0.8	1.3	0.9	7.8	8.6	7.4	7.1
1989	1.5	1.1	1.1	1.1	7.5	8.2	7.0	7.1

Sources: Projections based on intermediate (II-B) and pessimistic (III) assumptions in Social Security Administration, *1983 Trustees' Report;* SSA, Office of the Actuary, letter from John A. Svahn, commissioner of social security, to Daniel Rostenkowski, chairman of the House Committee on Ways and Means, February 10, 1983; and Data Resources Inc. and Chase Econometrics/Interactive Data Corp., based on data available before March 30, 1983.

a. The trustees' projection is based on the difference between the percentage increase in average annual wages in covered employment and the percentage increase in the annual consumer price index. Because the private forecasters do not project wages in covered employment, wage growth is calculated on the basis of wages and salaries of employed workers in the private sector. Chase made long-term forecasts of moderate growth; DRI, forecasts of trend.

In general the projections of the private forecasters in the table fall somewhere between the intermediate and pessimistic assumptions. Hence planning on a deficit between $117 billion and $198 billion for 1983–89 seems a reasonable strategy.

Financing Options in the Short Run

The options for restoring financial balance to the social security program fall into three categories: benefit reductions, tax increases, or transfers from other parts of the unified budget.[5] Because even an extension of interfund borrowing could ensure the timely benefit payments of the trust fund programs only through mid-1984, prompt legislative action was assumed.

BENEFIT REDUCTIONS. Although few would advocate abrupt changes in the level of social security benefits, several proposals have been advanced to modify the way in which benefits are increased to maintain a recipient's standard of living. Some of the specific options for indexing changes are listed in table 4-5. Savings over the

5. Inevitably the classification of the various proposals has taken on political importance. In fact, a reform such as the taxation of benefits can be characterized as a benefit cut or as a tax increase. The classification presented below is quite arbitrary and has been done solely for purposes of organizing the discussion.

Table 4-5. Social Security Savings for Different Cost-of-Living Adjustments, Intermediate Assumptions, 1983–89

Billions of dollars

Proposal	Total savings
Delay COLAs from July to October	23.3
Delay COLAs from July to January	39.4
Set COLAs at wage growth minus 1.5 percent[a]	51.5
Set COLAs at 75 percent of CPI increase	88.2
Eliminate 1983 COLA	93.5

Sources: National Commission on Social Security Reform, *Report of National Commission on Social Security Reform;* estimates of revenues are based on intermediate (II-B) assumptions in Social Security Administration, *1982 Trustees' Report,* except for the second proposal, which is based on data in SSA, Office of the Actuary, letter from Svahn to Rostenkowski, table 8.

a. This option would result in small savings in outlays in the short run because of the projected low productivity growth. Under the pessimistic assumptions, the short-run savings would be much greater, $142.5 billion over 1983–89; in the longer run, however, outlays could be either higher or lower than under current law, depending on the relative behavior of wages and prices.

next seven years would range from about $23 billion for a permanent shift in the cost-of-living adjustment (COLA) from July to October to about $94 billion for eliminating the COLA increase scheduled for July 1983.

Many argue that reductions in COLAs are justified as an offset to what they believe has been overindexing of social security benefits in the past few years. The overindexing is attributable to a soon-to-be corrected flaw in the consumer price index that gives excessive weight to mortgage interest rates and housing prices, components that have risen more rapidly than other prices in the recent past.[6] If COLAs had been computed using an index that included a rental equivalence measure of housing costs, for example, benefits would now be 5 to 6 percent lower.[7]

Even if a rental equivalence measure of housing costs had been used, however, benefit increases would still have outstripped the growth in wages in the past five years. Hence, social security beneficiaries have received more protection from inflation than have wage

6. Since January 1978 the Bureau of Labor Statistics has published official consumer price indexes for two groups: a new consumer price index for all urban consumers (CPI-U), about 80 percent of the noninstitutional population, and a revised CPI for urban wage earners and clerical workers (CPI-W), about 45 percent of the population. Despite its narrower coverage, the CPI-W is used to index social security benefits. In October 1981 the bureau announced plans to revise both indexes so that the cost of homeownership would be estimated on the basis of rental equivalence. The CPI-U was changed in January 1983; the CPI-W is scheduled for revision in January 1985.

7. See Congressional Budget Office, "Statement by Alice M. Rivlin before the National Commission on Social Security Reform," August 20, 1982, p. 12.

earners. Reductions in future COLAs are thus viewed by some as a means of equalizing the treatment of workers and retirees.

The disadvantage, of course, is that such reductions could lower the real value of social security benefits in time.[8] Even with the overadjustment, the average benefit for a retired person in 1983 is only $441 a month. Allowing the real value of this benefit to decline would increase the incidence of poverty among the disabled and among the aged, particularly the very old whose benefits tend to be lower than average.

TAX INCREASES. A second option that would improve social security trust fund balances is to increase tax revenues. Four separate approaches were under consideration: (1) raise the payroll tax rate; (2) increase the tax for the self-employed; (3) extend social security coverage to federal workers, the 30 percent of state and local employees currently without coverage, and the 20 percent of employees of nonprofit institutions without coverage; or (4) tax a portion of social security benefits under the personal income tax and transfer the receipts to the OASDI funds.

Raise payroll taxes. Under current law the OASDI payroll tax rate is scheduled to increase from the 1983 level of 5.4 percent each for the employee and the employer to 5.7 percent each in 1985 and 6.2 percent each in 1990. Moving the 1985 increases to January 1, 1984, would generate an additional $10 billion. Moving both scheduled increases to 1984 would generate about $133 billion by the end of 1989 (table 4-6).

Increase tax for self-employed. Another way to raise payroll tax revenues is to increase the social security tax for the self-employed to a rate comparable to that for other covered workers. Currently the self-employed pay about 1.5 times the employee rate, while the rate paid for most workers is the employee contribution plus a matching amount from the employer. Because all workers with social security coverage are entitled to the same benefits, the equity of the system would be improved by raising the tax on the self-employed to a level equal to the combined tax for employees and employers. Of course, to equalize the treatment between self-employed and salaried workers, the self-employed should be allowed a business

8. Another problem is that many new retirees who would receive less than full COLAs are not the same persons who benefited from the overindexing during the late 1970s and early 1980s.

Table 4-6. Additional Trust Fund Revenues for Various Tax Changes, Intermediate Assumptions, 1983–89

Billions of dollars

Proposal	Additional revenues
Increase payroll taxes	
Move 1985 increase to January 1, 1984	10.0
Move 1985 and 1990 increases to January 1, 1984	132.8
Increase tax rate for self-employed to combined employee-employer rate	18.5
Extend social security coverage to federal, state, and local government employees	
All federal, state, and local government employees and employees of nonprofit organizations	110.5
All new federal employees and employees of nonprofit institutions	21.8
All new state and local employees	13.3
Tax social security benefits	
Fifty percent of all OASDI benefits	53.3
Fifty percent of OASDI benefits for recipients with income above $20,000 (individuals) and $25,000 (couples)	26.6

Sources: National Commission on Social Security Reform, *Report of National Commission on Social Security Reform;* estimates of revenues are effective on January 1, 1984, and are based on intermediate (II-B) assumptions in Social Security Administration, *1982 Trustees' Report,* except for the third proposal, which is based on data in SSA, Office of the Actuary, letter from Svahn to Rostenkowski, table 8.

deduction under the personal income tax for the part of their payroll tax contribution that corresponds to the employer's share. Raising the rate for the self-employed would increase the income of the social security system by $18 billion between now and 1990.

Broaden coverage. Extending coverage to some or all workers not currently covered by social security is another way of increasing payroll tax revenues. This reform is also desirable. Under the present system employees without coverage can easily achieve insured status and receive social security benefits in addition to their regular pension. These dual beneficiaries profit from the progressive benefit formula, which was designed to help low-wage workers rather than workers whose second career entitles them to benefits. More fundamentally, it makes little sense to have a government insurance program from which government and nonprofit workers are excluded. Covering all federal civilian employees, state and local workers currently not under social security, and noncovered employees of nonprofit institutions as of January 1, 1984, would produce about $110 billion by 1989.

Tax benefits. Another method is to subject a portion of social security benefits—probably the half that is generally associated with the employer share of the payroll tax—to the personal income tax and to direct the new receipts to the social security trust funds. Such a reform would enhance the equity of the income tax—by equalizing the tax treatment of social security and private pension benefits, which are currently taxed in full to the extent they exceed the employee's own contributions.[9] Taxing benefits is equivalent, of course, to a benefit cut, but this approach protects the majority of the elderly with low and moderate incomes who do not pay taxes. Further protection could be gained for beneficiaries with moderate incomes by imposing taxes only on those with incomes above some threshold, as is done for the taxation of unemployment benefits.[10] Inclusion of one-half of social security benefits in adjusted gross income would yield $53 billion over the 1983–89 period, while an inclusion only for those individuals with income more than $20,000 and married couples with income above $25,000 would produce $27 billion by the end of the decade.

GENERAL REVENUES. The third possible approach to increasing social security revenues is to transfer some funds from other parts of the unified budget. Such a transfer would, of course, require either an increase in other taxes or a reduction in other expenditures to reduce the overall federal deficit.

9. A strict application of the principles of private pension taxation requires calculation of the portion of social security benefits attributable to employee contributions. In the aggregate, the Office of the Actuary of the Social Security Administration estimates that workers now entering covered employment will make payroll tax contributions totaling no more than 17 percent of the benefits they can expect to receive. Another 17 percent will be derived from employer contributions; the remaining 66 percent can be considered equivalent, for tax purposes, to the earnings on a funded pension plan. Therefore if social security benefits were given the same tax treatment as private pensions, only 17 percent of the benefits would be exempt from tax when received and 83 percent would be taxable. Similar calculations indicate that the self-employed will pay no more than 26 percent on average. See Advisory Council on Social Security, *Report of the 1979 Advisory Council on Social Security* (GPO, 1980), p. 75.

10. The Revenue Act of 1978 introduced the taxation of unemployment insurance benefits. Under its provisions, if income plus unemployment benefits exceeded $20,000 for single individuals and $25,000 for married couples, one-half of the excess amount, or the full amount of unemployment benefits, whichever was lower, was subject to tax. With the passage of the Tax Equity and Fiscal Responsibility Act of 1982, the taxable income levels for single individuals and married couples receiving unemployment benefits were reduced to $12,000 and $18,000, respectively.

The arguments for and against general revenue financing for social security rest in large part on one's view of the philosophical rationale of the social security system. Some argue that social security is best construed as an annual tax-transfer program to redistribute income from the relatively affluent wage earners to relatively poor retired persons. This view leads to an evaluation of the tax independent of the benefits, with the conclusion that the payroll tax violates the ability-to-pay criterion for equitable taxation. The tax is levied without provisions for the number of dependents; it excludes income from capital and exempts wages above the maximum. Advocates of the annual tax transfer favor a more progressive source of revenue to finance social security.

The more widely held position is that social security must be viewed in a lifetime framework in which payroll taxes are viewed as compulsory saving for retirement. When benefits and taxes are considered jointly, the payroll tax (with an earned credit for low-wage workers) can be seen as an appropriate method of financing a compulsory saving program. However, it could be argued that, because the social security system combines income redistribution with strictly wage-related saving, a rationale exists for supplementing payroll tax receipts with general revenues. Indeed, general revenues have been used several times on a limited basis to finance specific social security provisions, such as the gratuitous wage credit granted to servicemen, transitional benefits for certain uninsured people, and some hospital payments.

Support for the use of general revenues tends to divide along political lines. Liberals associated with social security during its formative years and members of organized labor have traditionally supported the idea of the limited use of general revenues to improve the equity of the system. Many of these people, however, recognize the value of a contributory program and would oppose exclusive reliance on general revenues lest a break in the perceived link between individual contributions and benefits create a situation in which social security would be transformed into a means-tested program.

Those who fear a tendency to expand social security without the countervailing constituency created by the payroll tax oppose the use of general revenues. This opposition reflects the judgment that increases in social security benefits might outbid more pressing needs for general revenues. The argument that general revenues should be used to finance components of the program unrelated to wages is also not very compelling to those who believe that the program should be divested of its welfare function and that benefits should be directly related to the earnings of each participant.

A limited use of general revenues has been advocated repeatedly in the proposal to transfer all or some financing of HI to general revenues and to credit the scheduled increases in the HI tax rate to the OASDI funds.[11] Because hospital insurance benefits bear no direct relation to contributions or earnings in covered employment, none of the underlying philosophies of the social security system would be violated. However, opposition exists even to this limited proposal because opponents fear that such a move might lessen the incentive to control the rapidly increasing costs of medicare.

The Commission's Recommendations

The National Commission on Social Security Reform rejected the explicit use of general revenues to solve the system's financial problems, and instead constructed a delicately balanced package of benefit cuts and tax increases that produces $165 billion over the next seven years, attempted to stabilize short-term financing, and eliminated two-thirds of the long-run deficit; two alternative proposals are included that eliminate the remainder of the long-run problems. General revenues, however, enter the commission's proposal in several indirect ways, and for this reason the package contributes somewhat less toward reducing the unified budget deficit than it does toward augmenting trust fund reserves.

Short-Run Revenues

The two largest amounts of short-run revenues are derived from the acceleration of payroll tax rate increases and from the six-month delay in the COLA, each contributing $39 billion (table 4-7). Both these proposals will have a smaller effect on the unified budget. The increase in the payroll tax rate in 1984 would be accompanied by a refundable income tax credit for the increase in employee's share

---

11. This proposal was advanced by the 1979 Advisory Council on Social Security. Moreover, previous advisory councils, beginning in 1965, have recommended the use of general revenues to finance some portion of the HI program.

Table 4-7. Effects of Recommendations of the National Commission on Social Security Reform on Trust Funds and Unified Budget, Intermediate Assumptions, 1983–2057

	Short-run effect, 1983–89 (billions of dollars)		Long-run effect on trust funds, 1983–2057 (percent of payrolls)
Recommended reform	Trust funds	Unified budget	
Accelerate scheduled rate increases	39.4	35.5	0.03
Delay COLA from July to January	39.4	33.4	0.30
Tax 50 percent of OASDI benefits for recipients with income above $20,000 (individuals) and $25,000 (couples)	26.6	26.6	0.63
Provide coverage to employees of nonprofit institutions and new federal employees	21.8	17.2	0.39
Increase OASDI tax rate for self-employed	18.5	7.4	0.19
Provide credit for the present value of benefits attributed to military service	17.2	0	0.01
Prohibit withdrawal of state and local employers	3.2	3.2	0.08
Change benefits[a]	−1.4	−1.4	−0.16
Total, all reforms	164.6	121.9	1.41[b]
Deficit	117.0	...	2.09

Sources: Based on intermediate (II-B) assumptions in Social Security Administration, Office of the Actuary, letter from Svahn to Rostenkowski, table 8; estimates of the short-run effects on the unified budget are based on the discussion in Congressional Budget Office, *Reducing the Deficit: Spending and Revenue Options: A Report to the Senate and House Committees on the Budget—Part III* (CBO, February 1983), pp. 63–95.

a. Changes in benefits include the following: eliminate windfall benefits for persons with pensions from employment without social security coverage; continue benefits for remarried disabled widow(er)s and for divorced widow(er)s; index deferred benefits for widow(er)s based on wages instead of prices; permit divorced, aged spouse to receive benefits when the husband would be eligible; and increase the benefit rate for disabled widow(er)s aged fifty to fifty-nine to 71.5 percent of a worker's basic benefit.

b. The total effect of reforms on the trust funds as a percentage of payrolls is not the sum of individual percentages; rather, the total reflects the interaction of individual reforms upon one another.

above the level in the current law.[12] Thus, although the 1984 increase would raise social security revenues by $9.9 billion, its effect on the federal budget would be only half as large.[13] Since no credit is scheduled for the 1988 and 1989 increase, $30.5 billion will be credited to both the trust funds and the federal deficit.

The proposal to delay the COLA for six months includes a recommendation that the supplemental security income (SSI) program be modified to allow beneficiaries receiving both SSI and social security

12. The commission proposed raising the OASDI payroll tax rate for employees and employers in 1984 from 5.4 percent each to 5.7 percent each (the rate scheduled for 1985) and to 6.06 percent in 1988 and 1989. In 1990 the rate will increase to 6.2 percent as scheduled under current law.

13. In fact, the net effect on the budget will be slightly smaller because the employer's portion of the payroll tax is a deductible expense under the corporation income tax. Hence an increase in the payroll tax leads to a slight reduction in corporation income tax revenues.

benefits to retain $30 more in monthly benefits to offset the effect of the delay in the social security COLA. Consequently, the OASDI savings for 1983–89 would be offset by an increase of about $6 billion in SSI spending.

Taxation of one-half of social security benefits is projected to produce $26.6 billion in additional personal income tax revenues.[14] Some argue that when this amount is channeled to the trust funds it should be considered general revenue financing, since the receipts from taxing unemployment insurance benefits in a similar fashion are not transferred to the trust fund of that program. On the other hand, the taxation could be viewed as a benefit reduction, with the savings properly accruing to the trust funds. In any event, the proposal contributes an identical amount to the trust funds and the unified budget.

The commission proposed that all employees of nonprofit institutions and *new* federal workers pay social security taxes. Although the commission acknowledged the desirability of including state and local workers, the majority of members felt that possible constitutional barriers precluded their mandatory coverage. The receipts from the coverage of nonfederal workers will represent a net addition to the federal coffers; in the case of federal employees, however, the federal government as the employer must pay half the tax. Hence only half of the $9.3 billion accruing to the trust funds from the coverage of federal employees will be credited to the unified budget.

14. The commission recognizes that taxation of benefits for individuals with income more than $20,000 or couples with income more than $25,000 involves a "notch" problem: persons with adjusted gross income of $19,999 would pay no tax on benefits, while those with income of $20,000 would be taxed in full. A similar problem arose in the taxation of unemployment insurance benefits. It was resolved by limiting the amount of benefits to be included in the income of individuals to 50 percent of the amount by which adjusted gross income plus unemployment insurance benefits exceed the base amount of $20,000 (or $25,000 for couples) or the amount of actual unemployment compensation, whichever was smaller. Adopting similar provisions for social security would involve limiting the portion of benefits to be included in income to the lesser of the actual amount of taxable social security benefits or 50 percent of the amount by which adjusted gross income plus the taxable portion of social security benefits exceeds the base amount. This approach eliminates the notch problem, although persons with income less than $20,000 or couples with income less than $25,000 will have to pay tax on a portion of their social security benefits.

An alternative approach would be to add one dollar of social security benefits to adjusted gross income for every two dollars of that income above the threshold, to a maximum of 50 percent of benefits. This approach limits taxation to incomes above the $20,000 and $25,000 thresholds, although the Congressional Budget Office estimates that it would also yield about 15 percent less in new revenues than would a phase-in plan like that of the unemployment insurance program.

The commission recommended that the self-employed be required to pay the combined employer-employee rate, but that one-half of the tax be allowed as a deductible business expense. This means that roughly twice the projected increase in revenues will be deductible (since the current self-employed level is 1.5 times the employee's rate). Assuming an average marginal rate of 30 percent, personal income tax revenues will decline by $11.1 billion, leaving a net contribution to the unified budget of $7.4 billion.

The commission proposed a credit to the OASDI trust funds of $17.2 billion to compensate for gratuitous wage credits for military service granted before 1983. The proposed lump-sum payment from general revenues also includes a reimbursement for social security checks issued but never redeemed. This transfer will provide the trust funds with additional reserves, but will have no effect on the federal deficit. On the other hand, the proposal to ban the withdrawal of state and local employers will produce a net increase of $3 billion.

Political support for the proposals stems from the commission's efforts to divide the burden of financing the deficits between workers and retirees by combining some tax increases with some benefit reductions. Moreover, many of the components—such as extending coverage, taxing benefits, and raising the tax rate on the self-employed—are desirable reforms even if additional revenues are not needed. The most serious opposition to the proposals came from the federal civilian employees who strongly resisted mandatory social security coverage. For this reason, a brief digression follows to outline the current provisions of the civil service retirement system and the changes required for new employees.

The Civil Service Retirement System

Virtually all federal civilian workers are covered under the civil service retirement system. The system is financed by contributions of 7 percent each from the employee and the employing agency plus an appropriation from the general revenues to meet the overall cost of the program, which is now roughly 35 percent of payrolls.

The civil service retirement system provides retirement, disability, and survivor pensions and also lump-sum refunds for those leaving government service. Full retirement benefits are payable under several combinations of age and service: age fifty-five with thirty years of service, age sixty with twenty years of service (or ten years as a member of Congress), or age sixty-two with five years of service. The basic employee pension depends on the number of years of service and the average salary during three consecutive years when salary was highest. The general benefit formula is 1.5 percent a year for the first five years, 1.75 percent a year for the next five years, and 2 percent a year thereafter, with a maximum of 80 percent possible (attained after forty-two years of service). Benefits for those over age sixty-two are adjusted annually to reflect changes in the consumer price index; benefits for retirees under age sixty-two are increased by one-half the change in prices.

The differentiation in the COLAs between those over and under age sixty-two was introduced on a temporary basis for fiscal years 1983–85 in the Omnibus Budget Reconciliation Act of 1982. This reform was an effort to mitigate the incentive for capable people to leave government service at the peak of their careers. Persons aged fifty-five with thirty years of service could retire with a benefit equal to 56.25 percent of their previous earnings and look forward to that initial amount increasing each year in line with the consumer price index. With government salaries capped during periods of rapid inflation, some retirees began to earn more than persons currently employed at their positions. Limiting the indexing for those under age sixty-two was designed to make early retirement a less desirable option. In the fiscal 1984 budget, President Reagan has proposed to make permanent the policy of limited indexing for younger retirees.

The 1984 budget contains four additional recommendations that would drastically alter the nature of the civil service retirement system. These include (1) reducing retirement benefits by 5 percent for each year before age sixty-five, phased in over ten years; (2) raising the employee's and the employing agency's contribution rates from 7 to 11 percent, so that each pays one-half the reduced total cost of the system once the proposed reforms are adopted; (3) basing benefits on five years of highest earnings instead of the highest three years; and (4) if the first three proposals do not lower costs sufficiently, reducing replacement rates to bring total costs down to 22 percent of payrolls. These reforms would dramatically change the benefit provisions for most current federal civilian workers.

The commission's social security proposals apply only to newly hired employees and do not require any reduction in benefit protection. For these workers, the commission recommends mandatory social security coverage and the establishment of a new supplementary retirement plan within the civil service retirement plan. The supplementary plan could be designed so that, when combined with social security, it provides the same protection as the civil service system does alone. That is, mandatory social security coverage implies nothing about the overall level of benefits for federal employees; the level of benefit protection will be determined by the combination of social security and the supplementary retirement program.

For many new federal employees this arrangement of social security plus a supplementary plan may well be better than the existing system. Social security with its progressive benefit formula is generally superior to civil service for low-paid employees, and is often better for those who move in and out of federal employment. Moreover, full survivor and disability protection is more quickly achieved under social security than under the current federal retirement system. In short, mandatory social security coverage will not only eliminate the windfall component of the benefit that arises when government workers gain minimum coverage under social security and profit from the progressive benefit formula, but will also improve certain benefits for many workers.

Stabilizing the System

As noted above, the short-term financing problem in social security is entirely the result of the poor performance of the economy during the past few years. The current system is very sensitive to economic conditions, particularly the relation between the rate of price increase and the rate of wage growth. Tax revenues vary with the growth of wages; benefits rise with increases in the consumer price index. Historically wages have risen faster than prices, and the resulting higher payrolls financed the more slowly rising growth in benefits. The recent deficits emerged when the relations between these key economic variables changed and benefit outlays exceeded payroll tax receipts.

To avoid this problem in the future, the commission proposed that (after 1988 when reserves have risen to more adequate levels) if the reserves of the OASDI funds ever drop below 20 percent of the following year's planned outlays, benefits will be indexed by the increase in wages or in prices, whichever is lower, until the 20 percent ratio is restored. When the reserves reach 32 percent of outlays, benefits would be adjusted to make up for any payments that were less than those called for by the price adjustment. The payback would occur only so long as reserves met the standard of 32 percent.

Although the commission's recommendation is likely to avoid a repetition of the recent difficulty, it does not necessarily protect the system from having long-run costs rise above those projected under the intermediate assumptions. Consider a period in which prices rise at an annual rate of 4 percent while wages increase at a rate of 3 percent. Indexing by wages or prices, whichever is lower, will mean that both tax revenues and benefits increase at 3 percent a year. With prices and wages increasing at the same rate, the cost of the program, measured as a percent of payrolls, would be substantially higher than it would be under the intermediate projections, which assume that wage growth will exceed price increases by 1.5 percent. Even if the situation changes and wages grow at 4 percent while prices increase at 3 percent, long-run costs will still be higher, since the differential between wages and prices would be only 1.0 percent, as against 1.5 percent under the intermediate assumptions.

Another indexing procedure considered by the commission was the proposal to adjust benefits by wages minus 1.5 percent. This approach would not only protect the system from unanticipated variations in the rate of wage increases and rate of price increases, but would also ensure that long-run costs will be in line with the intermediate assumptions. Stable long-run costs, however, would be achieved at the expense of great fluctuations in the welfare of beneficiaries. Periods of low or negative real wage growth, such as the recent past, would reduce real benefit levels. Under the circumstances just described, if prices increase at a rate of 4 percent and wages at 3 percent, nominal benefits (linked to wages minus 1.5 percent) would rise by only 1.5 percent, resulting in a 2.5 percent annual decline in their real value. On the other hand, the real wage differential, the difference between the rate of increase in average wages and the rate of increase in benefits, would remain constant at 1.5 percent. Thus under this proposal the beneficiaries rather than the trust funds would feel the consequences of poor economic performance. In contrast, the commission's recommendation to index by the lower of prices or wages can be viewed as an effort to divide the risks of a weak economy between trust funds and retirees.

The Long Run

In addition to increasing short-run revenues and stabilizing financing, the commission's specific recommendations make a substantial contribution toward eliminating the long-run deficit (table 4-7). The members of the commission also recommended bringing the deficit to zero and suggested two approaches for accomplishing this goal.

Specific proposals are relatively more important in reducing costs in the long run than they are in the short run. The most important proposal, which reduces long-run costs by 0.63 percent of taxable payrolls, recommends taxing one-half of social security benefits. Although the income limits initially restrict the tax to the 10 percent of individuals with higher incomes, as incomes rise with inflation and real wage growth, an increasing proportion of beneficiaries will be covered by the proposal.

The proposal to bring employees of nonprofit institutions and newly hired federal workers under social security also has a favorable long-run effect by contributing 0.39 percent of payrolls toward reducing the long-run deficit. The saving arises because an estimated 80 percent of those involved would have qualified for sizable social security benefits as a result of other employment even without the extension of coverage. Also, federal employees tend to have wages that are higher than average and, therefore, are entitled to less heavily weighted benefits.

The six-month delay in the COLA and the increase in the tax for the self-employed produce savings of 0.30 and 0.19 percent, respectively. Taken as a whole, the commission's recommendations result in a net reduction in long-run costs of 1.41 percent of payrolls or two-thirds of the 2.09 percent long-term deficit projected under the intermediate assumptions. The next section explores the outlook for the long run and examines the possibilities considered for eliminating the remainder of the deficit.

Long-Run Financing Problems and Options

In the absence of the commission's recommendations, the cost of the OASDI portion of the social security system was projected under the intermediate assumptions to rise from the current level of 11 percent of taxable payrolls to about 17 percent in the year 2030 and

Table 4-8. Long-Run Costs of the Combined OASDI Trust Funds as a Percent of Taxable Payrolls, Alternative Assumptions, and Scheduled Tax Rates, Selected Periods, 1983–2057[a]

| Period | Projected costs as percent of taxable payrolls | | | OASDI tax rate scheduled under current law |
	Optimistic assumptions	Intermediate assumptions	Pessimistic assumptions	
Twenty-five-year averages				
1983–2007	9.75[b]	10.46[b] 11.49	12.73[b]	12.07
2008–32	11.30	13.15 14.29	17.84	12.40
2033–57	11.88	15.65 17.36	25.66	12.40
Seventy-five-year averages				
1983–2057	10.98	13.09 14.38	18.74	12.29

Source: Based on optimistic (I), intermediate (II-A and II-B), and pessimistic (III) assumptions in Social Security Administration, *1983 Trustees' Report.*
a. The assumptions underlying the projections (in annual percentage rates of increase) are

	Optimistic	Intermediate		Pessimistic
Fertility rate	2.3	2.0	2.0	1.6
Real wages	2.5	2.0	1.5	1.0
Consumer price index	2.0	3.0	4.0	5.0

b. Data for average costs as a percentage of payrolls reflect twenty-five- and seventy-five-year periods beginning with 1982 and ending 2056, based on Social Security Administration, *1982 Trustees' Report.*

remain at that level through 2057 (table 4-8). The sharp increase in costs reflects the changing demographic structure of the population. The ratio of the beneficiary population to covered workers is projected to rise dramatically as the sizable post-World War II baby boom begins to reach retirement age after 2010. At that time the working population will be composed of the relatively small group born during the period of low fertility that began in the late 1960s. Assuming that the fertility rate will rise gradually from the current level of 1.8 to a long-run rate of 2.0, the Social Security Administration projects that the number of beneficiaries for every 100 workers with coverage will rise from 31 in 1983 to 57 by 2030, an increase of about 83 percent. Because the social security system is financed on a pay-as-you-go basis, with tax contributions by today's workers paying for benefits to today's beneficiaries, the projected increase in the aged population relative to workers implies a similar increase in OASDI costs from 11 to 17 percent of taxable payrolls.

For the entire seventy-five years (1983–2057) the average cost of OASDI, expressed as a percent of payrolls, is 14.38 percent below the intermediate assumptions. The scheduled payroll tax revenues average 12.29 percent, which leaves a long-run deficit of 2.09 percent of payrolls. Thus if the payroll tax rate were increased by 2.09

percent, about 1.41 percent each for employees and employers, the system would produce sufficient revenues to cover all costs for the next seventy-five years. The commission's recommendations, which contribute 1.41 percent toward reducing long-run costs, reduce the deficit from 2.09 to 0.68 percent of payrolls under the intermediate assumptions.

Of course, if the fertility rate drops or the growth in real wages falls, the deficit could be considerably larger. Conversely, an increase in birth rates or an acceleration of productivity growth would result in a smaller deficit or even a surplus. Under the pessimistic projections, which are based on the assumption of a long-run fertility rate of 1.7 and a real wage differential of 1.0, the long-run costs would rise as high as 18.7 percent of payrolls, leaving the system with a seventy-five-year deficit of about 6.5 percent of taxable payrolls. Such an outcome is unlikely, however, because the fertility assumptions, which drive the projections, are not consistent with the recent upward trend in the birth rate since 1977.[15]

Projecting costs seventy-five years from now is a risky exercise; the difficulties are apparent when one considers that it is equivalent to having made estimates for today in the year 1908. The entire demographic, economic, and social structure of the nation has changed in the past seventy-five years. Nevertheless, it is important for restoring confidence in the social security system to have the program in actuarial balance over the long-run as it is now envisaged. Hence Congress considered several possible alternatives for eliminating the 0.68 percent of the payroll deficit that remained once the commission's recommendations were adopted.

Proposals to Reduce the Long-Run Deficit

Three options exist for reducing long-run deficits: increasing payroll taxes, extending the retirement age, or reducing benefit levels.[16]

15. The fertility rate has increased during four of the past five years, and the data on expected births indicate that young women continue to expect to have more than two children during their lifetimes. See Bureau of the Census, *Current Population Reports*, series P-25, no. 922, "Projections of the Population of the United States: 1982 to 2050 (Advance Report)" (GPO, October 1982), p. 1; and *Current Population Reports*, series P-20, no. 369, "Fertility of American Women: June 1981 (Advance Report)" (GPO, March 1982), p. 3.

16. If the constitutional issue could be resolved, extending social security coverage to the 30 percent of state and local workers not currently included would also reduce the long-run deficit. Under the intermediate assumptions, the savings from this proposal would amount to 0.22 percent of taxable payrolls.

HIGHER PAYROLL TAXES. In a supplementary statement to the commission's report, the members selected by the Democratic leadership proposed that the remaining deficit be met by providing additional revenues starting in the year 2010, before the period when most of the deficit is projected to occur. The Democrats suggested that this revenue could be raised either by increasing employee and employer payroll tax by roughly 0.5 percent each or by transferring funds from general revenues. An OASDI payroll tax effective in the year 2010 of roughly 13.4 percent, or 6.7 percent each for the employer and the employee, would balance the system for the next seventy-five years; increasing taxes by half that amount and reducing benefits by roughly 5 percent would also achieve the balance. Proponents of higher payroll taxes argue that either reducing benefits or extending the retirement age would place the burden of the deficit on those most in need of benefits.

EXTENSION OF THE RETIREMENT AGE. The Republican designees to the commission recommended eliminating the long-run deficit by raising the age of first eligibility for full benefits to sixty-six by 2015 and thereafter allowing the age to rise automatically in accordance with increases in longevity, ultimately reaching age sixty-eight in about 2055 under the trustees' mortality assumptions.

The argument in favor of extending the retirement age is that as life expectancy increases and health improves, the retirement age should rise. If age sixty-five was the appropriate age for retirement when social security was established in 1935, a higher age will be appropriate in the future. Older workers will also be in greater demand as the growth in the labor force slows and as an increasing proportion of employment is generated by the service industries in which the work is less physically stressful.

On the other hand, many older workers will not be able to engage in gainful employment past sixty-two, the age at which reduced social security benefits are currently available, and they will need access to some form of income support. Some of the elderly may be prevented from working by physical disability and will require benefits under an expanded disability program that recognizes the interaction of age and physical impairments. Other older persons may not be able to find jobs because they have been displaced by technology. The latter will not be eligible for disability insurance and may face a severe loss of income as a result of extending the retirement age. Unless adequate provision is made for these workers, the costs of the 1983 legislation, which extended the retirement age to sixty-seven by 2027, will be borne by the most disadvantaged aged.

LOWER BENEFIT LEVELS. Several proposals have been advanced in recent years to introduce a gradual reduction of replacement rates, the ratio of benefits to preretirement earnings, as a means of eliminating the long-run deficit. Generally the proposals change the method for adjusting the benefit formula. In 1983 the basic benefit is 90 percent of the first $254 of the worker's average indexed monthly earnings (AIME), plus 32 percent of the next $1,274 of AIME, plus 15 percent of the AIME over $1,528. The amounts separating the individual's AIME into intervals—that is, $254 and $1,528 in 1983—are called bend points. Under current law these bend points are increased automatically each year to reflect the growth in average wages so that replacement rates remain constant over time. In other words, a worker with a history of average earnings retiring in the year 1990 will receive a benefit equal to the same percentage of his preretirement wages as a worker retiring today with a similar situation. Early proposals to reduce replacement rates have usually been couched in terms of adjusting the bend points by a smaller amount than the full increase in wages. This means that a greater portion of a worker's average indexed monthly wages will fall in the higher brackets of the benefit formula that provide lower levels of replacement.[17]

Recent discussions of reducing replacement rates have focused on changing the percentages in the benefit formula rather than the brackets. For instance, the social security subcommittee of the House Committee on Ways and Means approved a proposal to reduce the replacement rate by 5 percent through downward adjustments in the percentages over an eight-year period beginning in the year 2000. This proposal, combined with a 0.24 percent increase in the payroll tax for both employers and employees in the year 2015 and all the commission's other recommendations, would eliminate the remainder of the 2.09 percent deficit.

Proponents of lower benefit levels maintain that in the future

17. For example, if the indexing were changed beginning in 2010 so that the bend points were increased by, say, 75 percent of the increase in wages until the bend points were 80 percent of what they have been under full wage indexing, the long-run cost of social security would be reduced by 0.06 percent of payrolls.

private pensions and individual savings should fill the gap left by a reduced social security program. These assumptions may not be realistic, however, for large segments of the population. Past behavior indicates that workers with low pay will not save for retirement because they use all their income for current consumption. Many middle-income workers may not save for retirement because of the widespread myopic view of retirement needs that provided the initial justification for the social security program.

At first blush, a new emphasis on private pension plans may seem an appealing alternative to substantial increases in the payroll tax. Private pension benefits have increased dramatically as a source of retirement income, and private retirement plans may meet a larger portion of the income needs for some groups of future retirees. The private pension system should not be viewed as a panacea, however, since it is plagued with problems of its own. The private system as currently constituted is incapable of offsetting the effects of inflation or of protecting workers who change jobs frequently. Moreover, less than half of the private nonfarm work force is currently covered by private plans, and pension benefits are concentrated among highly paid people; low-wage workers receive few benefits from private pensions.

Because industries with traditionally high rates of pension coverage (such as manufacturing) are expected to employ a declining share of workers, a significant percentage of the work force may continue to lack pension coverage in the future. The people without pension coverage will be primarily low-wage employees, precisely those persons who find it difficult to save on their own. For these individuals, social security will remain the sole source of support in retirement. Lowering social security replacement rates for these workers, on the assumption that such a reduction will be acceptable because they will have higher real incomes, will force a large portion of future retirees to suffer a dramatic decline in economic well-being upon retirement.

Future Costs in Perspective

The long-run social security problem is one manifestation of a much larger economic and social issue, the aging of America. The social security program is not the source of the growing burden. Even if the social security program were abolished, tomorrow's

Table 4-9. Actual Past and Projected Future Dependency Ratios, Selected Calendar Years, 1940–2060[a]

Year	Age nineteen or younger	Age sixty-five or older	Total
1940	58.5	11.7	70.2
1960	74.1	17.4	91.5
1980	55.8	19.5	75.3
2000	47.9	22.6	70.5
2020	46.2	30.3	76.5
2040	47.6	38.0	85.6
2060	47.9	37.9	85.8

Sources: Testimony of Robert M. Ball in *Social Security*, Hearings before the Subcommittee on Retirement Income and Employment of the House Select Committee on Aging, 94 Cong. 1 sess. (GPO, 1975), p. 111; and Social Security Administration, *1982 Trustees' Report*, p. 79.

a. The dependency ratio is the total number of people under age twenty and over sixty-four per 100 people aged twenty through sixty-four.

workers would still need to provide support for the aged nonworkers in some way.

Higher social security costs will be offset somewhat by reduced spending for children. If the economic burden on active workers is measured in total number of dependents rather than merely aged retirees, the picture is less startling. The total dependency ratio (the ratio of the number of people under age twenty and over age sixty-five per 100 people aged twenty to sixty-four) will be lower in the twenty-first century than it was in 1960 (table 4-9). In other words, the increase in the number of aged persons will be more than offset by a decline in dependent children, thereby freeing resources that could be devoted to providing for the elderly.

Further, although projected tax rates are considerably higher than the current rates, they are substantially below the present payroll tax rates in many European countries. Austria, Italy, Sweden and the Netherlands all have rates for programs comparable to OASDI that cost more than 20 percent of payrolls (table 4-10). West Germany, with a tax equal to 18 percent of payrolls, also already has a rate that exceeds the rate projected for the United States as the baby boom population retires after the turn of the century.

It is also important to note that the U.S. payroll tax rate would be levied on a much smaller portion of the worker's total compensation than the amount that is taxable today. According to the trustees' projections, the ratio of cash wages to total compensation is esti-

Table 4-10. Employee and Employer Payroll Tax Rates for Old-Age, Invalids, and Survivors Insurance, Selected Countries, 1981

Percent

Country	Employer tax	Employee tax	Total
Austria	11.35	9.75	21.10
Belgium	8.86	6.25	15.11[a]
Canada	1.80	1.80	3.60
France	8.20	4.80	13.00[b]
West Germany	9.25	9.25	18.50
Italy	17.31	7.15	24.46
Japan	5.30	5.30	10.60
Netherlands	12.90	22.00	34.90[c]
Sweden	21.15	...	21.15
Switzerland	4.70	4.70	9.40
United States	5.35	5.35	10.70

Source: *Social Security in Europe: The Impact of an Aging Population*, Committee Print, Senate Special Committee on Aging, 97 Cong. 1 sess. (GPO, 1981), p. 13.

a. Pensions for invalids financed through sickness insurance.

b. Benefits for invalids and survivors financed through sickness insurance.

c. Disability insurance includes compensation for injury on the job.

mated to decline from 84.2 percent in 1980 to 62.2 percent by the year 2055.[18] Because the payroll tax is levied only on cash wages, the expansion of fringe benefits reduces the tax base and boosts the percentage of taxable payroll required for paying benefits. If fringe benefits remained a constant percentage of total compensation, the required tax rate for the OASDI portion of the program in the year 2055 would be roughly 25 percent lower than projected rates.

In short, if the costs of the social security program turn out to be close to those projected under the trustees' intermediate assumptions, the long-run financing of OASDI benefits should not be excessively burdensome. Although Congress has opted to eliminate the remainder of the long-run deficit by extending the retirement age to sixty-seven by 2027, it would be equally viable on economic grounds to maintain the current retirement age and raise taxes to remove the deficit.

Conclusion

Repeated short-run crises, a large impending deficit, and large increases in costs projected after the turn of the century have all

18. Yung-Ping Chen, "The Growth of Fringe Benefits: Implications for Social Security," *Monthly Labor Review*, vol. 104, (GPO, 1981), p. 3.

served to undermine public confidence in the social security system. The enactment of the recommendations of the National Commission on Social Security Reform, which the 1984 budget endorses, should go a long way toward restoring public confidence in the system.

The most significant aspect of the commission's proposals for social security is the acceptance by a group of bipartisan political leaders of the notion that abrupt and substantial restructuring of the program is unnecessary, undesirable, and politically unpalatable. The bipartisan proposals contain modest and desirable reforms that balance the interests of beneficiaries against those of current and future taxpayers, and it is encouraging that the proposals have received the support of the president and Congress.

CHAPTER FIVE

Medical Care

LOUISE B. RUSSELL

THE STALEMATE that characterized federal policy toward medical care in the 1970s has ended.[1] No longer deadlocked over what to do about the relentless growth in health programs, Congress in the 1980s has legislated some unprecedented changes in those programs to try to bring expenditures under control. The choices are no easier than before, but the pressure from rising costs is more intense. With the economy still weak and the budget deficit alarming, it has become necessary to reevaluate the goals and results of federal programs, and medical care programs are no exception.

The recent changes are important because they abandon the principle, in fact if not in rhetoric, that medical care should be provided whenever it is needed, that cost should not be considered when life or health is at stake. Congress has implicitly agreed that some medical services have benefits that are too small or too costly to warrant the necessary expenditure. This represents a fundamental change from the philosophy that has driven the system for a long time, and the beginning of a search for a new balance between the costs and benefits of increased spending on medical care.

THE AUTHOR is grateful to Henry J. Aaron, Thomas J. Buchberger, Paul B. Ginsburg, Julian H. Pettengill, Clifford S. Russell, and William J. Sobaski for their comments on drafts of this chapter; to Charlotte Kaiser for typing the manuscript; and to Joy O. Robinson for checking its factual content.

1. For a discussion of that stalemate, see Louise B. Russell, "Medical Care," in Joseph A. Pechman, ed., *Setting National Priorities: Agenda for the 1980s* (Brookings Institution, 1980), chap. 6.

111

Legislative Changes in 1981 and 1982

In 1981 Congress directed most of its attention to medicaid, the program that pays for medical care for those on welfare and, if a state chooses, for the medically needy, people whose incomes are not low enough to qualify them for welfare but who nonetheless need help with their medical bills. The program is financed jointly with the states, the federal matching rate depending on a state's per capita income. Well-to-do states like New York and California receive fifty cents of every dollar they spend from the federal government. Poorer states receive more: in 1979 Mississippi received seventy-eight cents of every dollar from the federal government.

Changes in Medicaid

Until the passage of the Omnibus Budget Reconciliation Act of 1981, matching funds for medicaid had been available without limit so long as the expenditures were for the kinds of people and services specified in the legislation. Congress rejected the Reagan administration's request for a straightforward ceiling on federal payments. Instead it passed a more complicated set of limits. The 1981 law requires that federal payments be reduced below what a state would ordinarily be entitled to on the basis of its total expenditures, by 3.0 percent in fiscal 1982, 4.0 percent in 1983, and 4.5 percent in 1984. The reduction would be less by one percentage point each if a state had an approved cost-review program, an unemployment rate 50 percent higher than the national average, or recovered payments from fraudulent claims equal to 1 percent of the federal payment. Potentially, then, a state could completely offset the reduction for 1982, though not for the later years.

Stated that way, the limits are essentially retrospective. A state spends according to the benefits and beneficiaries it has specified for its program, the federal matching payment is calculated and then reduced as required, and the state ends up supplying a larger proportion of the total than in preceding years. But Congress added a further provision to encourage cost containment and make it possible for states to budget prospectively if they so choose. The law established 1981 expenditures plus 9 percent as the "target" for 1982. Any state whose total costs were less than the target by 3 percent, that is, whose 1982 expenditures were only 6 percent above

1981, received federal funds at the same matching rate as before, with no reduction in payments. Similar rules apply to 1983 and 1984, and the secretary of health and human services is directed to set new targets for each year, using the medical component of the consumer price index.

Even before the 1981 law, the states had been trying to restrain the growth in medicaid expenditures simply because their own share was becoming burdensome. To help them deal with the new pressure, the 1981 law loosened several medicaid requirements. Services offered to some of the medically needy no longer must be offered to all of them. On receipt of appropriate waivers from the secretary of health and human services, states may limit the recipient's freedom to choose a doctor, hospital, or other provider; this means a state can require recipients to use providers it has selected as low-cost. Congress made this new flexibility subject to a general requirement that the quality of services and a recipient's access to them should not be substantially impaired. States may now offer home health and community-based services through medicaid, to reduce the cost of caring for people who would otherwise require care in a nursing home. Medicaid recipients may be enrolled in health maintenance organizations in which medicare and medicaid beneficiaries make up as much as 75 percent of the total enrollment; the limit used to be 50 percent. And no longer must states base their hospital payments under medicaid on reasonable costs as determined by the federal medicare program. States have always had considerable freedom to set reimbursement rates for other providers and to limit the amounts of service the program would cover, for example, the number of days in the hospital.

Many states have taken advantage of the changes, some to launch experiments that differ sharply from the previous state program. Perhaps the most notable is the new plan in California, under which hospitals must negotiate contracts with the state in order to participate in the medicaid program. The contracts specify the rate to be paid, usually a flat rate per day, and require the hospital to accept all medicaid patients who come to it. Hospitals that fail to get a contract in the first round cannot try again until the state decides that more medicaid beds are needed in the area.

Changes in Medicare

The Omnibus Budget Reconciliation Act of 1981 made only minor changes in medicare, the federal program that helps pay the medical expenses of the elderly and disabled, including those with end-stage kidney disease. For the most part they consisted of modest increases in the deductibles and coinsurance required of beneficiaries and the tightening of several reimbursement limits—for example, reimbursement for a hospital's routine operating costs was limited to no more than 108 percent of the average cost for similar hospitals, down from the 112 percent set earlier by the Department of Health and Human Services (HHS).

In 1982 the situations were reversed. Only a few changes were made in medicaid: the states were given more freedom to impose small amounts of cost sharing on beneficiaries and to take over the property of medicaid recipients in nursing homes. But medicare was changed in important ways by the Tax Equity and Fiscal Responsibility Act of 1982.

By far the most important change was in the method for paying hospitals. The principle with which medicare began, a principle still largely intact in 1982, was that the program would pay the costs actually incurred by hospitals in caring for medicare beneficiaries. This approach, it was believed, would interfere least with the practice of medicine. The approach was modified over the years in minor ways. Most notably, in 1972 Congress gave the Department of Health, Education, and Welfare (now HHS) authority to limit payments to hospitals whose costs were substantially higher than those of similar hospitals. Until 1982, however, the limits were applied only to routine costs, including nursing. Only a few hospitals were affected by the limits, and those few managed to shift some of the disallowed amounts to the costs they reported for ancillary services, such as x-rays and laboratory tests, or to other payers, particularly private insurers.

In the 1982 tax act Congress abandoned the traditional approach and replaced it for fiscal years 1983–85 with a system in which maximum rates of payment would be set in advance and hospitals would be at risk for the difference if their costs exceeded the maximum rate. First, the law officially extended the reimbursement limits legislated in 1972 to include ancillary services, except in rural hospitals with fewer than fifty beds and certain specialty hospitals, such as children's hospitals. With this provision to rein in hospitals that have especially high costs, Congress then described the new system of payment. Beginning in fiscal 1983, a target rate would be calculated for each hospital. That rate is the allowable operating cost per admission in 1982, for both routine and ancillary services, adjusted upward by the rate of inflation in hospital wages and prices plus 1 percentage point. Each year thereafter, the target rate would be increased in the same way. Hospitals whose costs were less than the target would keep half the savings up to a maximum of 5 percent of the target. Hospitals whose costs exceeded the target would be paid 25 percent of the difference in 1983 and 1984, but none of it in 1985. Capital costs and the costs of medical education would be paid separately.

Congress viewed this system as temporary, to be replaced by a more sophisticated method of prospective payment as soon as possible, and directed that the secretary of health and human services design a permanent system and report back to the Congress before the end of 1982. The secretary's proposal, which would establish separate rates for admissions with different diagnoses, is described later in the chapter.

The 1982 tax act made several other changes worth noting, though none of such fundamental importance to the program as the change in hospital reimbursement. It required employers with twenty or more employees to offer those aged sixty-five through sixty-nine the same health insurance benefits as younger workers, which makes medicare the second payer whenever the employee accepts the offer. It authorized payment of health maintenance organizations either on the basis of a flat annual rate per enrollee or on the existing basis of incurred costs, and directed that premiums for part B (physicians' services) coverage be increased faster than permitted by earlier legislation. And it brought federal employees under medicare starting January 1, 1983.

The Continuing Pressure of Costs

Congress has slowed the rate of increase in medicare and medicaid expenditures somewhat, but those expenditures are still projected to grow substantially in the 1980s. Again this year, the government will have to look for new ways to trim costs or add to

Table 5-1. Federal Outlays for Health, Selected Fiscal Years, 1970–88[a]

Billions of dollars

Program	1970	1975	1980	1981	1982	Projected 1983	1984	1985	1986	1987	1988
Medicare[b]											
Under existing law	7.1	14.8	35.0	39.1	46.6	53.0	61.5	70.6	79.1	89.9	101.8
With proposed savings	...	...	...	...	...	53.0	59.8	67.5	74.5	83.4	93.1
Medicaid, federal share											
Under existing law	2.7	6.8	14.0	16.9	17.4	19.3	21.1	24.0	26.1	28.5	31.2
With proposed savings	...	...	...	...	...	19.3	20.8	23.1	25.3	27.8	30.6
Other[c]											
Under existing law	3.1	6.0	9.1	9.9	10.1	10.0	10.1	9.9	10.1	10.3	10.6
With proposed savings	...	...	...	...	...	10.0	10.0	9.8	9.7	9.8	9.9
Total											
Under existing law	13.0	27.6	58.2	66.0	74.0	82.3	92.7	104.5	115.3	128.7	143.6
With proposed savings	...	...	...	...	...	82.4	90.6	100.5	109.6	121.0	133.5

Sources: *Budget of the United States Government, Fiscal Year 1984,* and earlier budgets; and unpublished data provided by the Office of Management and Budget. Figures are rounded.

a. Fiscal 1970 and 1975 end June 30; later fiscal years end September 30. Health outlays by the Department of Defense and the Veterans Administration are excluded.

b. Total outlays less the premiums paid by enrollees for physicians' coverage.

c. Other health services, research, education and training, and consumer and occupational health and safety, less deductions for offsetting receipts.

revenues, and to consolidate the savings already legislated. Further, the administration and Congress must settle on more permanent structures to consolidate the changes legislated in medicare and medicaid.

Even with the changes that have been made, total federal health outlays are projected to rise from $74 billion in 1982 to $144 billion in 1988 (table 5-1), or by an average of 12 percent a year. Other federal health programs, always a small fraction of the total, have been pared so sharply that medicare and medicaid will account for 90 percent of expenditures. The growth in outlays is thus primarily the growth projected for these two programs as the costs of serving their beneficiaries continue to rise within the limits set by Congress; most of the growth is due to medicare, which is larger and growing faster than medicaid.

Health outlays are the fourth largest item of expenditure in the federal budget, after income security, national defense, and interest on the public debt. They are important not only because they are big but because they have grown so rapidly over the years, absorbing a larger and larger proportion of federal outlays. In 1970 health accounted for less than 7 percent of the federal budget. In 1980 it accounted for about 10 percent. When medical care expenditures for the armed services and for veterans are added—in the budget these are included with national defense and veterans' benefits, respectively—the share of all health outlays in the federal budget was 12 percent in 1980.

A large chunk of health outlays, the hospital insurance part of medicare (part A), is financed not through general revenues but through a payroll tax especially earmarked for the purpose. These revenues are handled in the same way as the payroll tax revenues for social security cash benefits: they are kept in a separate hospital insurance trust fund, and funds are withdrawn as needed to pay benefits; general revenues may not be used for the purpose. The earmarked tax has been raised several times over the course of the program, to levels well above those projected when medicare began, and stands at 2.6 percent of taxable payroll in 1983 (for employers and employees combined). Early in 1982 the trustees of the fund projected that taxes would need to be raised again if expenditures continued to grow as they had in the past, but that the current schedule of rates would probably be adequate for the next few years.

The most recent projections are more pessimistic than earlier ones because, late in 1981, Congress passed legislation permitting the financially troubled social security retirement program to borrow from the hospital insurance and disability trust funds. In 1982 the retirement program, in need of ready cash to meet benefit payments, did borrow from the hospital insurance fund, and though the original authorization expired December 31, 1982, it was renewed by the 1983 social security legislation. Until the loans are repaid, the hospital insurance fund is thus itself nearer depletion than it would otherwise be. The financial problem is primarily a technical one. The federal deficit is simply the difference between all outlays and all revenues, without regard for the niceties of earmarked taxes and special trust funds. But Congress will have to address additional problems raised by the particular way this part of the program is financed—whether to continue financing it this way and, if so, what rates to set if medicare outlays continue to rise more rapidly than the current tax schedule can support.

The gap between federal revenues and federal expenditures is affected not only by what Congress decides to spend and to tax but also by what it decides not to tax. In recent years the growing use of tax incentives and exclusions from taxation as conscious instruments of policy has led to the realization that some important "programs" are reflected not in outlays, but in tax expenditures. These are defined as revenues forgone because certain items are taxed less heavily than others or not at all.[2]

In the 1982 tax act, Congress reduced tax expenditures for health by eliminating the $150 deduction for health insurance premiums paid by individuals and raising from 3 percent to 5 percent the amount of adjusted gross income that must be spent out-of-pocket on medical care before the taxpayer can deduct further expenses. The most important tax expenditure, the exclusion from tax of employer contributions for health insurance premiums and medical care, was considered but left unchanged. Most private insurance is provided by employers as a fringe benefit of employment. The Congressional Budget Office estimates that this exclusion alone will save taxpayers, and cost the Treasury, $18 billion in income taxes in 1983. All tax expenditures for health will total about $24 billion in 1983, up from less than $3 billion in 1967 and about $5 billion in 1974.[3]

The Basic Problem Revisited

It is obvious at a glance that the changes made in medicare and medicaid in the last two years are significant. But to understand their full import, and the context in which future changes will be made, it is necessary to review the reasons why expenditures have risen so rapidly year after year.

General inflation accounts for a large part of the growth in expenditures, of course. The consumer price index rose 134 percent between 1970 and 1981. Medical expenditures would have had to more than double simply to keep up. But though inflation is the largest single reason for higher expenditures, it is the least important. Had

2. For an analysis of tax expenditures, see appendix C.
3. Payroll taxes, which are not considered a tax expenditure since they are offset by future liabilities for benefits, were lower by almost $8 billion in 1983 because of the exclusion.

health outlays merely risen with the price level, they would not be absorbing a larger share of the federal budget and the gross national product, and there would be no cause for particular concern about them.

Instead, health outlays have risen much faster than inflation, primarily because the beneficiary populations of federal programs have grown and because they are receiving more medical care per person. Medicaid grew especially fast during the late 1960s and the early 1970s as the number of people on welfare grew; the number eligible for welfare increased somewhat, but the proportion of those eligible who actually applied for it rose sharply, from 60 percent to more than 90 percent.[4] Since the mid-1970s the number of medicaid recipients has fluctuated around a level of 22 million. Despite high unemployment, the number is not likely to rise, because in the 1981 budget act Congress placed new restrictions on the eligibility for welfare of families with dependent children.

The number of elderly people in the medicare program has increased gradually over the years along with the elderly population. About 95 percent of those sixty-five and older are enrolled. A big jump in enrollment occurred in 1973, when disabled people under sixty-five and those with end-stage kidney disease were added to the program. Medicare enrollees currently number more than 29 million: 26 million sixty-five and older, and 3 million disabled people under sixty-five.

With the help of medicare and medicaid, the elderly and the poor received much more medical care in the late 1970s, the most recent period for which data are available, than they did before the programs came into being. Poor people visited doctors about as often as people with higher incomes, and their rates of surgery were about the same; before medicaid, their use of both kinds of care was much lower.[5] Only about half the elderly had any hospital insurance before medicare, and their use of hospitals has increased substantially since its passage. The proportion of elderly people in nursing homes rose even more sharply, from 23 per 1,000 people aged sixty-five or older in 1963 to 48 per 1,000 in 1977. This rise put particular strain on the

4. Karen Davis and Cathy Schoen, *Health and the War on Poverty: A Ten-Year Appraisal* (Brookings Institution, 1978), chap. 3.
5. Ibid., chap. 2.

medicaid program, which now spends forty cents of every dollar on nursing home care.

The steadiest contributor to federal expenditures, and to private expenditures as well, has been increases in the cost of a day in the hospital. Most other sources of growth have been important for a few years, or from time to time, but the cost of a hospital day has gone up year after year by substantially more than the rate of inflation. Almost all of the difference has been due to the increasing amounts of resources used in hospital care. Hospitals have upgraded old services and added new ones—intensive care, which has mushroomed since the 1960s, open-heart surgery, kidney dialysis, CT scanners, and more—hiring more employees, buying new equipment, and renovating facilities or building new ones in the process.[6] Between 1965 and 1978 cost per day rose more than 12 percent each year on average, and about half that increase—6 percentage points —represented additional resources. The level of real resources per day in 1978 was approximately double the level of 1965.

The increases in resources devoted to the medical care of the poor and the elderly have been accompanied by some impressive gains in health. The life expectancy of people aged sixty-five has grown much faster since 1965 than it did in the fifteen years between 1950 and 1965. The infant mortality rate eased downward in the years before medicare and medicaid; it has fallen sharply since then, from 25 deaths per 1,000 births for all races in 1965 to 13 per 1,000 in 1980. The gains for nonwhites have been especially remarkable. The infant mortality rate for nonwhites stood at 45 per 1,000 in 1950 and was still 40 per 1,000 in 1965. By 1979 it had fallen to 20 per 1,000. No one can say exactly to what degree better medical care has contributed to these gains, but it is unquestionably an important part of the explanation.

The rapid growth in expenditures has not been limited to federal programs, of course. Total national expenditures for medical care have been growing faster than the rate of inflation for many years (table 5-2). The percent of gross national product spent on medical care, a measure that reflects the increasing amounts of real resources absorbed by the medical care sector, free of the effects of general inflation, rose from 4.4 percent in 1950 to 6.0 percent in

6. See Louise B. Russell, *Technology in Hospitals: Medical Advances and Their Diffusion* (Brookings Institution, 1979).

Table 5-2. National Health Expenditures, Selected Calendar Years, 1950–81
Billions of dollars unless otherwise specified

Type of expenditure	1950	1965	1980	1981
Hospital care	3.9	13.9	100.4	118.0
Physicians' services	2.7	8.5	46.8	54.8
Drugs	1.7	5.2	19.3	21.4
Dentists' services	1.0	2.8	15.4	17.3
Nursing-home care	0.2	2.1	20.6	24.2
All other[a]	3.2	9.3	46.2	50.9
Total	12.7	41.7	249.0	286.6
Addendum:				
Percent of gross national product	4.4	6.0	9.5	9.8

Source: Robert M. Gibson and Daniel R. Waldo, "National Health Expenditures, 1981," *Health Care Financing Review,* vol. 4 (September 1982), tables 1 and 2. Figures are rounded.

a. Other services, appliances, administration, public health activities, program administration and net cost of insurance, research, and construction.

1965. The rate of increase has been considerably faster since the passage of medicare and medicaid: in 1981 medical care expenditures were almost 10 percent of the GNP.

The reasons for the growth in total expenditures are similar to the reasons for the growth in federal programs. A summary of the expenses for care in community hospitals concluded that general inflation accounted for 52 percent of the growth between 1971 and 1981. Increases in the wages and prices paid by hospitals, over and above general inflation, accounted for another 12 percent. The rest reflected additional resources required by a growing population (7 percent), more hospital stays per capita (8 percent), and more services per stay (21 percent).[7]

The mechanism that has made the growth in expenditures possible is third-party payment—not only medicare and medicaid, but private insurance and other, smaller public and private programs. In the late 1970s more than 90 percent of the population was covered by at least one of these programs. Drawing on tax revenues or insurance premiums, the latter often paid by employers, third-party programs pay much of the cost of medical care, especially hospital care. Most patients today, and their doctors on their behalf, do not have to

7. Mark S. Freeland and Carol Ellen Schendler, "National Health Expenditure Growth in the 1980s: An Aging Population, New Technologies, and Increasing Competition," *Health Care Financing Review,* vol. 4 (March 1983), pp. 1–58. This analysis uses the GNP deflator to measure general inflation. Had the consumer price index, a more limited but better-known measure, been used instead, the share attributed to general inflation would have been larger and that attributed to additional inflation in the hospital sector smaller.

worry whether they can afford the care they need. They have only to decide what services will be best from a medical point of view.

Third-party payment has come in for much criticism in recent years. It has been accused of changing the incentives of patients and doctors, of making them insensitive to the cost of care and encouraging them to make use of services whose benefits are small or problematic. Often these services are enormously expensive, as when heroic efforts are made to save a patient with severe injuries or terminal disease.

The critics are right, but they miss the point. It is no accident that third-party payment makes patients and doctors insensitive to cost. That is exactly what it was designed to do. Third-party payment puts into practice the philosophy that no one should have to forgo medical care that might save his life or preserve his health because he cannot afford to pay. Part and parcel of that philosophy is the principle that medical care should be provided whenever it is needed, whenever there is a chance it can help. With extensive third-party payment, patients and doctors do not have to consider whether the benefit of a medical service is worth the resources it draws from other uses.

The economic consequences of this philosophy, especially in the modern era of ever-improving medical technology, have become much clearer as expenditures have continued to grow. Even for a country as rich as the United States, to provide medical care on the basis of need alone is enormously expensive. At the level of the aggregate economy, it has proved impossible to maintain the fiction, encouraged at the individual level by third-party payment, that resources are unlimited. Resources used for medical care are resources taken from some other purpose. There is no completely satisfactory solution to the dilemma. Trying to do everything worthwhile means rapidly escalating expenditures; slowing the growth in expenditures means going without.

The dilemma is not peculiar to the United States or its system of medical care. In the mid-1970s a number of countries, such as Sweden, West Germany, the Netherlands, and France, were spending as much of their national resources on medical care as the United States. Scattered data for more recent years indicate that this is still true, and these countries have debated, and sometimes adopted, the same kinds of cost-control measures debated and adopted in the United States.

Canada and Great Britain both spend markedly lower proportions of their national products on medical care than the United States. But they have not somehow escaped the dilemma. They have simply chosen a different point on the continuum between high costs and abundant medical care at one end, and low costs and limited medical care at the other. Both countries control expenditures by setting overall budgets, at the national level in Britain and the provincial level in Canada. The strains and deprivations are greater and more obvious in Britain, where the Health Service receives a smaller share of a smaller GNP and where spending has been restrained for much longer than in Canada.

Again, the recent changes in medicare and medicaid are significant because they abandon the principle that cost should not be considered when life or health is at stake. By placing absolute limits on what medicare will pay for a hospital stay and on how much the federal government will contribute to state medicaid programs, Congress has implicitly agreed that some medical benefits are too small or too costly. It is hard to overemphasize the importance of the new limits. They represent a fundamental change in philosophy, one that will require difficult, even painful, choices as the nation tries to strike a new balance between the benefits and costs of more spending on medical care.

The Basic Options

The basic dilemma is the same one that has bedeviled the country and its elected representatives for years. The basic options for cutting expenditures are also the same and can be grouped under two broad headings: cost sharing and budget limits. Congress could raise additional revenues as well, as it has in the past. But in the current climate, options for cutting expenditures will be getting most of the attention.

The important question about the various proposals is not whether they can succeed in controlling the growth in expenditures. Given the political will, they can. The choice among them, then, depends on how well each one works—its costs and benefits, quirks and foibles—and on the compatibility of each with the emerging national philosophy about medical care. How are limited funds to be rationed among specific uses and individuals? How does each approach square with principles of equity, efficiency, and personal and social responsibility?

Cost Sharing

Cost sharing includes any proposal to make people individually responsible for more of the cost of the medical services they receive or of their insurance premiums. The crucial feature is that how much a person pays is linked to the quantity and price of the services he or she uses, either directly through charges for the services themselves, or indirectly through the charges for third-party coverage.

SERVICES. Cost sharing for services encourages the patient to consider the cost of care, and whether the possible benefits outweigh those costs, before accepting a doctor's advice. Similarly, it encourages the doctor, on the patient's behalf, to weigh the costs as well as the benefits of additional care. In the process, doctor and patient may individually or jointly decide to go without some services that they would have used had the patient been responsible for less of the cost or none of it.

Cost sharing comes in various forms. Programs of third-party payment, both public and private, specify that the program will cover some services but not others, making the individual responsible for the full cost of uncovered services. Payment for covered services is usually subject to deductibles and coinsurance: a deductible is a dollar amount of expenditures that the patient must pay before the program will pay anything; coinsurance is the percentage of further expenditures for which the patient is responsible. For example, under part B of medicare, the enrollee must pay the first $75 of covered expenditures in a year. After that, medicare pays 80 percent of any further expenditures, and the enrollee pays the remaining 20 percent. In some plans the enrollee must pay set dollar amounts, called copayments, for each service, say $5 for each visit to the doctor, and the plan covers the rest.

The patient's share of the cost is also greater when the plan disallows certain expenditures. For example, medicare has what it calls reasonable-charge limits for doctors' fees. If the fee charged exceeds the limit, the patient is responsible for all the excess; medicare pays 80 percent of only the amount it has determined to be reasonable. Many private plans have similar limits on charges. Unless both patient and doctor are kept well informed of these limits, they have less effect than other forms of cost sharing on the use of services, because expenditures are disallowed after the fact, when decisions have already been made. If the pattern of disallowances is consistent, the participants may alter their choices the next time. If not, they simply find themselves paying more than expected.

No one proposes to do away with third-party payment and have patients pay the full cost of care. The debate is over whether patients should pay a larger share, how they should pay it, and what effects the change will have. Some people have argued that cost sharing has no effect on the use of services, indeed can have no effect because doctors, not patients, make the decisions. Others have worried that if cost sharing has an effect, people will forgo beneficial services and their health will suffer. Still others believe that cost sharing is simply immoral, and that if care must be rationed, more collective approaches should be used.

The factual issues have remained in dispute despite some good, small studies showing that cost sharing does reduce the use of services.[8] But some of these disputes should be finally settled by the results now beginning to appear from an important social experiment conducted by the Rand Corporation under the sponsorship of HHS. The experiment, which began in the early 1970s, is far larger than any previous study, encompassing more than 2,700 families (7,700 people) living in six different areas across the country. Medicare enrollees and families with incomes over $25,000 in 1973 were excluded. The families were assigned to health insurance plans that differed in their coinsurance rates (0, 25, 50, and 95 percent) and in the maximum amount the family had to pay before the insurance plan assumed full responsibility for further expenditures; this amount was higher for families with higher incomes, but never exceeded $1,000. The families assigned to the different plans were matched as closely as possible on the basis of a large number of characteristics.

Preliminary results, published late in 1981, confirmed that cost sharing reduces expenditures on medical care.[9] The families subject

8. Anne A. Scitovsky and Nelda M. Snyder, "Effect of Coinsurance on Use of Physician Services," *Social Security Bulletin*, vol. 35 (June 1972), pp. 3–28; and Anne A. Scitovsky and Nelda McCall, "Coinsurance and the Demand for Physician Services: Four Years Later," *Social Security Bulletin*, vol. 40 (May 1977), pp. 19–30.

9. Joseph P. Newhouse and others, "Some Interim Results from a Controlled Trial of

to higher amounts of coinsurance had fewer visits to the doctor, and the adults had fewer hospital stays, than families that received free care; there was no difference in the number of hospital stays for children. The total expenditures on hospital and physicians' care of families subject to 95 percent coinsurance were less than 70 percent as large as the expenditures by families that faced zero coinsurance. Put another way, the families that received free care spent 50 percent more. The differences in amounts of service, rather than in prices for those services, accounted for most of the difference in total expenditures.

The study should lay to rest the argument that cost sharing cannot affect use because doctors make the decisions, not patients. Cost sharing does affect use substantially. Whoever makes the decisions, whether the patient, the doctor on his behalf, or the two together, is paying attention to the costs facing the patient and responding to them. Not only visits to the doctor but admissions to the hospital, important decisions often thought to be left to the doctor, were reduced by cost sharing.

The study has also been following the health of the families in each insurance plan, but the results have not yet been published. Two points should be kept in mind about these results when they do appear. First, families were enrolled in the study for only three to five years. If no differences in health appear during this period, this does not necessarily mean that no differences would occur over a longer period. Second, if the study finds that families who used fewer services because of cost sharing had poorer health, it does not follow that cost sharing is an unacceptable way to ration care. Any mechanism for controlling the growth in expenditures will result in fewer medical services than otherwise and may have detrimental effects on people's health. The issue, then, becomes whether the health effects of one approach are preferable to those of another—whose health is affected in each case, and by how much?

There are some issues that the study will not be able to settle. The early results showed virtually no difference between plans in the costs incurred once a patient was admitted to the hospital. A likely explanation is the low limit on the maximum amount payable by the family. With a limit of $1,000 or less, the main possibility for saving money is in the decision whether to enter the hospital in the first place. Once in, it is the rare patient whose expenditures, however carefully watched, would not pass the point at which the insurer took full responsibility, and from that point, regardless of the plan, further expenditures cost the patient nothing; 70 percent of the patients hospitalized during the study did exceed the maximum. The study will not be able to show whether the cost of hospitalization would have responded had cost sharing been more extensive. The alternative possibility is that hospitals establish a general style of care, which they then apply to each patient who enters, regardless of the patient's financial situation.

More important, the study cannot show what happens to medical expenditures when most or all of the people in an area are subject to substantial cost sharing. It seems reasonable to believe that the style of care offered by hospitals and physicians and the prices they charge reflect the finances of the average patient. If the average patient is well insured, the style of care and prices will be higher than if the average patient pays a good part of the bill directly. This general effect could easily be as important to total expenditures as the responses of individual patients to cost sharing. But the families participating in the study were only a small part of the population in each of the six study sites. Thus the results show only the effect of individual responses to cost sharing, not general market responses.

The low limit on expenditures by patients in the Rand study reflects a more general philosophy about the use of cost sharing for medical services. Even its advocates believe there should be limits on the patient's liability. While some would set the maximum higher than $1,000, all propose a fairly low limit, often one scaled to income. Low limits on cost sharing mean that it cannot be the sole, or even the major, mechanism for controlling expenditures. A substantial proportion of expenditures will always fall above the limit. With no cost sharing to hold these expenditures in check, some form of budget limit will have to be applied. Given the current consensus, cost sharing is necessarily only part of a strategy for controlling expenditures, not the whole strategy.

INSURANCE PREMIUMS. Contributions made by employers toward health insurance provided as a fringe benefit of employment are free of tax. Employers deduct the contributions as a business expense, and employees do not pay income or payroll taxes on them. As a result, health insurance is a better bargain than other items, such as food and clothing, that must be bought with after-tax dollars. The tax advantages of receiving an extra dollar in the form of health insurance rather than as income encourage employees, and their employers, to choose more generous insurance plans than they otherwise would. And as has already been explained, more generous plans drive up medical care expenditures.

Proposals have been put forward to tax contributions above a certain amount as part of an employee's income. This increase in the cost of health insurance would encourage employers and employees to settle on less expensive plans. But a plan could be made less expensive in only one of two ways: by making the deductibles and coinsurance larger, so that the amount paid by the insurer was smaller (in the extreme case, some services might be dropped from the plan altogether); or by providing services through organizations that operate under budget limits, such as health maintenance organizations, and that have limits stringent enough to keep premiums within the tax-free allowance. Thus this kind of cost sharing would operate indirectly by inducing individuals to choose plans that ration at the point of service more than current plans do, either through cost sharing for services or through budget limits.

High-income people would be affected most. Not only do a greater percentage of high-income families receive health insurance as a fringe benefit of employment but the contribution is larger. The Congressional Budget Office estimates that in 1983, 13 percent of households with less than $10,000 in income, and 31 percent of those with incomes between $10,000 and $15,000, will receive health insurance as a fringe benefit, compared with more than 70 percent of households with incomes between $30,000 and $100,000. Employer contributions for those receiving them will average $640 and $970 for the two low-income groups, respectively, and almost $2,000 for the high-income group. Since high-income households pay a higher marginal rate of income tax, they save far more in taxes than low-income households—between $700 and $800, compared with $130 and $270 for the two low-income groups.

The Congressional Budget Office has estimated the effects on insurance premiums and medical care expenditures of several possible plans for changing the tax exclusion. As an example, their projections indicate that taxing employer contributions above $150 a month for a family and $60 a month for an individual (1983 dollars) would mean that total premiums would be 13 percent less by 1987 than if insurance remains tax-free. The lower coverage would reduce expenditures under these plans by approximately 9 percent. In addition, of course, taxing employer contributions would raise substantial amounts in taxes. The plan indicated would add $3 billion to income and payroll taxes in 1983 and more than $9 billion in 1987.

The treatment of insurance policies purchased by individuals deserves brief mention. Until the end of 1982 taxpayers could deduct $150 of the cost of such policies from their taxable income, but they can no longer do so. A major type of individual policy is medigap coverage, which pays the deductibles, coinsurance, and other items not paid by medicare. Enrollees who have these policies spend more on medical care than other enrollees, and collect more from the program, thus raising its costs. Proposals have been made to tax medigap policies to reflect these extra costs. The Congressional Budget Office estimates that such a tax would add about 35 percent to the cost of a policy.

Budget Limits

Budget limits include any proposal to limit the amount paid on behalf of an individual by a third-party payer for a package of medical services. For example, a state government, or a third-party payer acting alone, may set the rates it will pay for a day in the hospital or for an entire stay. Some state governments fix the maximum total revenues a hospital can receive. Health maintenance organizations offer to provide a broad range of services to their enrollees, all they will need in the course of a year, in return for a single annual fee set in advance. (This is not strictly a budget limit because the same organization sets and receives the limit, a point that is discussed later.) Like cost sharing, budget limits can be applied indirectly through insurance premiums. An employer may offer to pay a fixed amount toward the premium of any health insurance plan selected by the employee, with the rest of the cost to be paid by the employee. A public program could make a similar offer to its beneficiaries.

Through a budget limit, the payer essentially tells the provider of services: "Here is all the money you can have—for this patient, or this hospital stay, or this year. Do the best you can with it and don't come back for more." In direct contrast to cost reimbursement, the payer's liability is limited and does not go up with costs. The onus is on the provider to keep the cost of the package of services within the limit if it wants to survive. Analogously, a person buying an insurance policy with the help of a fixed payment from an employer or public program will have to pay more money out-of-pocket the more expensive the policy. The liability of the employer or program is fixed and the risk falls on the buyer.

SERVICES. The states have been experimenting with budget limits for several years in the form of prospective reimbursement for hospital care. The term *prospective reimbursement* emphasizes that the amount to be paid is supposed to be set in advance; like any good budget limit, it should not vary with the costs actually incurred by the hospital. In practice, of course, hospitals that cannot stay within the limit sometimes appeal and win extra payments.

As of 1982 eight states had mandatory rate-setting programs. Most of them had been in operation since the mid-1970s, the New York program even longer. Under mandatory programs hospitals must participate in the program and must accept the limits set on their revenues by the rate-setting authority (subject to the possibility of appeal). The states differ in how broadly they define the package of services for which rates are set. New York has set rates for a day in the hospital, New Jersey for a stay, and Maryland, Connecticut, Massachusetts, and Washington control the entire hospital budget. Rhode Island has experimented with setting a budget for hospital care throughout the state. States differ also in how many third-party payers are included in the program. Only in the fall of 1982, for example, did New York and Massachusetts receive permission from HHS to include medicare patients in their programs.

Although these programs have been constantly changing—expanding to include new payers, adopting new methods for calculating rates, responding to lawsuits brought by hospitals—they appear to have had some success in controlling the growth in hospital expenditures. The Congressional Budget Office reports that between 1976 and 1981 inpatient hospital expenses per capita in seven rate-setting states rose 11 percent a year, compared with 14 percent in all other states; it is worth keeping in mind, however, that controlling the growth of expenditures may have been easier for these states than it would be for others, because most of them started with levels of expenditure above the national average. The international evidence presented earlier also confirms the effectiveness of budget limits. Both the United Kingdom and Canada have used them to control the growth of total expenditures for medical services.

There is nothing magical about the way budget limits work. Whatever their precise form, budget limits provide less money than providers and patients would like. In common with cost sharing, they force providers to ration, to omit services with small benefits or extremely high costs. They differ from cost sharing in that the pressure to ration is on the provider; the patient's incentives are not changed. Some of the omitted services will scarcely be noticed, while others will cause doctors and patients to make painful choices.

The administration's proposal for medicare. In December 1982 HHS sent a report to Congress proposing a permanent system of prospective reimbursement for hospitals under medicare to replace the temporary system included in the Tax Equity and Fiscal Responsibility Act. Although it was introduced early, the plan is an important component of the administration's proposals for health in the 1984 budget. Its early introduction permitted early action by Congress, and the plan, largely intact, was passed by both houses in late March as part of the 1983 social security legislation.

Under the plan, medicare would pay hospitals fixed amounts per admission. To reflect differences in the costs of caring for patients with different problems, separate rates would be set for each of 467 diagnosis-related groups (DRGs). The rate would be the same for every patient in a given group, regardless of what was done for the patient or how long he or she stayed in the hospital,[10] and would be considered payment in full for the cost of inpatient care, except capital costs and costs associated with medical education. Hospitals whose costs were less than the rate could keep the difference; those whose costs were greater would have to absorb the loss. Patients could not be charged extra amounts to cover the losses, though they would still be responsible for the deductibles and copayments specified by medicare. The rates would be updated every year to reflect inflation and other factors.

Computation of the rates would start with the national average costs of care for medicare patients in the 467 diagnosis-related groups; separate averages would be calculated for urban and rural

10. In some instances, however, major surgical procedures are used to define a group.

hospitals. These averages would be adjusted to reflect wage levels in each standard metropolitan statistical area and in the nonmetropolitan area of each state, resulting in rate schedules for about 300 different areas. The schedule would be the same for all the hospitals in an area. Each hospital would still be paid its incurred costs for capital (interest, rent, and depreciation) and the direct expenses of medical education, principally the salaries of interns and residents. The indirect costs of medical education, reflecting the higher cost of caring for patients in teaching hospitals, would be estimated by HHS and paid as a lump sum. Payments under the system are projected to be about the same, and save about as much, as those under the temporary plan included in the 1982 tax act.

The new payment system would apply to all hospitals except long-term, psychiatric, and pediatric institutions. Health maintenance organizations that are paid for their medicare enrollees on the basis of incurred costs would automatically be included in the system; those that accept annual payments per enrollee could join the system if they wished.

Diagnosis-related groups, on which the proposed system is based, were developed at Yale University in the late 1960s. Their purpose is to sort patients into groups according to cost. Patients in the same group are reasonably alike, and the remaining differences between them may be due as much to variations in the way different physicians choose to treat the same patient as to differences in their medical condition. DRGs have been used in Maryland to adjust hospital budgets for the kinds of patients the hospital treats. New Jersey has based its prospective reimbursement system directly on DRGs, much as would the medicare plan, and sets a separate payment rate per admission for each group.

In 1979 HHS awarded Yale a grant to develop an improved set of DRGs that built on experience with the original set. Groups were included in the new set only if they made medical sense to an advisory panel of physicians and differed significantly in cost from other groups when tested against data on hospital admissions. The new DRGs are based on the patient's principal diagnosis, the principal surgical procedure if surgery was performed, whether substantial complicating conditions are present, the patient's age, and the type of discharge. Diagnoses and procedures are identified by the standard International Classification of Diseases codes used by all hospitals.[11]

Prospective payment issues. The main issues involving the new payment system, indeed any system of budget limits, fall into two categories: the choice of unit of payment and the level at which rates will be set.

Any of the three possible ways to set budget limits—by prescribing payment per day, payment per admission, or total payments to the hospital—has its advantages and disadvantages. Setting total payments, an approach rejected by Congress under the Carter administration, requires that all third-party payers be included in the system and effectively puts the rate-setting authority in the position of deciding when and where new hospitals will be built and old ones allowed to close. Of the two other possibilities, the payment system for medicare would use the more comprehensive unit, the admission. There are concerns, as there would be for any other choice, that hospitals may respond by cutting costs too much for the unit itself (the admission in this system), possibly endangering the patient's health, and by artificially increasing the number of units (admissions). The hospital can also gain by shifting costs to parts of its operation that are not subject to limits.

These perverse incentives mean that the payment system cannot be left to run by itself if the government is concerned not only about expenditures but about how well medicare serves its beneficiaries. The effects of the system must be monitored. HHS proposes to monitor admissions to check whether they increase in response to the new system. It also plans to verify a sample of the DRG codes reported to it, to guard against the possibility that hospitals will try to get higher payments by classifying patients in more expensive groups. The new DRG system has reduced the opportunities for profitable reclassification; for example, by automatically choosing the most expensive surgical procedure as the principal one. Congress added a requirement that hospitals contract with peer review organi-

11. Some examples will illustrate the nature of DRGs. The new system includes respiratory neoplasms (DRG 82); simple pneumonia and pleurisy, patient aged eighteen through sixty-nine, with no complicating conditions (DRG 90); simple pneumonia and pleurisy, patient seventy or older, or complicating conditions (DRG 89); coronary bypass without cardiac catheterization (DRG 107); chest pain (DRG 143); and fractures of hip and pelvis (DRG 236).

zations, which would review the quality of care provided medicare patients.

The new system may actually help teaching hospitals shift costs out from under the limits and give them an advantage. Teaching hospitals will be paid the full cost of employing interns and residents, although interns and residents perform some services that in nonteaching hospitals are performed by staff whose salaries must be paid out of the fixed rate. HHS plans to keep an eye on the possibilities that hospitals may shift some costs to the reports of outpatient departments, which are not included in the new system. Congress added restrictions on hospitals' freedom to charge for inpatient hospital services under part B, to reduce the opportunities for shifting costs to that part of the program.

The level at which rates are set will influence the hospitals' interest in exploring these escape routes. Commercial insurers are concerned that if rates are set low, hospitals may also raise charges to privately insured patients to cover their losses. Even before the prospective reimbursement plan legislated in the 1982 tax act and the one just passed, commercial insurers complained that the cost-cutting policies of medicare (and Blue Cross–Blue Shield in some states) added several billions of dollars a year to their patients' bills. They fear that the new plan will cost them still more. Cost shifting of this kind is always possible when payers act separately, and in some states commercial insurers have supported state rate-setting programs in order to put an end to it.

The possibility of diverging rates of payment—low rates for medicare and medicaid, higher rates for privately insured patients—concerns other groups who worry that it will lead to inferior care for the beneficiaries of public programs. One purpose of these programs has been to ensure that the elderly and the poor receive the same quality of care as most Americans. If rates of payment diverge, some hospitals may choose not to participate, and others, whether by choice or accident of location, may specialize in treating the elderly and the poor, tailoring the quality of their care to the level of payment. There is no way to avoid this possibility so long as payers, and the citizens they represent, do not agree that they should be subject to a single system of payment and a single (or at least, less diverse) quality of care.

Some effects of the new payment system will depend less on the overall level of rates than on how accurately the rates reflect differences in the costs of treating patients. Advocates argue that hospitals will have to develop accounting systems that parallel the DRGs, to discover how costs compare with revenues for each type of patient, and that this change in itself will be a significant step toward better management. They argue further that since the rate is the same no matter how many patients of a particular type are treated, hospitals will specialize more than they do now—dropping some services for which their volume is low and their average cost is high, and expanding those they produce more efficiently. Greater specialization could improve the quality of care: high volume is associated with lower mortality for some surgical procedures.[12]

But if the rates do not accurately reflect the costs of treating patients, they could send the wrong signals. Rather than encouraging hospitals to produce those services at which they are efficient, they might penalize hospitals whose patients were more severely ill than average, and even encourage them to avoid accepting such patients. HHS calculates that inequities in the rates will usually average out for a hospital with more than fifty medicare admissions a year and leave total revenues unaffected; however, they may distort the incentives for specialization. The plan has two mechanisms to help ease problems caused by inequitable rates. One is the extra payments to teaching hospitals, which are thought to care for more severely ill patients. The other is a special process for handling cases with extraordinarily long stays: additional payments will be made for these cases, which are expected to amount to only a few percentage points of the total.

A preliminary analysis by the Congressional Budget Office indicated that, even with these adjustments, the amounts paid to different hospitals are likely to change dramatically under the new system: about a third of all hospitals, mostly small ones, would receive at least 25 percent more in medicare payments than under the current system, and 4 percent, mostly large ones, would receive at least 25 percent less. In response to these findings, Congress directed HHS to increase the lump-sum payments to teaching hospitals and devised a system for phasing in the new plan over a period of three

12. Harold S. Luft, John P. Bunker, and Alain C. Enthoven, "Should Operations Be Regionalized?" *The New England Journal of Medicine*, vol. 301 (December 20, 1979), pp. 1364–69.

years. During the transition period, payments would continue to be based in part on a hospital's actual costs.

If they are to remain reasonably accurate, the DRG rates will have to be adjusted from time to time for changes in technology. These adjustments will necessarily be made with a lag. HHS must first recognize that an adjustment is required and then determine whether the new technology is cost-effective enough to justify a new rate. The lag should encourage the adoption of money-saving technologies, since hospitals will earn extra profits until the rate is reduced. It may slow the spread of beneficial technologies that add significantly to costs, since hospitals will not be able to recover those costs until the rate is increased.

As with cost sharing, some critics argue that regardless of the design of the system, budget limits for hospitals will not work, precisely because they put the pressure on hospitals rather than on doctors. But the evidence shows that budget limits do slow the growth of expenditures. Doctors are not isolated from the pressures on the institutions for which they work. Indeed, American doctors may well be more responsive than those in Britain, where budget limits have been applied for decades. Several observers of the American system of hospital accreditation later visited British hospitals to discuss the introduction of a similar process there, and reported: "By American standards . . . the medical staffs that we visited were very loosely structured, with relatively little understanding of, or commitment to, the goals of the organisation of which they formed a vital part."[13]

Taken all in all, the payment system is a reasonable one. It is not based on a great deal of experience, but neither are any of the alternatives except the more global approaches used in Canada and the United Kingdom. Like any of the alternatives, the system will be imperfect. It will have effects that are less than ideal and will require close watching, frequent minor adjustments, and occasional major revisions. Only time can show all the problems that will develop when it is applied on a large scale. In the meantime, it is worth trying.

HEALTH MAINTENANCE ORGANIZATIONS. HMOs offer a comprehensive set of medical services for a fixed annual fee per person or

13. Robert Maxwell and others, "Seeking Quality," *The Lancet*, January 1, 1983, pp. 45–48.

per family enrolled.They sometimes charge small copayments for outpatient services, but other services are covered in full, no matter how much care the enrollee uses. For the most part, then, an HMO works under a self-imposed budget limit, a limit that differs from other kinds of budget limit in not being set by an outside party. The level at which the limit is set depends on the philosophy of the HMO and on external pressures such as competition. When its competitors are not concerned about costs, as when most patients are well insured by conventional plans, an HMO need not be concerned either. When its competitors are very conscious of costs, an HMO must be conscious of them too.

Historically, the two main types of HMO have been prepaid groups, in which services are offered at one or a few central clinics, and independent practice associations, in which participating doctors practice in smaller groups or alone, just as fee-for-service doctors do. Several studies, most of them of plans run by Kaiser-Permanente, show that total expenditures per enrollee, including expenditures made out-of-pocket by the enrollee, are 10 to 40 percent lower in prepaid groups than in conventional insurance plans; independent practice associations do not appear to have lower costs.[14] The reasons for the lower costs in prepaid groups are not well understood and may have something to do with the kind of people who choose these plans. Some studies indicate that people who enroll in HMOs used less care than average even when they were covered by conventional insurance. Nonetheless, HMOs clearly have the ability to control expenditures, depending on the pressure from outside. Since they do not ration by price, but on the basis of judgments about costs and benefits by their staff doctors, they offer an alternative to price rationing for those who prefer it.[15]

VOUCHERS. Vouchers have been proposed as a way for programs like medicare and medicaid to control their expenditures and, at the same time, allow their beneficiaries to buy medical coverage through private plans. The program would offer each beneficiary a voucher for a fixed amount, which might be related to income, toward the cost of any one of several approved plans. Faced with responsibility

14. Harold S. Luft, *Health Maintenance Organizations: Dimensions of Performance* (Wiley, 1981), chap. 4 and p. 387.

15. For more on HMOs, see Luft, *Health Maintenance Organizations*; and Lawrence D. Brown, *Politics and Health Care Organization: HMOs as Federal Policy* (Brookings Institution, 1983).

for paying the difference between the full cost of the plan and the voucher, the beneficiary would have a strong incentive to consider lower-cost plans, and these would necessarily be ones that controlled expenditures through cost sharing for services or through other means.

Strictly speaking, vouchers have never been tried. They are analogous, however, to fringe benefit plans in which the employer offers the same amount toward any of several medical insurance plans.[16] The reasoning behind them is essentially the same as that behind the tax limit on employer insurance contributions. Like the tax limit, they put the pressure on the individual at the point of choosing a plan rather than at the point of service. Assured of a basic level of care by the voucher, the beneficiary can then choose from among plans that control expenditures in different ways the one whose methods best match his or her preferences.

The Administration's Proposals

The main proposals for federal health programs presented in the 1984 budget are the prospective payment plan for hospitals under medicare, just discussed; additional cost sharing for medicare enrollees; required cost sharing for medicaid beneficiaries; and a plan to make employer contributions for health insurance above a certain limit subject to income and payroll taxes. In addition, the administration will try once again to persuade Congress to make the family planning, migrant health, and black lung clinic programs part of a block grant to the states for primary care. It also proposes to change the health insurance program for federal employees by requiring all plans to include catastrophic coverage and by reducing the federal contribution and making it the same for all plans.

Under medicare the administration proposes to introduce cost sharing for the second through sixtieth days in the hospital and eliminate it for days beyond the sixtieth. Currently, enrollees pay nothing for the second through sixtieth days and increasing amounts for days beyond that. The new plan would require enrollees to pay a deductible, estimated at about $350 for 1984, for the first day in the hospital, as they do now; 8 percent of the deductible amount for each day from the second through the fifteenth; and 5 percent for each

16. Alain C. Enthoven, *Health Plan: The Only Practical Solution to the Soaring Cost of Medical Care* (Addison-Wesley, 1980).

Table 5-3. Estimated Savings in Federal Outlays for Health under the New Reagan Proposals, Fiscal Years 1984–88

Billions of dollars

Item	1984	1985	1986	1987	1988
Medicare					
Changes in hospital cost sharing	0.7	1.2	1.3	1.5	1.7
Higher part B premiums	−0.2	0.2	1.3	2.6	4.2
Elimination of 1 percent increase in hospital payment rates and freeze on doctors' fees	0.8	1.1	1.2	1.4	1.6
New hospital payment system[a]	(1.5)	(2.6)	(4.0)	(5.3)	(6.9)
Other	0.3	0.4	0.5	0.8	0.9
Medicaid	0.3	0.8	0.7	0.8	0.9
Tax on health insurance premiums paid by employers	2.3	4.4	6.0	8.0	10.7

Source: *Budget of the United States Government, Fiscal Year 1984*, p. 3-35.

a. Estimates are in parentheses because they are the same as the savings already expected from the temporary plan included in the Tax Equity and Fiscal Responsibility Act of 1982.

additional day through the sixtieth. Thus many enrollees with relatively short stays would pay more for hospital care than under the current system, while some with extremely long stays would pay less. Since no more than two deductibles would be required in a year, regardless of the number of times the enrollee was admitted to the hospital, the most an enrollee would have to pay would be approximately $1,500 (one admission) to $1,850 (two or more admissions) in 1984. Cost sharing for the twenty-first through hundredth day of skilled nursing facility care would be reduced from 12.5 percent of the hospital deductible, its current level, to 5 percent. Since medicare covers skilled nursing facility care only in very limited circumstances, this change would not affect many people. Together the net savings from these changes in cost sharing under part A of the program are estimated at $700 million for 1984 (table 5-3).

The administration proposes that premiums for coverage under part B of medicare, which pays for physicians' services, should be increased to provide 35 percent of the revenues required for this part of the program by 1988; the remaining revenues would be drawn, as they are now, from general tax receipts. The share of premiums in total part B revenues has dropped from 50 percent, required when the program began but later rescinded, to less than 25 percent. Congress recently passed a new requirement that premiums supply 25 percent of the total. The administration's proposal to push this requirement to 35 percent would necessitate even greater increases in part B premiums over the next four years. In addition, the administration proposes that the part B deductible, now $75 a year, be indexed to inflation and that physicians' fees paid by medicare be frozen at 1983 levels during 1984. Enrollees would continue to pay 20 percent of charges above the deductible, plus any extra charges by physicians who do not accept medicare fees as payment in full. There is no limit on out-of-pocket payments by enrollees under part B.

In a proposal of primarily symbolic importance, the administration is also requesting the introduction of a voluntary voucher under medicare. Enrollees would be allowed to withdraw from the program and purchase private insurance policies with the help of vouchers equal to 95 percent of the average medicare payment per enrollee in their area. Private plans would be required to offer a package of benefits similar to medicare. Because private insurers have high marketing costs and are less able to negotiate reduced rates with hospitals than medicare, they are expected to be able to offer an attractive alternative only to the healthiest people.

Under medicaid the administration proposes that the states be required to charge recipients small amounts for care, rather than permitted to do so if they wish, as they are now. Welfare recipients would be charged $1.00 a visit to a physician and $1.00 a day in the hospital. For the medically needy the charges would be $1.50 a visit and $2.00 a day. The administration also proposes to cut federal matching payments by 3 percent in 1985 and later years, when the plan passed as part of the Omnibus Reconciliation Act of 1981 will have expired.

As the last of its major proposals, the administration would tax employer health insurance contributions above a certain limit beginning January 1, 1984. The limit would be $175 a month for a family and $70 a month for an individual in 1984 and would rise with inflation in later years. Contributions above this amount would be considered part of the employee's taxable income and would be subject to income and payroll taxes. The administration estimates that this tax limit would bring in $2.3 billion in revenues in 1984 and $11 billion in 1988.

As in previous years, the administration's primary focus is on cutting federal outlays and, more generally, on reducing the budget deficit. The package of proposals includes a bit of everything: higher

revenues, more cost sharing, and stricter budget limits in the form of
the new system for paying hospitals under medicare and the continu-
ation of cuts in medicaid matching funds. These general approaches
were analyzed individually earlier in the chapter. The hospital payment system was also analyzed in some detail.

Each proposal taken by itself is reasonable enough. Each reflects
an approach that can succeed if the political will and consensus exist
to make it succeed. The important questions about the package of
proposals are: how well do the parts fit with each other and with
existing conditions in medical care? And when they are added to the
changes of the last few years, where will they take medical care in
the United States?

The changes suggested for medicare do not fit well together. The
effect of cost sharing on the decisions of medicare enrollees is severely limited because so many of them, approximately 60 percent,
buy supplementary policies from private insurers to cover the deductibles and copayments. Medicaid pays these amounts for some of
the poor elderly. The Congressional Budget Office estimates that, as
a result, no more than one-third of enrollees pay the cost-sharing
amounts themselves. Consequently, cost sharing has little influence
on decisions about care and is almost purely a transfer of costs from
the federal government to enrollees. It can be argued that such a
transfer should be shared as fairly as possible by spreading it over as
many enrollees as possible. The premiums and deductibles for part B
serve this purpose better than cost sharing for hospital care, which is
used by relatively few people.

Cost sharing is also of less value when used in conjunction with
budget limits, particularly the type of budget limits in the new hospital payment plan. Since the rates are fixed for an admission, hospitals already have strong incentives to shorten stays; there is no need
to reinforce that effect with daily charges to the patient. Charging
the enrollee a percentage of the bill, as has been proposed by other
administrations, would not influence the choice of hospital, because
the DRG rate is the same for all hospitals in an area and the patient
would gain nothing by choosing a less expensive one. (Of course, the
enrollee could seek out care in another area.) By encouraging the
enrollee to resist hospitalization, cost sharing could be used to
counter the incentive for hospitals to increase admissions, but a simple increase in the deductible would serve this purpose best. Again,

however, relatively few enrollees would be affected since few pay the deductible themselves.

What about the larger pattern of the proposed changes, not only those that would affect medicare but those that would affect other federal programs and the private sector? This pattern can be compared with the standards offered by any of several comprehensive and philosophically consistent approaches the administration might have chosen to pursue.

One of these is a collective, regulatory approach in which the federal government sets budget limits of some sort that apply to all payers, whether public programs or private insurers. This approach would minimize the use of economic incentives directed at individuals and would put the main burden of rationing on hospitals and doctors. Since it would apply to all, it would ration all and, as a side benefit, would prevent the sort of cost shifting that occurs now.

Another alternative, more oriented to individuals and markets, is the "competition" approach favored by some members of the administration.[17] Under this alternative the government would give the beneficiaries of public programs—the poor, the elderly, and the disabled—vouchers with which to buy private insurance. The government's liability would be controlled by raising or lowering the voucher amounts, with the beneficiary paying any difference between the voucher and the premium. Public beneficiaries would be put on a roughly equal footing with other insured citizens if employers were required to offer a choice of plans and contribute the same amount to each, and if contributions above a certain limit were prohibited or taxed.

Either of these approaches has its problems, and neither offers a painless solution. In practice, each would be modified—there would be more regulation under a competition plan and more market incentives under a regulatory plan than their respective advocates would like to see. But each has the virtue that it proposes a mutually consistent set of changes and would attempt to spread the burden of cost containment with considerable equity.

By contrast, the attempts to control costs in the last few years and the administration's new proposals do not add up to a unified or particularly equitable approach. They are a collection of efforts to

17. Competition plans are outlined in ibid.

deal with specific problems one at a time, limited by immediate concerns and the unwillingness of the parties to act together. Some of the pieces, such as the tax limit, are taken from the competition approach; others, such as prospective reimbursement, from the regulatory approach. The focus is very much on the public sector. Although the tax limit will encourage further private initiatives and may help to increase the resistance to cost shifting, its primary purpose is to raise revenues, and nothing about it encourages private efforts to mesh in any way with public ones. Similarly, medicare and medicaid are dealt with separately. For example, no attempt is made to simplify hospital reimbursement by designing a common system for both programs. The 1981 budget act even moved away from a common system by dropping the requirement that medicaid base its payments on reasonable costs as determined by medicare.

Increasingly for the last decade attempts to control expenditures have been carried on in this spirit of each against each. What has changed in the last few years is that the cuts proposed by the federal government, and state governments, have become larger. Somebody has to lose out in each round. Recently, the losers have been private insurers and individuals. Commercial insurers complain that they are being charged for costs medicare and medicaid refuse to pay. Blue Cross–Blue Shield, a major writer of supplementary policies for the elderly, finds itself covering more and more of their expenses as medicare cuts back. The elderly in turn pay more for those policies or pay more directly in cost sharing.

In the longer run, perhaps only a few years, the struggle of each against each could lead to a more unified approach to expenditure control as the parties involved recognize more clearly the dangers of acting alone. Already, private insurers increasingly support state regulation of hospital rates as a way to protect themselves against cost shifting. But since medicare joins these plans only at the discretion of the federal government, the parties may eventually find themselves bargaining for some sort of federal coordination of rates.

What has been lost in the battle of each against each is the issue of coverage. In the late 1970s more than 90 percent of the population was covered by some program of third-party payment, public or private. This may prove to be a high-water mark for a while. Medicaid never covered more than two-thirds of the poor, and some people were cut from the rolls when the eligibility rules for welfare were tightened in 1981. Because unemployment is now so high, almost 11 million people have lost the health insurance that used to be provided by employers. As programs fight to control expenditures, more people will find themselves without adequate coverage, or without coverage at all.

CHAPTER SIX

Jobs and Training

DANIEL H. SAKS

NOT SINCE the Great Depression have so many workers been without employment or the prospect of finding employment. In December 1982, 12 million people reported that they had sought work and could not find any. Almost 2 million more said they had stopped looking because they did not think there was any chance of finding work. Among the employed, 2 million regular full-time workers reported that they could only find part-time jobs. Among the unemployed, 39 percent had been trying for more than fourteen weeks to find work. The adult male unemployment rate, which has exceeded 6 percent in only three years since the 1940s, approached 9 percent in 1982.[1] Yet the proportion of the unemployed receiving unemployment compensation was smaller than in the worst previous postwar recession. In 1975 more than three-quarters of the unemployed got unemployment benefits. Now, only half are getting such benefits.

With unemployment likely to remain high for several years, the president announced in his State of the Union address new initiatives to "offer both short-term help and long-term hope for our unemployed." Yet his 1984 budget reduces federal outlays for employment and training programs. His plan to aid those exhausting their unemployment benefits provides only a fraction of the relief ex-

THE AUTHOR wishes to thank Henry J. Aaron, Martin Neil Baily, Barry P. Bosworth, Gary T. Burtless, Sar Levitan, and Isabel Sawhill for their comments and suggestions. Charlotte Kaiser typed the manuscript.

1. The adult male unemployment rate was 6.2 percent in 1958, 6.7 percent in 1975, and 6.3 percent in 1981.

tended in the 1975–76 recession. And he proposes little federal help to encourage job creation in either the public or private sectors—far less than in the last major recession. The president is depending on economic recovery to generate jobs for the unemployed, but he is not pushing for as fast a recovery as in past recessions because he fears an acceleration in inflation. His approach is consistent with his domestic goals of reducing the size of government, reducing inflation, and reducing income maintenance for those who can work.

This chapter analyzes the administration's strategies to relieve the high unemployment associated with the current state of the business cycle. It also examines programs to help those with structural unemployment problems that are likely to outlast the recovery.

Cyclical Unemployment

A strong, long-lasting economic recovery is the surest way to reduce unemployment to acceptable levels. However, even a strong recovery will leave unemployment at unprecedented levels for several years. For example, if the economy grows by 6 percent a year, half again as fast as the administration assumes, it will take four to five years to reduce the unemployment rate to 6 percent. The high unemployment projected for the interim will compel some kind of policy response to help reduce its painful side effects.

Recent Trends

During the the 1970s the American economy experienced a trebling of real oil prices, a doubling of international trade's share of economic activity, the maturing of the baby boom generation, a rapid rise in labor force participation among women, and a sharp decline in productivity growth. Labor market analysts generally agree that these structural changes have caused a rise in the unemployment rate consistent with nonaccelerating inflation. Virtually all of the rise in unemployment since 1979, however, has been cyclical. The short, sharp recession in the first half of 1980 led to the first large rise in unemployment since the deep 1975 recession. Unemployment leveled off for a time in mid-1980 with the end of the recession, but resumed its upward movement in mid-1981. Recovery from the 1980 recession had hardly started when the 1981–82 recession began.

By the end of 1982 unemployment had diffused broadly among all

Table 6-1. **Unemployment Rates for Various Demographic and Occupational Groups, Selected Months, 1979–82**

Percent, seasonally adjusted

Group	July 1979	July 1981[a]	December 1982
All workers	5.7	7.2	10.8
Adult men	4.1	5.8	10.1
Adult women	5.5	6.7	9.2
Teenagers	15.8	18.7	24.5
Whites	5.0	6.3	9.7
Blacks	11.0	13.8	20.8
White-collar workers	3.3	4.0	5.6
Professional and technical workers	2.5	2.8	3.7
Managers and administrators	2.0	2.6	4.0
Sales workers	3.5	4.9	6.4
Clerical workers	4.5	5.7	8.0
Blue-collar workers	6.8	9.5	16.3
Craft and kindred workers	4.4	6.9	11.9
Operatives, except transport	8.3	11.1	20.5
Transport equipment operatives	5.1	7.3	13.4
Nonfarm laborers	11.0	14.4	20.4
Service workers	7.1	8.0	12.2
Farm workers	4.2	4.8	7.7

Source: Data supplied by the Department of Labor, Bureau of Labor Statistics.
a. Month corresponding to the most recent period of low unemployment.

groups and regions (see table 6-1). Unemployment rates for white-collar and service workers were 70 percent higher than in mid-1979; the rate for blue-collar workers was 140 percent higher. Although the population over sixteen years old grew 7 percent during this period, the increase in unemployment was not concentrated among new entrants to the labor force. The proportion of the unemployed who were job losers rose from 41 to 61 percent. Overall employment declined 1.5 percent from mid-1979 to the end of 1982. Employment in durable goods manufacturing declined 18 percent, and even service industry employment, which normally grows even during recessions, posted only minuscule gains over the period.

Although virtually all groups have felt the downturn, blacks have been more affected than whites. While white unemployment was five percentage points higher at the end of 1982 than in mid-1979, black unemployment was ten percentage points higher than it had been (table 6-1). This unequal impact is also reflected in incomes. Past recessions suggest that, for every percentage point rise in the unem-

Table 6-2. President Reagan's Economic Projections for Calendar Years 1982–86, as of February 1981 and February 1983

Percent

Item	1982	1983	1984	1985	1986
	Year-to-year change				
Real gross national product					
1981 projection	4.2	5.0	4.5	4.2	4.2
1983 projection	−1.2	3.1	4.0	4.0	4.0
Implicit price deflator					
1981 projection	8.3	7.0	6.0	5.4	4.9
1983 projection	6.0	5.2	5.2	4.9	4.6
	Annual average				
Unemployment rate					
1981 projection	7.2	6.6	6.4	6.0	5.6
1983 projection	9.5	10.7	9.9	8.9	8.1

Sources: The White House, "America's New Beginning: A Program for Economic Recovery," February 18, 1981, p. 25; and *Budget of the United States Government, Fiscal Year 1984*, pp. 2-9, 2-10.

ployment rate, the income of stable working families declines on average 1 percent.[2] But poor white families suffer more than twice that percentage decline in income, and poor black families suffer more than three times that percentage decline.

The majority of those who become unemployed during a recession either find jobs or leave the labor force fairly quickly, but one-fifth of the unemployed are out of work more than six months.[3] These long-term unemployed suffer about half of all the reported weeks of unemployment. While high unemployment imposes severe hardships on the long-term unemployed and their families, it confers the benefits of lower price inflation on those who remain employed.

When the Reagan administration sent its initial "Program for Economic Recovery" to Congress in February 1981, it promised its plan would "stimulate growth, productivity, and employment at the same time that we move toward the elimination of inflation."[4] Table 6-2 compares the administration's economic forecast in early 1981 with the forecast made two years later in the 1984 budget. Inflation has dropped even faster than the administration predicted, but this

2. Edward M. Gramlich, "Short- and Long-Run Income Losses from Recession: A Summary" (Washington, D.C.: National Commission for Employment Policy, July 1981).

3. This was the case in the 1975 recession. *Economic Report of the President, February 1982*, p. 36.

4. The White House, "America's New Beginning: A Program for Economic Recovery," February 18, 1981, p. 26.

gain has come at the cost of an unemployment rate much higher than was forecast in 1981.

Much of the gain in achieving a lower overall inflation rate reflects changes in world prices for energy and food, which are only indirectly affected by U.S. domestic policy. But, in addition, domestic wage and price increases have slowed by about four percentage points over the last three years (from 10 to 6 percent annually). This decline is due in large measure to the deep recession and the associated high level of unemployment. In fact, the deceleration of underlying inflation is about in line with the historical short-run response of inflation to unemployment.[5]

The underlying inflation rate may well continue to decline for a number of years, reflecting an economy operating below capacity. In its 1984 budget the administration predicts the unemployment rate will remain above 8.5 percent until 1986. Thus for several years output and employment can grow without any significant threat of labor shortages. Economists disagree about how low the unemployment rate can fall before it stimulates inflation, but the projected rates will be substantially above the highest estimate of that threshold for several years. Any continued reduction in underlying inflation will thus be won at the expense of the small portion of individuals who bear the costs of prolonged unemployment. Unemployment insurance and job creation programs can assist these casualties of disinflation.

Unemployment Insurance

Unemployment insurance is the principal program providing cash benefits to regular workers who are laid off. In fiscal 1983 benefits

5. Underlying inflation is the change in prices of all goods and services excluding mortgage interest rates, food prices, and energy prices.

One model based on experiences during the late 1960s and the 1970s predicts to within two- or three-tenths of a percentage point wage and price deceleration during the first two years of the Reagan administration. Furthermore, 60 percent of the predicted wage deceleration and 27 percent of the predicted price deceleration is due to the high unemployment since the beginning of 1981. Import price deflation (including oil and the appreciation of the dollar) since then accounts for nearly one-fifth of the deceleration in inflation. Most of the remaining predicted deceleration is caused by events before 1981. The simulated model is described in Stephen G. Cecchetti and others, "OPEC II and the Wage-Price Spiral," in Richard F. Zeckhauser and Derek Leebaert, eds., *What Role for Government?* (Duke University Press, 1983). It is a simple dynamic model with wage and price inflation simultaneously determined by adult male unemployment and other factors; farm, housing, and import price inflation; productivity; and social security taxes. David McClain of Boston University performed the reported simulations.

under all federal and state unemployment insurance programs will cost about $35 billion. Unemployment insurance is a complicated federal-state program with rules that vary from state to state. To become insured a worker must typically work for six to nine months in a job covered under the program. Consequently, new entrants to the labor force and reentrants who cannot find jobs are not eligible for benefits. An unemployed worker who qualifies for regular unemployment insurance benefits is entitled to a weekly grant averaging 35 to 40 percent of previous gross earnings, with payments normally available for twenty-six weeks. The system is financed by a payroll tax collected by the federal government but determined (within federal regulations) by each state. This unique financing arrangement implies that the entire cost of the regular unemployment insurance program appears in the federal budget, even though benefits and the payroll tax used to support the system are largely determined by state legislatures and vary considerably from state to state.

When insured unemployment in a state rises above some trigger level, insured unemployed workers in the state become eligible for extended unemployment benefits (EB). The EB program is jointly financed out of the state payroll tax and the federal unemployment insurance payroll tax. It typically raises the maximum duration of unemployment insurance by thirteen weeks, to a total of thirty-nine weeks. The program formerly had a national as well as a state unemployment rate trigger, so that all states became eligible when the insured unemployment rate for the nation exceeded 4.5 percent.[6] In 1981 President Reagan proposed and Congress approved elimination of the national trigger and an increase in the state trigger rate. These changes have markedly reduced the scope of the EB program. At the end of 1982 only fourteen states with particularly high unemployment were offering extended benefits. By contrast, under the pre-1981 law extended benefits would have been available in all fifty states, as they were during the 1975 recession.

During both the 1975 and the current recessions, temporary legislation has extended the number of weeks an unemployed worker can receive benefits beyond thirty-nine weeks (or beyond twenty-six weeks in those states not qualifying for EB). In the 1975 recession,

6. The insured unemployment rate is based on administrative data from the regular unemployment insurance program and is usually far below the much better known total unemployment rate published monthly by the Bureau of Labor Statistics.

the maximum duration was lengthened by twenty-six weeks under the temporary federal supplemental benefit (FSB) program, which created a maximum potential duration of sixty-five weeks. Last year Congress enacted a temporary federal supplemental compensation (FSC) program slated to expire on March 31, 1983. This program, as later amended, provides from eight to sixteen weeks of additional benefits for those qualified for full regular benefits. The number of weeks of additional benefits depends on the level and history of insured unemployment in a state. In January 1983 thirty-six states were eligible for fourteen to sixteen additional weeks. Seven states were eligible for eight weeks. Counting benefits under all three programs—regular unemployment insurance, EB, and FSC—potential eligibility for unemployment insurance ranged from thirty-four weeks in eight states to fifty-five weeks in twelve states with the remainder of states somewhere in between. In his 1984 budget, the president has proposed extending the FSC program by an additional six months through the end of fiscal 1983. An extension of the current program would cost about $310 million a month.

Unemployment insurance provides far less income support and countercyclical stimulus in the current recession than it did in the last major recession in 1975. This is illustrated in table 6-3, which compares actual and proposed real expenditures for unemployment insurance in the two recessions. In an average week in 1976 approximately two-thirds of the unemployed were recipients of regular, extended, or supplemental unemployment insurance. In 1982 only about one-third were recipients. (The fraction of the unemployed covered by unemployment insurance rose to one-half by the end of 1982, after the FSC program began in October.) Since unemployment levels have been high longer in the current recession than in the 1975 recession, a larger portion of job losers in 1982 have probably exhausted all unemployment insurance benefits. In addition, the persistence of high unemployment levels has probably prevented many current job losers from establishing a work history sufficient to gain entitlement to program benefits. But another reason for the difference between the two recessions has been the conscious choice of current policymakers to reduce the generosity of the EB and FSC programs in relation to the corresponding programs available in 1975. Since the legal maximum duration of benefits is lower in 1982–83 than in 1975–76, while the actual duration of unemploy-

Table 6-3. Unemployment Insurance Outlays and Beneficiaries, Selected Fiscal Years, 1975–84

Item	1975	1976	1982	1983[a]	1984[a]
Federal outlays for unemployment insurance (millions of 1983 dollars)	23,703	32,318	24,945	36,870	27,327
Civilian unemployment rate (percent)	8.5	7.7	9.7	10.7[b]	9.9[b]
Average civilian unemployment (millions)	6.84	7.58	10.00	11.45[b]	10.45[b]
Average weekly recipients of unemployment insurance (millions)[c]	3.74	5.01	3.66	5.40	4.60
Percentage of unemployed receiving benefits[d]	54.7	63.5	36.6	...	...

Sources: *Budget of the United States Government, Fiscal Year 1977; Fiscal Year 1978;* and *Fiscal Year 1984;* Department of Labor, *Employment and Earnings* (various issues); and administrative data supplied by the Department of Labor, Unemployment Insurance Service.

a. Projected.

b. Calendar year rather than fiscal year.

c. Number of weekly recipients of regular and extended unemployment insurance under (1) state programs, (2) unemployment compensation for federal employees (UCFE) and for ex-service personnel (UCX), (3) federal supplemental benefit programs, and (4) special unemployment assistance programs. Data include a small number of recipients in Puerto Rico and in the Virgin Islands.

d. Ratio of figures in the preceding two rows.

ment is about 10 percent higher, a higher fraction of the unemployed have no entitlement to benefits.

The administration's rationale for curtailing the EB and FSC programs was to limit program costs and to reduce the adverse incentives arising out of the unemployment insurance program.[7] Eliminating the national trigger for the EB program, for example, removed the requirement that states with low unemployment rates offer extended benefits just because unemployment had risen in some other region of the country. Raising the state unemployment trigger for EB benefits is more difficult to justify, however. The higher trigger prevented Indiana from offering extended benefits in the last quarter of 1982, although that state's total unemployment rate exceeded 11 percent in every month after November 1981.

The effectiveness of the EB program could be improved by reducing the stringency of the current insured unemployment rate trigger

7. By providing income protection during spells of unemployment, unemployment insurance reduces the incentive to actively search for a job and to accept a job if one is offered. Of course, the latter incentive may contribute to economic efficiency if it encourages unemployed workers to reject clearly unsuitable employment. By prolonging the job search period, unemployment insurance may improve the match between employers' needs and employees' qualifications. For estimates of the impact of benefit duration on unemployment duration, see Walter Corson and Walter Nicholson, *The Federal Supplemental Benefits Program* (Kalamazoo, Mich.: W. E. Upjohn Institute for Employment Research, 1982), pp. 117ff, and Robert Moffitt and Walter Nicholson, "The Effect of Unemployment Insurance on Unemployment: The Case of Federal Supplemental Benefits," *Review of Economics and Statistics* (February 1982), pp. 1–11.

while also reducing the increments by which the maximum duration of benefits is now raised. Instead of extending benefits by a full thirteen weeks (or 50 percent) whenever the insured unemployment trigger conditions are met, the program should raise the maximum duration of the benefits by smaller increments. For example, duration could be raised by a small number of weeks for each percentage point by which the insured rate exceeds the trigger rate. This reform would tie program benefits more closely to the principle that unemployment insurance should offer a reasonably constant level of relative income protection irrespective of the state of the economy. As the state of the economy worsens and the expected duration of involuntary unemployment lengthens, the maximum duration of benefits should lengthen correspondingly in order to maintain relative income protection.

Many of the differences between the current FSC program and the earlier FSB program available in 1975–76 were introduced to improve effectiveness. The current program is, of course, less generous and hence less costly than the 1975 program, but it targets benefits more closely to states where labor-market conditions are poor, and its design ensures that the potential duration of benefits declines as a state's employment situation improves. One serious inequity in the FSC program, however, is that, while costs are entirely paid out of general federal revenues, benefit levels are essentially determined by the states (since payment levels are the same as those set in the states' regular unemployment insurance programs). Thus the maximum weekly benefit ranges from $90 in Alabama to $258 in Massachusetts. There is no obvious justification for federal support for such unequal benefit awards. A simple reform that would eliminate this inequity would be for the federal government to limit FSC benefits to a fixed weekly maximum but permit states to supplement this award out of their own funds.

Aside from technical differences in the generosity of the earlier FSB and current FSC programs, the main way in which the two programs differ is the comparatively short life of the latter. The FSB payments became available in January 1975, only seven months after unemployment began its rapid rise in 1974. A large number of the unemployed were still being helped by the program in 1977, three years later. By contrast, FSC did not begin until October 1982, two and a half years after the initial rise in unemployment in 1980 and more than a year after the start of the most recent rise in 1981. The president proposes not to extend the FSC program beyond September 1983, at which point unemployment is forecast to be higher than it was at the *peak* of the 1975–76 recession. Clearly, the administration is proposing a considerable reduction in the income protection offered to the long-term unemployed, in comparison to benefits available in the 1970s. Given the depth of the recession and the likely persistence of long-term unemployment, the FSC program should be extended or the EB program liberalized or both.

In light of the cutback in social insurance benefits, it is reasonable to ask whether means-tested programs such as food stamps, medicaid, and welfare can be expected to help maintain consumption levels among the unemployed. Because of the high and sharply rising cost of medical care, one of the most pressing problems for the unemployed may be paying for preventive or emergency care. Since health insurance is so frequently linked to employment in the United States, almost 11 million Americans have lost health insurance coverage because they or someone in their household lost a job.[8] The income and assets tests to qualify for medicaid are so stringent in many states that the unemployed must become destitute before qualifying for public aid in paying for health care. Some publicly supported mechanism is desirable to allow the unemployed to maintain their health coverage by permitting them to purchase either their former employers' plans or some federal or state plan.

Even more serious problems face that half of the unemployed who are not covered by unemployment insurance. These are new entrants or reentrants to the labor force, job losers who have not worked long enough to become insured, and unemployed workers who have exhausted all benefits. For the families of these workers, assets other than a house and car must be depleted to $1,500 and income must fall below the poverty line if they are to qualify for benefits under the largest means-tested program—food stamps. Since 1980 the number of food stamp recipients has remained at 20.5 million even though unemployment has risen sharply. Stricter eligibility requirements have offset at least part of the increase in participation ex-

8. Alice M. Rivlin, "Health Insurance and the Unemployed," testimony before the Subcommittee on Health and Environment of the House Committee on Energy and Commerce, January 24, 1983.

pected from higher unemployment.[9] As a result, many of those who exhaust unemployment insurance benefits do not qualify for help under food stamps or other means-tested programs. This group would be a logical target for special jobs programs.

Job Creation

In addition to fiscal and monetary stimulus, governments have used direct methods to create extra jobs during periods of high unemployment. These methods fall into three categories: wage subsidies, public service employment, and public works. The administration has proposed activities of two types: a small wage subsidy for the long-term insured unemployed and an accelerated schedule of public construction projects. (The latter program was proposed some weeks after the president's regular budget message.)

WAGE SUBSIDIES. In undertaking a wage subsidy program, the government offers to reimburse employers for some portion of the cost of hiring workers. The government can subsidize the wages of all employees or, more commonly, a more limited group, such as new hires. General wage subsidies of this type reduce employment costs on the margin, so employers are induced to hire more workers than they otherwise would. Since costs are lowered, the subsidy can also result in higher profits, lower product prices, and increased output.

A somewhat different kind of subsidy is one that is targeted on certain types of workers, for example, the long-term unemployed. Under this form of subsidy the employer is induced to hire a larger number of targeted workers, so their job prospects improve relative to unsubsidized job applicants. Obviously, some unsubsidized job holders or job applicants may be displaced by such a program because the targeted subsidy provides employers an incentive to expand targeted rather than general employment. Employers will naturally try to use wage subsidies to pay for employment they would have undertaken even in the absence of the program, so a certain amount of the subsidy will amount to a windfall gain to the employer and will have little effect on unemployment. These are unavoidable side effects of any subsidy scheme and must be taken into account in evaluating its potential costs and usefulness. The relative size of these different effects depends on the design of particular programs

9. Participation rose by almost 30 percent from 1974 to 1975, but some of that increase reflects the fact that 1974 was the first full year of the program.

and on the responsiveness of employers to reductions in labor costs for particular categories of workers. Past wage subsidies have included the work incentive program (WIN) tax credit (targeted on recipients of aid to families with dependent children, or AFDC), the new jobs tax credit (providing a tax subsidy on net employment growth in 1977 and 1978), and the targeted jobs tax credit (targeted on seven categories of generally disadvantaged job applicants, including poor youths and welfare recipients).

The wage subsidy proposal in the 1984 budget is targeted on those unemployed who are eligible for federal supplemental compensation. The subsidy program is expected to cost $642 million in fiscal 1984. Under the administration's proposal, an FSC recipient will be able to convert any remaining entitlement to FSC benefits into a wage subsidy, which is payable to the employer who hires him or her. The FSC recipient would be given a voucher identifying him or her as eligible under the subsidy program, and the subsidy would be paid in the form of a tax credit equal to the amount of the worker's remaining potential FSC benefits. This voucher option would be available to those who exhaust their extended unemployment benefits before April 1984.

The administration's proposal has some attractive features. As the recovery proceeds, it starts providing benefits to potential employers of the long-term unemployed. The idea is to get these unemployed workers to the head of the reemployment queue. The incentive, however, is not large, averaging less than 20 percent of weekly labor costs and at most some 12 percent of annual labor costs.[10] If the long-term unemployed were identical to other job seekers, that would represent a considerable incentive to many potential employers. But if the long-term unemployed are regarded by employers as less attractive substitutes for other job applicants, a temporary incentive of that magnitude may not be effective.[11]

10. The wage replacement ratio of 0.45 for the last FSB program (as estimated by Corson and Nicholson) was adjusted by 20 percent for fringes and divided by two to get the weekly percentage subsidy.

11. The subsidy will be a larger percentage of the normal wages of low-wage eligible workers because unemployment insurance replaces a larger fraction of their wage losses during unemployment. Some states replace a larger fraction of earnings than others—the percentage subsidy is substantially higher in New Jersey, for example, than in Michigan. Wayne Vroman, "State Unemployment Insurance Replacement Rates in 1980," working paper 1280-5 (Washington, D.C.: Urban Institute, August 1980). This adds an arbitrary variation to the scheme.

Experience with such credits in the past has shown relatively low participation rates for programs with even more generous subsidy rates.[12] For example, during the first eighteen months of the targeted jobs tax credit program, only 4 percent of the eligible new hires from the target groups were hired by an employer who applied for the tax credit. Thus target group members who became employed during that period overwhelmingly did so without the aid of the subsidy. The net impact of the subsidy on job prospects in the target group was almost certainly negligible. It is not obvious why experience under the administration's proposed program should be any better.

The United States has tended to use tax credits as the instrument to subsidize employment—a result of the often-mistaken notion that tax expenditures require less administration than other expenditures. The consequence is unfortunate. States, localities, nonprofit organizations, and firms without tax liabilities are excluded from participation in the program. Because all these employers, contrary to certain preconceptions, provide real jobs, the restriction of the credit to taxable firms is an undesirable limitation. A refundable tax credit to subsidize employment is one solution, but a direct expenditure would be simpler, would probably be more effective, and would not clutter up the tax system.

PUBLIC SERVICE EMPLOYMENT AND PUBLIC WORKS. The potential success of general or targeted wage subsidies in helping the long-term unemployed is very uncertain. Nonetheless, it is desirable to extend public aid to these victims of the recession, especially when they have exhausted all potential unemployment insurance benefits. One simple kind of assistance, without the stigma associated with means-tested income maintenance programs, is to offer countercyclical publicly funded jobs. Two types of jobs programs have been used in the past: public service employment and public works projects.

Under public service employment programs, state and local governments receive payment from the federal government for hiring certain employees, usually low-wage employees who have suffered long-term unemployment or who are otherwise disadvantaged. In

12. For several useful discussions, see Robert H. Haveman and John L. Palmer, eds., *Jobs for Disadvantaged Workers* (Brookings Institution, 1982). See also National Commission for Employment Policy, *Sixth Annual Report* (Government Printing Office, 1981), section A, pp. 21–48.

essence, these programs provide a 100 percent wage subsidy. The administration has proposed imposing work requirements on able-bodied recipients of food stamps and welfare, compelling beneficiaries to "work off" their public aid grants in community work experience programs. However, since this type of "workfare" program does not pay regular wages, it does little to improve the situation of the unemployed. The administration has made no proposals, aside from its workfare plan, to expand public service employment and has generally been opposed to such programs.

Countercyclical public works programs employ workers in public construction or reconstruction projects. Because these programs typically do not impose stringent eligibility criteria on participants and because wages paid on the jobs are reasonably high, public works projects are a more expensive way to help the long-term unemployed than are public service employment programs. In his 1984 budget the president proposed no new public works program and recommended a 9 percent real cut in fiscal 1984 for programs designed to assist local governments with public works projects.[13] But Congress is certain to consider a variety of such projects, and the administration has indicated its willingness to discuss them. In fact, after the formal budget was submitted, the president actually proposed spending $4.3 billion for accelerated construction projects.

Public works "jobs" bills can be a cover for supplemental appropriations to support the favorite local project of each member of Congress. But with unemployment likely to remain high over the next several years, a well-designed temporary public employment program could be useful in reducing the burdens imposed on the long-term unemployed. What might distinguish a well-designed program? The best statement of those principles is contained in President Franklin D. Roosevelt's 1935 State of the Union address.

1. All work undertaken should be useful—not just for a day, or a year, but useful in the sense that it affords permanent improvement in living conditions or that it creates future new wealth for the Nation.

2. Compensation on emergency public projects . . . should be larger than the amount now received as a relief dole, but at the same time not so large

13. The programs are community development block grants, urban development action grants, rural development, economic development assistance (currently being phased out), and local public works. The administration proposes outlays of $5.26 billion for these programs in fiscal 1984.

as to encourage the rejection of opportunities for private employment or the leaving of private employment to engage in government work.

3. Projects should be undertaken on which a large percentage of direct labor can be used.

4. Preference should be given to those projects [for which]. . . there is a reasonable expectation that the government will get its money back at some future time.

5. The projects undertaken should be selected and planned so as to compete as little as possible with private enterprises. This suggests that if it were not for the necessity of giving useful work to the unemployed now on relief, these projects in most instances would not now be undertaken.

6. The planning of projects would seek to assure work during the coming fiscal year to the individuals now on relief, or until such time as private employment is available. In order to make adjustment to increasing private employment, work should be planned with a view to tapering it off in proportion to the speed with which the emergency workers are offered positions with private employers.

7. Effort should be made to locate projects where they will serve the greatest unemployment needs. . . . Our ultimate objective being the enrichment of human lives, the government has the primary duty to use its emergency expenditures as much as possible to serve those who cannot secure the advantages of private capital.[14]

Most of the direct government job creation programs during the 1970s would get rather poor marks from President Roosevelt. Public service employment under the Comprehensive Employment and Training Act (CETA) typically provided services rather than "permanent improvements in living conditions." Instead of being set between welfare and regular wages, wages on countercyclical construction projects usually met federal prevailing wage requirements (often union scale). Regular public works construction projects required considerable capital per worker. The long-term rate of return on the government's investment was rarely considered. There was little direct competition with private enterprises, but the late initiation of the projects did result in competition with the private sector for resources during economic expansion. Most outlays under the local public works program of 1976 and 1977 did not occur until 1978, three years after the worst part of the 1975 recession. Public service employment also peaked in 1978. Finally, the targeting of funds under these programs ensured that benefits were widely distributed across states and congressional districts, though areas of high unemployment did get a larger share.

14. Franklin D. Roosevelt, State of the Union address, January 4, 1935.

President Roosevelt's principles do not address one important issue: the substitution of subsidized workers for regular workers under a public service employment program. Almost all such programs involve payments by the federal government to state, local, or community sponsors to hire people. If these sponsors are smart, they will try to get the federal taxpayer to pay for the things they think most important to do. Naturally, some of those valuable things would have been done anyway. The more flexible such programs are, the more they become simple intergovernmental revenue sharing. Unfortunately, it is difficult to know the degree to which federal job creation programs are only subsidizing employment that states and localities would have supported anyway. Plausible estimates of substitution range from 20 to over 60 percent.[15]

If job creation is the goal, an important question is the net cost of each job created under alternative programs. One study estimated that a $3 billion public service employment program started in 1981 could have created some 384,000 person-years of extra employment over three years at a cost of $7,800 a job.[16] It assumed a 40 percent substitution rate and included the indirect employment effects from stimulating the economy by the amount of the program. By contrast, a local public works program limited to small ($250,000) projects that spent 30 percent of funds for wages would have cost about $21,000 for each new job. Thus, unless society valued the output of a public service job at less than one-third the value of the output of a local public works job, public service employment was the cheaper program for job creation.

Creating jobs through simple revenue sharing to the states was more than twice as expensive as local public works, though that result is sensitive to assumptions about the degree to which local governments use such revenues to reduce taxes. With states under severe financial pressure now, they may not be so inclined to cut taxes, and revenue sharing may not be quite so unattractive a device for job creation.

15. For a review of the public service employment program and low estimates of the substitution issue, see Richard P. Nathan and others, *Public Service Employment: A Field Evaluation* (Brookings Institution, 1981), p. 13. Higher estimates are in George E. Johnson and James D. Tomola, "The Fiscal Substitution Effect of Alternative Approaches to Public Service Employment Policy," *Journal of Human Resources*, vol. 12 (Winter 1977), pp. 3–26.

16. David Brazell, "Employment Effects of Alternative Countercyclical Spending Programs," paper presented at the Southern Economic Association meeting, January 1981.

To the extent that Congress wants to create as many jobs as possible for each dollar of extra direct expenditures, public service employment is the better program. Local public works are superior only if the value of such projects is several times higher than the value of output under public service employment—not an impossibility if valuable public capital is being created. Either program creates new jobs more cheaply than a grab bag of typical supplemental appropriations for nondefense programs.

IMPLICATIONS FOR COUNTERCYCLICAL POLICY. The most basic responsibilities of government during a severe economic contraction are to extend help to the hardest-hit victims of recession and to provide macroeconomic stimulus to reverse the slide. The unemployment insurance system is the most important source of public income support for the unemployed, but instead of strengthening this system during the worst postwar recession, the administration and Congress have reduced its generosity. The first requirement of a better countercyclical policy during severe recessions would be to improve the income protection now offered to the unemployed, especially those with family responsibilities.

But an indefinite extension of unemployment insurance benefits would be inequitable as well as inefficient. Since these benefits are not means-tested, there is no necessary correlation between their level and family needs. Because both taxpayers and potential recipients have a strong aversion to means-tested programs, it may be desirable to offer help to the long-term unemployed in the form of publicly funded jobs, either in public service employment or public works projects. Public service employment is more efficient than public works because it can be more easily targeted on the long-term unemployed, because a greater portion of the budget is spent on wages, and because in theory the program can be started and stopped on shorter notice. However, the "output" of many public service employment projects is often of questionable worth. The choice between public service employment and public works programs must be based on a broad appraisal of their relative advantages in providing help to those most in need and in producing output of real value to the community.

Policymakers should not be under the illusion that government job creation of the scope currently contemplated will make a serious dent in unemployment. The size of the proposed program is simply too small. (Furthermore, depending on the design of the program, a significant fraction of those hired might come from the currently employed or from the population outside the labor force.) The main objective of such a program, then, should be to help those victims of the recession who have suffered exceptionally long spells of unemployment or who have exhausted their family resources.

The administration's proposal to provide a wage subsidy for employment of the long-term unemployed has merit, but it is unlikely that this plan will be more successful than past targeted subsidy programs, such as the targeted jobs tax credit. If experience provides any guide, program participation will be low, and the effect on job prospects will be minor.

Structural Unemployment

Even in the relatively buoyant labor market of the late 1970s, many workers were unemployed for long periods, others found their normal earnings insufficient to take them out of poverty, and yet others were unable to find jobs at their normal wages. In 1979 some 10.5 million Americans in the work force for at least part of the year did not earn enough money to lift their families out of poverty.[17] Two-thirds of these suffered no unemployment during their time in the labor force, reminding us that low wages and limited hours of work can cause poverty as surely as unemployment.

Serious as the structural labor market problems were in the late 1970s, the administration expects them to be even worse through the 1980s as a result of slow economic recovery and a modest unemployment rate target. In spite of this grim forecast, outlays for the major employment and training programs aimed at the disadvantaged will decline about 15 percent after inflation between 1983 and 1984 (see table 6-4).

In no other domestic area has the administration accomplished its objectives more completely than in employment and training. Federal outlays for employment and training programs have declined by two-thirds in real terms since 1980 (see table 6-4). The funds have also been refocused to eliminate job creation programs for the disadvantaged and to curtail stipends and support services for partici-

17. Based on tabulations from the March 1980 Current Population Survey; see Robert Taggart, *Hardship: The Welfare Consequences of Labor Market Problems* (Kalamazoo, Mich.: W. E. Upjohn Institute for Employment Research, 1982), p. 43.

Table 6-4. Outlays for Employment and Training Activities, Fiscal Years 1980–84
Millions of dollars

Activity	1980	1981	1982	1983	1984
Grants to states and localities for training and work experience[a]	3,238	3,381	2,374	2,039	1,851
Dislocated workers[b]	7	8	7	47	204
Job Corps	470	540	570	605	589
Public service employment[c]	3,697	2,399	108	0	0
Summer youth employment[d]	721	769	679	653	638
Work incentive (WIN)	395	381	235	315	26
Older workers[e]	235	263	269	278	211
Other national programs	737	603	412	304	228
Total	9,500	8,344	4,654	4,241	3,747

Source: Data supplied by the Office of Management and Budget.

a. For 1980–83, Comprehensive Employment and Training Act (CETA) titles II-BC, IV-A, VII; for 1984, Job Training Partnership Act (JTPA) title II-A.

b. For 1980–82, Trade Act activity only; for 1983–84, Trade Act and JTPA title III.

c. CETA title II-D, VI.

d. For 1983–84, net of savings realized through establishing a differential minimum wage for summer youth employment; no change in number of youths served.

e. For 1984, outlays are from 1983 authority.

pants in the programs (from more than half of expenditures under CETA to perhaps 15 percent or so under the 1982 Job Training Partnership Act). The major activity the administration wishes to support is training, both on the job and in the classroom. According to the administration, the consequence of these changes is that real funding for job training activities will increase, notwithstanding the overall reduction in budgets for employment and training.

The Job Training Partnership Act, passed last year, requires a considerable change in federal, state, and local relations in the administration of federal employment and training programs. Most of the regulatory and oversight responsibilities formerly vested in the federal government have been passed on to state governors. The business-dominated local private industry councils (set up by the Carter administration in 1978) have been expanded and given greater responsibility. These arrangements are likely to renew conflict between federal authorities and local program operators. Their long-standing conflict arises because the employers often want to screen out the least desirable program applicants while the federal government wants to help the worst-off people get stable jobs. CETA was criticized for not paying enough attention to the needs of employers. The balance has now shifted, though the program is still targeted on the disadvantaged. If the new balance takes the form of employer-set standards for skills and a commitment to teach these skills to the disadvantaged, the new programs will be an advance. If it takes the form of screening the difficult cases out of the program, it will accomplish little that the market would not do anyway.

Since different programs tend to work better for particular groups, the following discussion will center on three distinct groups: disadvantaged youths having trouble starting careers, disadvantaged adults with low regular earnings, and dislocated workers who are having trouble adjusting to reduced demand for their skills.

Disadvantaged Youths

Youth unemployment rates in the United States tend to be two or three times higher than adult unemployment rates. Youths have a harder time finding work because they are searching for careers and first jobs and because employers normally prefer to hire experienced workers. Of major industrial countries, only West Germany managed (until recently) to avoid high youth unemployment by arranging for most school leavers to enter directly into apprenticeships with employers. The high youth unemployment rates in the United States decline sharply as a cohort ages, and it is hard to argue that there is a serious unemployment problem among youths in general. There is, however, highly concentrated unemployment among poor, black, and other minority youths. Three-fourths of the weeks of unemployment experienced by youths in 1977 were concentrated among the 8 percent of the youth labor force unemployed more than fourteen weeks.[18] In 1977 approximately 750,000 sixteen- to twenty-four-year-olds lived in low-income families and suffered more than fourteen weeks of unemployment. These youths are not just job shopping; they are in serious trouble. Furthermore, there is mounting evidence that sustained unemployment among school leavers results in lower earnings later in life. Thus troubled youths often become troubled adults.[19]

The labor market problems for black youths who are not college

18. Robert Lerman, "An Analysis of Youth Employment Problems," in Vice President's Task Force on Youth Employment, *A Review of Youth Employment Problems, Programs and Policies* (GPO, 1980), tables 2, 3, and 11.

19. See the chapters by David T. Ellwood and Mary Corcoran in Richard B. Freeman and David A. Wise, eds., *The Youth Labor Market Problem: Its Nature, Causes, and Consequences* (University of Chicago Press, 1982), pp. 349–425.

bound are especially severe. In 1980 the black teenage unemployment rate was 39 percent. Young black men aged twenty to twenty-
four have suffered the most dramatic fall in employment-population
ratios of any group in the labor force over the past decade or so. As
one indication of how their opportunities compare with those of
young white men, young black men who qualify for military service
are three times as likely as qualified white men to enlist.[20] Since
military service is identical for both groups, young black men must
be facing worse alternatives than their white counterparts. The
black youth unemployment problems will probably persist during
the 1980s, as their share of the youth population rises slightly over
the decade. The persistence of high cyclical unemployment over the
1980s will more than offset the small employment gains expected
because of smaller youth cohorts.[21]

Among the reasons employers give for failing to hire disadvantaged youths are their lack of basic skills and their poor attitudes.
Proper attitudes may merely reflect employers' prejudices or may
represent the good work habits that many youths eventually pick up
simply by being steadily employed. There is some evidence that
youths who work while in school do better in the labor market later,
either because they are inherently more motivated or because the
work experience increases their productivity.[22]

There have been a number of proposals and programs to address
the youth employment problem. Many European countries use the
period from ages sixteen to eighteen to mix work and general vocational education for those not going on to a university. The West
German "dual system" is the best known example—a mixture of
vocational training and apprenticeships for some two-thirds of a
German youth cohort. The program is not without its problems. A
system in which young workers enter firms at the bottom of the job
ladder is under tremendous strain in a weak economy, when employers do not like to lay off valuable experienced workers to make room
for more apprentices. That is why German youth unemployment has
been rising rapidly in the current recession.

In the United States cooperative education programs mixing

20. Martin Binkin and others, *Blacks and the Military* (Brookings Institution, 1982), p.
66.
21. For discussion of the baby boom effects, see Louise B. Russell, *The Baby Boom
Generation and the Economy* (Brookings Institution, 1982).
22. Freeman and Wise, *Youth Labor Market Problem*, p. 12.

work and schooling are run by the vocational education system and can have some short-term success in improving the labor-market performance of non–college bound youths.[23] A federal experiment in the late 1970s offered part-time jobs to disadvantaged youths who attended school. Although the regular school dropout rate was not greatly affected, the program did seem to get a substantial number of those who had already dropped out into "alternative" schools. Whether it was the job or the alternative school that caused the effect is unknown.[24]

A good deal of the federal funds spent in the 1970s on disadvantaged youths went into work experience programs, such as the summer jobs program. Careful evaluation of the most intensive and well-designed work experience program, the supported work experiment, showed that the program had no effect on the subsequent labor market experience of young participants.[25] The administration has made cuts in such activities, though it maintains $638 million in fiscal 1984 for the summer youth employment program. Various other part-time programs to provide preemployment skills to youths seem to produce only small transitory gains in the relative earnings of participants. These programs will probably expand under the Job Training Partnership Act.

One of the most successful programs for seriously disadvantaged dropouts has been the Job Corps—boarding schools that provide a mixture of skills training, remedial education, and health care. Job Corps seems to provide a payoff both to those youths who stay in the program and to society;[26] it is expensive but worthwhile. Job Corps is probably the archetype of an effective program for the seriously disadvantaged, since a major effort is required to offset a lifetime of problems. Reducing unemployment by focusing resources on those who will likely experience so much of it costs more than some other strategies. But the expenditures ultimately enlarge the economy.

23. For example, see Ernst Stromsdorfer and others, "An Economic and Institutional Analysis of the Cooperative Vocational Education Program in Dayton, Ohio," final report to the U.S. Department of Labor (March 1973).

24. George Farkas and others, "Early Impacts from the Youth Entitlement Demonstration: Participation, Work, and Schooling" (New York: Manpower Demonstration Research Corporation, 1980).

25. Rebecca Maynard, *The Impact of Supported Work on Young School Dropouts* (New York: Manpower Demonstration Research Corporation, 1980).

26. Charles Mallar and others, "Evaluation of the Economic Impact of the Job Corps Program" (Princeton, N.J.: Mathematica Policy Research, Inc., 1980).

The administration has made modest cuts in the Job Corps program for fiscal 1984. If it is as successful as the studies imply, Job Corps should be expanded and perhaps even given some opportunity to develop programs for young adults.

The 1984 budget contains three new proposals relevant to youth problems. First, the administration proposes to give states and localities the option of offering vouchers to disadvantaged elementary and secondary school students in place of current federal compensatory education aid. The details are not available yet, but most of the current federal compensatory funds have been used for basic skills in the primary grades. How a full-time elementary school student with basic reading or math deficiencies would use a voucher of a few hundred dollars to buy a dose of compensatory education in the marketplace is unclear. It is also unclear how the proposal would affect school-aged youths who are nearest to becoming labor force participants—high school students.

Second, the administration proposes to reduce expenditures on vocational and adult education from $820 million in 1982 to $600 million in 1985 and to convert this aid into an unrestricted block grant. Secondary school vocational education is more expensive than other high school curriculum, and graduates appear to have virtually no gain in relative earnings.[27] Since the average gain is inconsequential, it is unclear why the federal government should subsidize the increased production of an average unit of more expensive vocational education. About 90 percent of the costs of vocational education are currently paid at the state and local levels. If the federal government could use its resources exclusively to increase the return on vocational education, it might make a substantial contribution to the preparation of youths for the labor market, and it might then justify even larger federal expenditures. If it simply subsidizes the overproduction of typical vocational education, the government will be hard-pressed to justify any federal expenditures at all.

Third, the administration hopes to improve the summer employment prospects of youths by lowering the summer minimum wage for persons less than twenty-two years old from $3.35 an hour to $2.50 an hour. The Minimum Wage Study Commission recently

27. Exceptions include transitory gains for men who study industrial arts and women who study clerical skills.

estimated that a 25 percent decline in the regular minimum wage of teenagers would generate a net increase in total employment of 250,000 to 350,000 jobs.[28] To the extent that the lower minimum wage for youths would cause them to be hired over the more numerous adults willing to work at the regular minimum wage, there might be an even larger gain in teenage employment. A *summer* youth subminimum would probably have a substantially smaller effect on employment since it is costly for firms to adjust their work force for such short periods (though many do it). Although fewer youths would find jobs, fewer adults would be likely to be displaced under such a scheme. There will be some federal budget savings from a summer subminimum, since youths hired under federal summer youth programs would be paid at a lower rate. The program is likely to help students get summer jobs but is unlikely to improve the career opportunities of severely disadvantaged youths. If they need a 25 percent wage reduction to be hired for the summer, they are likely to need a wage differential lasting more than three months to begin a career.

Disadvantaged Adults

A small group of men and women appear to constitute a stable class of extremely low earners. One study of low-wage adults followed a group of workers through the 1970s.[29] While the study found a certain degree of movement between low and high earnings, 5 percent of all the male workers in the sample were in the lowest tenth of the male earnings distribution seven out of ten years. Twenty-one percent of women who headed households had earnings comparable to the lowest tenth of the male earnings distribution every year of the decade. The study found that the best predictor of low earnings in any year was not race, sex, or education, but rather low earnings in the previous year. Some persistent and unmeasured personal characteristics seem largely responsible for continually low earnings.

Might it not be more effective to try to raise the earnings of those at the bottom of the earnings distribution through employment and

28. *Report of the Minimum Wage Study Commission*, vol. 1 (Washington, D.C.: MWSC, 1981), pp. 31–60.

29. Richard B. Freeman, "Troubled Workers in the Labor Market," in National Commission for Employment Policy, *Seventh Annual Report: The Federal Interest in Employment and Training* (GPO, 1981), appendix A, pp. 103–73.

training programs rather than through transfer payments? Many employment and training programs, including classroom training, have been effective for women with chronic labor market problems, but few programs have been effective for seriously disadvantaged men.[30] This may be because work and training programs are most effective for those entering or reentering the labor market.

Evidence from the supported work program suggests that well-designed work experience is effective in improving the earnings of welfare mothers.[31] The administration wants to make workfare for welfare mothers more general, but there is likely to be a difference between fairly expensive and well-designed work experience programs, such as supported work, that provide a bridge to unsubsidized work, and make-work schemes that are intended to make welfare less pleasant.

The main question for disadvantaged adults, however, is whether the Job Training Partnership Act's almost exclusive reliance on *training* for the disadvantaged can work during a serious recession. Targeted subsidies for employers may be required as well to get participants jobs in either the public or private sectors.

Dislocated Workers

The third group that suffers structural unemployment consists of permanently or temporarily dislocated experienced workers. This group is small. Only about 90,000 of the prime-age workers who were unemployed more than twenty-six weeks in 1980 came from industries with declining employment.[32] The magnitude of the dislocated worker problem is difficult to judge; many blue-collar workers in industries where sales are sensitive to interest rates are out of work because of business cycle conditions. It is uncertain how many will be rehired if real interest rates decline and the economy recovers.

Dislocated workers tend to be better educated and to have both more assets and greater access to public programs, such as unem-

30. Congressional Budget Office and National Commission for Employment Policy, *CETA Training Programs—Do They Work for Adults?* (CBO and NCEP, 1982), pp. 24–26.

31. Stanley H. Masters and Rebecca Maynard, "The Impact of Supported Work on Long-Term Recipients of AFDC Benefits" (New York: Manpower Demonstration Research Corporation, 1981).

32. Marc Bendick, Jr., and Judith Radlinski Devine, "Workers Dislocated by Economic Change: Do They Need Federal Employment and Training Assistance?" in NCEP, *Seventh Annual Report*, appendix B, pp. 175–226.

ployment insurance, than do other unemployed workers. Surprisingly, unemployment in a declining industry or a declining occupation does not increase the probability of long-duration unemployment. However, the unemployed who reside in declining regions tend to have longer spells of unemployment.

For dislocated workers, the administration is proposing to provide some $200 million to the governors under title III of the Job Training Partnership Act. This is being financed by reductions in outlays for other titles of the Job Training Partnership Act and Job Corps. It could provide about $2,000 for each worker from a declining industry who is unemployed more than six months. The funds, however, are not targeted on dislocated workers who have strong attachments to particular industries or regions with declining employment. Furthermore, the governors have considerable flexibility and may end up using the funds to support normal job search activities within the federal Employment Service. The hope is that some governors will do something inventive and effective.

Retraining and relocation assistance for dislocated workers has not been very effective, but past failures may have been due to defects in particular programs. One model that some claim is useful in dealing with dislocation is that of the Canadian labor-management committees that go into plants before they close and enlist the help of the current employers in relocating the workers. Such a system requires giving employers strong incentives for advance notification of closings. Currently, U.S. employers gain little from advance notification and some do not do it. Retraining and wage subsidies might also be used to induce plants to relocate in declining regions, though experience suggests such adjustments cannot occur quickly.

Conclusion

With unemployment higher than at any time since the Great Depression, the president has set a priority on providing jobs "for all Americans who want to work." Unlike his two predecessors, however, he has outlined a strategy that makes little use of active labor market policies—public service employment, public works, employment subsidies, or even unemployment insurance. True to his philosophy of less government, he is depending on recovery to generate jobs, arguing correctly that economic expansion is the best "jobs program." But even that "program" will be modest because of his continuing concern about inflation: unemployment is projected to exceed its previous post-depression peak for the next three years. Furthermore, only about 50 percent of the unemployed are receiving unemployment insurance benefits and, were it not for the federal supplemental compensation program (slated by the administration to expire next fall), the proportion would be closer to 40 percent.

What more could be done? Take each strategy in turn:

FASTER RECOVERY. If the administration were willing to accept the economic recovery path set out in its first message on the economy in 1981, at least a million more jobs could probably be created over the next two years. Recent progress against commodity inflation provides even more room to maneuver. Such a strategy, however, requires convincing the financial markets that the long-term federal budget deficit will be brought under control (see chapters 2 and 8).

INCOME SUPPORT AND WAGE SUBSIDIES. For those unemployed who are covered by unemployment insurance, the potential duration of benefits should only be reduced as it becomes easier to find a job. That will help offset the adverse incentives of the program yet provide needed help when it is especially hard to find a job. The federal supplemental compensation program has this feature, and it should be kept in place at least until unemployment returns to more normal levels. Thought should be given to modifying the extended benefit program to be more like the FSC program. In the FSC program, cost sharing with the states should take the form of a uniform federal benefit formula, with states adding benefits if they wish to be more generous and are willing to tax their employers more. Income support should be available to those needy job seekers who either have just entered the labor force or have exhausted their unemployment benefits. For such persons, help in the form of a public or private job subsidy may be the best way of testing their labor force attachment. The administration's proposed wage subsidy voucher is a good example of such a scheme, but the subsidy is too low to have much effect. Moreover, the subsidy does not affect the hiring decisions of the large number of employers who have no tax liability.

DIRECT JOB CREATION. Targeted wage subsidies can generate new jobs, though the cost and problems of these programs make them more helpful in getting jobs for those most in need than in lowering the overall unemployment rate. Unfortunately, experience with such programs does not suggest that wage subsidies will be very effective in the short run. Public service employment is probably the least expensive direct way to create jobs for the long-term unemployed not covered by unemployment insurance. Public works is a more expensive alternative but would be justified if the value of the output greatly exceeded that of public service jobs.

TRAINING AND JOBS FOR THE STRUCTURALLY UNEMPLOYED. For those whose labor-market problems will outlast the recovery, effective programs are known to exist, but such programs are expensive. Job Corps is an example for disadvantaged youths; long-term earnings gains of participants in this program exceed the $8,000 spent on each participant. Many programs work for disadvantaged women, few for disadvantaged men. The recent reforms of the employment and training system are promising, but the weakness of the labor market means that more extensive job subsidies may be required in addition to training. Unfortunately, targeted subsidy programs have not worked well in the past. For many of the structurally unemployed, it may be that income transfers are the best form of help until the labor market improves.

CHAPTER SEVEN

Tax Policy

HARVEY GALPER

THE NEED to raise taxes is a major policy focus of the 1984 budget. This is hardly surprising in view of the truly staggering deficits—approaching $300 billion—that the budget otherwise projects for fiscal years 1986–88. Nonetheless, raising taxes represents a considerable change in emphasis for an administration that two years ago committed itself to massive tax cuts in order to reduce the role of the federal government in the national economy. The Reagan administration now proposes to increase revenues by $46 billion in 1986 and $51 billion in 1988 by means of a standby tax package: a surtax of 5 percent of individual income tax liability and an excise tax of $5 per barrel on domestically produced and imported oil. The specifics of the standby taxes, however, are less important than the administration's acknowledgment that the tax reductions in 1981, even after the increases subsequently enacted in 1982, may have gone too far.

By recommending new taxes, President Reagan has set the stage for a reexamination of the tax policies of the last two years and indeed of the whole tax structure. The purpose of this chapter is to analyze these policy issues. First the tax increases contained in the budget for the years after fiscal 1985 are placed in the context of the historical trends in tax burdens. Then, after a review of the current

THE AUTHOR gratefully acknowledges the helpful suggestions of Henry J. Aaron, Barry P. Bosworth, Stephen B. Cohen, Richard Goode, John Karl Scholz, Emil M. Sunley, and Eugene Steuerle, the research assistance of Lisa James, and the preparation of the manuscript by Jane R. Taylor.

173

Table 7-1. Social Security Taxes and Non–Social Security Taxes as Percent of GNP, Selected Fiscal Years, 1955–88

Year	Social security taxes	Non–social security taxes	Total receipts
1955	1.3	16.0	17.3
1960	2.1	16.5	18.7
1965	2.5	15.2	17.7
1970	3.9	16.0	19.9
1975	5.0	13.9	18.9
1980	5.3	14.8	20.1
1981	5.6	15.3	20.9
1982	5.9	14.5	20.4
1984[a]	6.0	12.9	18.9
1986[a]	6.2	14.1	20.3
1988[a]	6.5	14.1	20.6

Source: *Budget of the United States Government*, selected years.

a. Assumes enactment of the president's tax proposals. Receipts from taxing 50 percent of social security benefits—$1.1 billion, $4.7 billion, and $6.4 billion respectively in 1984, 1986, and 1988—are classified here as non–social security taxes. Railroad retirement figures are not included in social security receipts.

state of the tax system, alternative strategies for raising revenues are presented. These alternative strategies are based on the idea of broadening the tax base rather than increasing tax rates.

Tax Receipts in the 1984 Budget

The 1984 budget proposes to reduce the 1986 deficit by 3.0 percent of GNP (from 6.5 percent under the administration's current services projection to 3.5 percent). Equal weight is given to tax increases and expenditure cuts (each 1.5 percent of GNP). By fiscal 1988 budget receipts are projected to be 20.6 percent of GNP, well in excess of the president's target of 19.5 percent announced in March 1981 and only slightly below the 20.9 percent level in fiscal 1981. This last figure in turn was the basis for the administration's original belief that taxes were spiraling out of control.

To gain a proper perspective on these recommended tax increases, it is useful to examine aggregate tax burdens more closely. Total receipts have indeed increased over the past twenty-five years, from 17.3 percent of GNP in fiscal 1955 to 20.9 percent in 1981. This growth has been particularly pronounced in recent years, despite the decline to 20.4 percent of GNP in 1982 (see table 7-1). However, the sharp rise in social security taxes—from 1.3 percent of GNP in 1955 to 5.9 percent in 1982—is the sole reason for the increase in the overall tax burden. Receipts from all other sources declined over this same period from 16.0 percent to 14.5 percent of GNP.[1]

Even with the standby taxes, budget receipts from non–social security sources would amount to only 14.1 percent of GNP in 1986 and 1988.[2] The administration's tax program, therefore, would keep nonpayroll taxes as a percentage of GNP somewhat below that of recent years and roughly equal to that experienced in 1971–80 (an average of 14.2 percent of GNP). If the social security system is regarded as a separate self-financed program, the president can legitimately claim that taxes for supporting general public programs have not been increased over the levels of the past decade.

Apart from the social security tax increases recommended by the National Commission on Social Security Reform,[3] the 1984 budget raises revenues by $53.8 billion in 1986 and $61.6 billion in 1988 through the standby tax increase and other tax changes. These revenue increases may be compared to the net tax cuts enacted in the last two years in the Economic Recovery Tax Act of 1981, the Tax Equity and Fiscal Responsibility Act of 1982, and the Highway Revenue Act, enacted later in 1982. The revenue effects of these three pieces of legislation are shown in table 7-2. The 1981 act provided major tax reductions for households and businesses beginning in calendar 1981.[4] The first 1982 act offset part of these tax cuts, particularly by repealing the acceleration of depreciation scheduled for 1985 and 1986. The Highway Revenue Act will raise receipts by approximately $4 billion annually in fiscal years 1985 through 1988 by increasing the existing excise tax on gasoline and diesel fuel from 4 cents to 9 cents per gallon. On a net basis, these three tax acts would cut taxes $146.3 billion in 1986 and $210.6 billion in 1988. The revenue increases proposed in the budget—the

1. Payroll taxes in this chapter refer only to those taxes that support old-age, survivors, disability, and health benefits and not to all taxes levied on payrolls. Therefore, this measure of receipts is somewhat less comprehensive than the budget receipts category of social insurance taxes, which also includes taxes for unemployment insurance, contributions by federal civil servants to their own retirement fund, and other functions.

2. For these calculations and those that follow, receipts from taxation of 50 percent of social security benefits, estimated in the budget to reach $4.7 billion in 1986 and $6.4 billion in 1988, are treated as income tax rather than social security tax receipts.

3. See chapter 4 for a discussion of the social security issues in the 1984 budget.

4. For a review of the major provisions of the Economic Recovery Tax Act directly affecting households, see John Karl Scholz, "Individual Income Tax Provisions of the 1981 Tax Act," in Joseph A. Pechman, ed., *Setting National Priorities: The 1983 Budget* (Brookings Institution, 1982), pp. 251–62.

Table 7-2. Tax Effects of 1981 and 1982 Tax Legislation, Fiscal Years 1985–88
Billions of dollars

Legislation	1985	1986	1987	1988
Economic Recovery Tax Act of 1981	−158.2	−202.3	−246.7	−282.2
Individual taxes	−121.4	−151.7	−185.9	−215.6
Corporate taxes	−31.3	−43.2	−51.9	−56.3
Other taxes	−5.5	−7.4	−9.0	−10.4
Tax Equity and Fiscal Responsibility				
Act of 1982	42.2	52.1	63.6	67.6
Individual taxes	12.8	16.0	18.7	20.8
Corporate taxes	19.3	30.1	39.7	42.8
Other taxes	10.0	6.0	5.1	4.0
Highway Revenue Act of 1982[a]	3.9	3.9	4.0	4.0
Total	−112.1	−146.3	−179.1	−210.6

Sources: *Budget of the United States Government, Fiscal Year 1984;* and Department of the Treasury, Office of Tax Analysis. Figures are rounded.
a. Revenue effect of increase of five cents per gallon in the gasoline tax after accounting for lower income tax receipts.

standby tax along with other smaller tax increases—would take back 37 percent of the net tax cut in 1986 and 29 percent in 1988. There is now general recognition that the tax cutting of the past two years has been excessive.

Current State of the Tax System

The tax system is not only generating too little revenue, but it suffers from a number of structural deficiencies as well. Chief among them are a narrow tax base that forces high marginal rates on taxable income; the unfavorable interaction of the tax system with inflation, which arbitrarily increases real tax burdens; and the wide array of corporate and individual tax preferences that distort economic choices and misallocate resources. It is not surprising, in these circumstances, that the public has become increasingly dissatisfied with the tax system.

Dissatisfaction with the Income Tax

Growing disenchantment with the income tax in recent years is documented by the annual surveys on public attitudes toward government published by the Advisory Commission on Intergovernmental Relations.[5] In the 1972 survey, 19 percent of the public se-

5. Advisory Commission on Intergovernmental Relations, *Changing Public Attitudes on Governments and Taxes: 1982* (Government Printing Office, 1982), p. 4.

lected the federal income tax as the most unfair tax, far below the 45 percent choosing the local property tax. By 1982, 36 percent of the respondents regarded the federal income tax as least fair, greater than the 30 percent selecting the local property tax. The decline of public support for the federal income tax over the last ten years has been substantial and persistent.

To some degree, public dissatisfaction with the tax system may reflect general unhappiness with the state of the economy, particularly because current economic woes of lagging growth and productivity have been blamed on deficiencies in the income tax system. It is also no coincidence that resentment of the income tax has grown since the rate of inflation started to accelerate substantially in 1972.

Inflation interacts adversely with the tax system in two separate ways. The first is its effect in moving individual taxpayers to higher marginal tax brackets, thereby increasing effective tax rates when real incomes have not increased. Of perhaps greater significance is the mismeasurement of capital income during periods of inflation. For example, gains from the sale of assets may be purely inflationary rather than real gains, but they are subject to tax nonetheless. Similarly, the value of both nominal interest receipts (or payments) and depreciation deductions based on the original cost of an asset is eroded as a result of inflation. The public may increasingly regard the tax system as out of touch with real economic values in an inflationary environment.[6]

To some degree—perhaps as a result of widely publicized cases of tax evasion and of high-income taxpayers who pay little or no tax— negative public attitudes toward the tax system may reflect concerns that the progressivity of the individual income tax has been substantially reduced.[7] Despite such examples, the individual income tax in fact has retained a moderate degree of progressivity.[8] Nonetheless, the tax base has been narrowed as the tax system has come to be employed as an instrument of selective social and economic policy rather than solely as a means of collecting revenues. People have

6. For a discussion of the interaction of inflation and the tax system, see Henry J. Aaron, ed., *Inflation and the Income Tax* (Brookings Institution, 1976).

7. See Department of the Treasury, Internal Revenue Service, *Estimates of Income Unreported on Individual Income Tax Returns* (GPO, 1979); and Department of the Treasury, Office of Tax Analysis, *High Income Tax Returns: 1975 and 1976* (GPO, 1978).

8. See Joseph A. Pechman and John Karl Scholz, "Comprehensive Income Taxation and Rate Reduction," *Tax Notes*, vol. 17 (October 11, 1982), p. 84.

become increasingly familiar with the term *tax expenditures*, meaning favored treatment for certain industries and households in the form of tax concessions rather than direct outlays, as this mechanism has been more widely used for implementing government programs.[9] Tax expenditures rose from the equivalent of 24.8 percent of federal revenues in 1971 to 40.8 percent in 1982.[10] In addition to narrowing the tax base, the use of tax expenditures as a substitute for direct spending has complicated tax computations and rendered the ordinary citizen increasingly at a loss as to how to comply with the tax law.

The myriad of special tax preferences also leads to distortions in economic choices as taxpayers undertake transactions to maximize the benefits from these preferences. For example, the tax exemption of interest on private industrial revenue bonds lowers the cost of finance for those firms eligible to issue such instruments and expands the scope of their activities beyond what purely market considerations would otherwise dictate.[11] Similarly, tax preferences for housing in the form of tax exemption of the implicit rental income accruing to homeowners increases the size of the housing stock relative to industrial plant and equipment.[12] In the case of labor income, compensation in the form of untaxed fringe benefits, such as employee health and retirement plans, reduces the tax base and causes distortions in payroll arrangements.[13]

9. See appendix C.

10. Congressional Budget Office, *Tax Expenditures: Budget Control Options and Five-Year Budget Projections for Fiscal Years 1983-1987* (CBO, 1982), table 3, p. 12. The percentage for the earlier year is based on calendar-year data and for the later year on fiscal-year data.

11. See Harvey Galper and Eric Toder, "Modelling Revenue and Allocation Effects of the Use of Tax-Exempt Bonds for Private Purposes," in George G. Kaufman, ed., *Efficiency in the Municipal Bond Market: The Use of Tax Exempt Financing for "Private" Purposes* (JAI Press, 1981), pp. 85–116.

12. Implicit rental income refers to the flow of service benefits or income in kind that homeowners receive from living in their own dwellings. Tax exemption of this income in kind, combined with deductibility of mortgage interest, provides a substantial tax preference to homeowners. See Frank de Leeuw and Larry Ozanne, "Housing," in Henry J. Aaron and Joseph A. Pechman, eds., *How Taxes Affect Economic Behavior* (Brookings Institution, 1981), pp. 283–319; and Patric H. Hendershott and Sheng-Cheng Hu, "Government-Induced Biases in the Allocation of the Stock of Fixed Capital in the United States," in George M. von Furstenberg, ed., *Capital, Efficiency, and Growth* (Ballinger, 1980), pp. 323–60.

13. See Charles T. Clotfelter, "Equity, Efficiency, and the Tax Treatment of In-Kind Compensation," *National Tax Journal*, vol. 32 (March 1979), pp. 51–60.

Taxation of Capital Income under Current Law

The structural problems of the tax system are most pronounced in the taxation of income from capital. Capital income is subject to three main forms of taxation: the corporate income tax, the individual income tax, and the estate and gift tax. In the aggregate, capital income taxation is not as onerous as commonly perceived, especially since the passage of the Economic Recovery Tax Act in 1981.

MAJOR TAXES. The corporate income tax over the last twenty-five years has declined more or less continuously as a relative share of non–social security receipts, from 29.6 percent in fiscal 1955 to 20.2 percent in 1978 and then sharply to 11.2 percent in 1982. This decline reflects in large measure a similar decline in corporate profits as a share of GNP. For nonfinancial corporations, profits on a calendar-year basis fell from 9.6 percent of GNP in 1955 to 6.6 percent in 1978 and 4.0 percent in 1982.

But this decline in corporate profits is somewhat misleading. An increasing share of the return to corporate capital has gone to holders of corporate debt rather than equity. The before-tax return to combined debt and equity for nonfinancial corporations has fallen more slowly than profits, from 10.0 percent of GNP in calendar 1955 to 8.3 percent in 1978 and 6.3 percent in 1982. Compared to total capital income generated by corporations, therefore, the corporate tax is taking a smaller share now than in the mid-1950s.

The effective degree of corporate taxation on new investment may be calculated by determining the real before-tax return to capital required to provide corporate investors with a given real after-tax return. The lower the before-tax return required to generate a given after-tax return, the smaller the effective corporate tax rate. This type of calculation has been performed by a number of researchers using somewhat different assumptions, but the overall trends in the effective corporate tax rate on new depreciable capital are quite similar. This tax rate declined from above 50 percent in the late 1950s to 25 to 35 percent in the mid-1960s, rose again to over 50 percent in the high-tax years of 1968–70 (when taxes were increased to pay for the war in Vietnam), and has since generally declined to about 30 percent in 1979 and 1980.[14] With the passage of the 1981

14. The figures reported here have been taken from Charles R. Hulten and James W. Robertson, "Corporate Tax Policy and Economic Growth: An Analysis of the 1981 and 1982 Tax Acts" (Washington, D.C.: Urban Institute, 1982), p. 18. For similar analyses, see Dale

and 1982 tax acts, the effective corporate tax rate will continue to fall to 16 percent or less in 1983 and thereafter.[15]

At the individual household level, the return from corporate business is taxed when dividends and interest are received and capital gains are realized. Income from unincorporated enterprises is taxed directly to individuals, but with corresponding tax benefits such as accelerated depreciation and the investment tax credit. The return in kind to owner-occupied housing is not taxed at all, although mortgage interest is deductible. When the various kinds of capital income in the economy are considered in the aggregate, the individual income tax burden is not very heavy. Before the 1981 act the average marginal rate of federal individual income tax on all capital income —taking into account both fully taxed income such as interest on corporate bonds and income not in the individual income tax base at all—was calculated to be only 9 percent. In contrast, when the corporate tax is included, the combined tax rate on such income was found to be 28 percent.[16]

The low marginal rate of individual taxation reflects the fact that less than one-third of all real capital income in the economy (and an even smaller proportion of nominal income) shows up on individual tax returns, in part because of earnings that are retained at the corporate level and in part because of various tax preferences given to the income received by households. The rate cuts and savings incentives enacted in 1981 have reduced the individual tax burden on capital income even more.

Estate and gift taxes never bulked large in the U.S. tax structure, and the avenues of escape from these taxes are well known and widely used.[17] Nonetheless, the 1981 act will greatly decrease this tax, cutting revenues in 1986 from $11.5 billion to $5.0 billion and (assuming 1982 wealth levels) reducing the number of taxable estates from 2.8 percent of decedents to 0.3 percent when the law is

W. Jorgenson and Martin A. Sullivan, "Inflation and Corporate Capital Recovery," in Charles R. Hulten, ed., *Depreciation, Inflation, and the Taxation of Income from Capital* (Urban Institute, 1981); and Martin F. Feldstein, James Poterba, and Louis Dicks-Mireaux, "The Effective Tax Rate and the Pretax Rate of Return," working paper 740 (Cambridge: National Bureau of Economic Research, 1981).

15. See Hulten and Robertson, "Corporate Tax Policy and Economic Growth," p. 32; and *Economic Report of the President, February 1982*, pp. 122–25.

16. Eugene Steuerle, "Is Income from Capital Subject to Individual Income Taxation?" *Public Finance Quarterly*, vol. 10 (July 1982), pp. 283–303.

17. See George Cooper, *A Voluntary Tax? New Perspectives on Sophisticated Estate Tax Avoidance* (Brookings Institution, 1979).

fully effective.[18] Even estates of fairly substantial size ($600,000 in 1987 and subsequent years) can avoid tax completely.

STRUCTURAL DEFECTS. Beyond the major reductions in recent years, the entire structure of taxing capital income is very much confused under current law. This confusion takes two forms. The first is the enormous disparity in the taxation of income from different industries. Second is the inconsistent treatment of the income from capital—in the form of profit, interest, dividends, or rents— and the interest costs of borrowing to finance the acquisition of capital assets.

The disparity in taxation across industries results from a range of industry-specific tax preferences combined with depreciation deductions allowed under the accelerated cost recovery system (ACRS) in the 1981 tax act. These depreciation deductions for tax purposes bear little if any relationship to the actual economic depreciation of capital assets. As tax depreciation deductions become more accelerated compared to actual depreciation, the effective tax rate imposed by the tax system falls. However, the disparity between tax and economic depreciation varies widely across industries, and so do effective tax rates. According to the 1982 *Economic Report of the President*, the ACRS provisions generate effective tax rates across industries that range from a high of 30.6 percent for utilities and 37.1 for services and trade to −11.3 percent for motor vehicles.[19] A negative tax rate means that the tax system is actually providing a subsidy to the corporation. The economic significance of these wide variations in tax rates by industry is that capital becomes allocated according to where the tax benefits are greater, rather than where its productivity is highest. As a result, resources are misallocated and real economic output is lost.[20]

The inconsistency between the taxation of earning assets and the deduction for interest expenses stems from the range of tax preferences accorded to the return to saving and investment combined

18. For an analysis of the estate tax provisions of the 1981 act, see Harry L. Gutman, "Federal Wealth Transfer Taxes after the Economic Recovery Tax Act of 1981," *National Tax Journal*, vol. 35 (September 1982), pp. 253–68.

19. See *Economic Report of the President, February 1982*, p. 124, and Jane G. Gravelle, "Effects of the 1981 Depreciation Revisions on the Taxation of Income from Business Capital," *National Tax Journal*, vol. 35 (March 1982), pp. 1–20.

20. Gravelle estimates this efficiency loss from the Economic Recovery Tax Act to be $3.5 billion to $3.8 billion at 1980 price and income levels ("Effects of the 1981 Depreciation Revisions," p. 1).

with full deductibility generally available for the interest costs of borrowed funds.[21] The results are unintended subsidies and economic distortions induced strictly by the tax structure itself.

There are numerous examples of preferred tax treatment of saving, investment, and the return to capital under current law. Saving and investment are not included in the tax base in the case of employee contributions to individual retirement accounts, employer pension contributions on behalf of the employee, deductions for the depreciation of physical assets (which along with the investment tax credit is equivalent to expensing, or more, for many assets), and expensing of intangible drilling costs for oil and gas.

Similarly, the return to capital is partially or fully exempt from tax in the case of interest on state and local bonds; in-kind rental income from owner-occupied housing; the deferral of tax on interest from U.S. savings bonds; the treatment of capital gains (deferral of gain for appreciating assets until realized, exclusion of 60 percent of realized gain, and forgiveness of unrealized gains at death); the exemption of accrued interest on life insurance reserves; percentage depletion for oil, gas, and hard minerals; the deferral of tax on domestic international sales corporations (so-called DISCs, intended to promote U.S. exports); and a new provision to take effect in 1985, the exemption of 15 percent of net interest income.

This array of tax preferences for capital income yields the equivalent of full tax exemption in many cases. The combination of zero or partial taxation of the income from earning assets and fully deductible interest expenses provides major opportunities for using the tax system for private gain even where there is no social gain whatsoever. A taxpayer who can borrow with full deductibility of interest in order to hold tax-sheltered assets (pensions, life insurance, housing, corporate stock) can earn a positive after-tax return in circumstances where the before-tax return (the measure of return to society) is negative.

To illustrate this kind of "tax arbitrage,"[22] consider a taxpayer in

21. The major exceptions to full deductibility are the denial of interest deductions for borrowing incurred to hold tax-exempt bonds and the limitation of deductible expenses for investment purposes to the sum of net investment income plus $10,000. This latter limitation applies to very few taxpayers. Also, since there are no restrictions on business borrowing, either limitation can be avoided by taxpayers who are able to use trade or business assets as collateral for borrowing.

22. See David F. Bradford, "Issues in the Design of Savings and Investment Incentives," in Hulten, *Depreciation, Inflation, and the Taxation of Income from Capital*, pp. 13–47.

the 50 percent tax bracket who borrows $100,000 at a 12 percent fully deductible interest rate to purchase an asset yielding an 8 percent nontaxable return. The after-tax return (8 percent) minus the after-tax cost (6 percent) is 2 percent. The taxpayer therefore realizes a net after-tax gain of $2,000 generated solely by the inconsistent tax treatment of the return and the interest expense. In the absence of taxes, borrowing at 12 percent for the purpose of lending at 8 percent would yield a negative return of 4 percent.

This inconsistent tax treatment of the return to earning assets and the cost of borrowed funds finds its most important application in the case of business investment. For many business assets, rapid depreciation plus the 10 percent investment tax credit approximates immediate write-off of the asset. This tax rule effectively exempts from taxation the return to capital. But the deduction of borrowing costs at the marginal corporate tax rate of 46 percent can reduce the after-tax cost of funds to considerably below the after-tax gross return. The net effect is a direct subsidy that goes beyond tax exemption and induces borrowers to undertake investments that would be unprofitable if there were no income tax whatsoever. As long as there is other income against which interest expenses may be deducted, the tax system in many instances has reached the point where the private gain or after-tax return on an asset exceeds the economic before-tax return or social gain.[23]

The distributional consequences of such a tax structure are not easy to measure. The reason is that tax preferences not only reduce the liabilities of those eligible to receive them, but they may reduce before-tax incomes that can be claimed in the market as well. The net effect of both lower tax burdens and lower before-tax incomes on the distribution of after-tax incomes is not always clear.[24] In general, however, tax preferences reduce effective tax rates compared to the structure of nominal rates and can also give rise to arbitrary differences in tax burdens among taxpayers in essentially the same economic circumstances.

23. Similar examples for the United Kingdom may be found in the Institute for Fiscal Studies, *The Structure and Reform of Direct Taxation*, report of a committee chaired by Professor J. E. Meade (London: George Allen and Unwin, 1978), chap. 4, "The Existing Base for Direct Taxes in the United Kingdom," pp. 49–73 (henceforth referred to as the Meade report).

24. See Harvey Galper and Eric Toder, "Transfer Elements in the Taxation of Income from Capital," presented at a National Bureau of Economic Research Conference on Income and Wealth, Madison, Wisconsin, May 14–15, 1982.

Broadening the Tax Base to Raise Revenues

The natural instinct of the tax reformer in response to the tax-payer concerns noted above is to broaden the tax base in order to improve the equity and efficiency of the tax structure. This instinct is even more justified when substantial revenues must be raised. The alternative of raising tax rates on the current base, as in the president's proposed tax surcharge, not only forgoes an opportunity for significant reform, but actually exacerbates the two structural deficiencies of current tax law. With higher nominal rates, discrepancies in effective tax rates across industries and activities would be further widened, as would the gap between private and social returns resulting from the inconsistent treatment of the return on assets and interest expenses. In general an increase in the tension between taxable and nontaxable income has a negative impact on tax equity and efficiency.[25] On these grounds, with due regard for those few cases where other policy considerations may compel the use of special tax provisions, the tax structure should be as broadly based as administrative feasibility allows in order to have the lowest practicable marginal tax rates.

Recent Legislative Actions

The view that base broadening is a desirable approach to raising revenues may not be confined to those with a merely academic interest in tax reform. There is some evidence, although of recent vintage, that base-broadening measures are politically attractive as well. The main exhibits are the Tax Equity and Fiscal Responsibility Act enacted by Congress in 1982 and two of the tax proposals in the 1984 budget. As shown in table 7-3, the 1982 act would increase receipts by $17.3 billion, $38.3 billion, $42.2 billion, and $52.1 billion in the fiscal years 1983 through 1986.

With the exception of the acceleration of the payment of corporate taxes, virtually all the provisions of that act relating to individual income taxes, corporate taxes, and pensions and insurance expand the tax base. At the individual level, the 1982 act broadened

25. The tension between taxable and nontaxable income can induce taxpayer responses that have adverse consequences for simplification of the tax structure as well. See Harvey Galper and Michael Kaufman, "Simplification and Comprehensive Tax Reform," in Charles H. Gustafson, ed., *Federal Income Tax Simplification* (American Law Institute, 1979), especially pp. 165–68.

Table 7-3. Revenue Gains from Major Provisions of the Tax Equity and Fiscal Responsibility Act of 1982, Fiscal Years 1983–86

Billions of dollars

Item	1983	1984	1985	1986
Individual income tax	1.0	3.9	3.8	4.1
Medical and casualty loss deductions[a]	0.3	2.4	2.5	2.7
Increase in the minimum tax	*	0.7	0.8	0.9
Increased tax on unemployment compensation	0.7	0.7	0.6	0.5
Business taxes	5.2	13.5	16.4	28.1
Cutback of business tax preferences	0.4	0.7	0.7	0.7
Modification of safe-harbor leasing rules	1.0	2.6	4.3	5.5
Accelerated corporate tax payments	0.9	3.3	0.8	1.2
Modification of investment tax credit[b]	0.5	1.6	2.9	4.4
Reduction of accelerated depreciation	...	...	1.4	9.5
Construction period interest and taxes[c]	0.6	1.2	1.2	1.1
Accounting for long-term contracts[d]	0.9	2.2	2.5	2.4
Other[e]	0.9	1.8	2.6	3.4
Compliance	4.5	11.1	10.5	11.2
Withholding on interest and dividends	0.8	5.8	4.0	4.6
Other[f]	3.6	5.3	6.5	6.6
Insurance and pension provisions[g]	2.2	2.9	3.6	4.0
Employment taxes[h]	1.9	3.1	3.5	2.8
Excise taxes[i]	2.7	3.8	4.4	1.9
Total	17.3	38.3	42.2	52.1

Sources: Department of the Treasury, Office of Tax Analysis. Also see *General Explanation of the Revenue Provisions of the Tax Equity and Fiscal Responsibility Act of 1982*, Committee Print, Joint Committee on Taxation, 97 Cong. 2 sess. (Government Printing Office, 1982). Figures are rounded.

* Less than $500,000.

a. Increase in the floor for medical deduction from 3 to 5 percent of adjusted gross income, repeal of the separate deduction for one-half of health insurance premiums up to $150, limitation of deductibility of drugs to the cost of prescription drugs and insulin, and introduction of a floor of 10 percent of adjusted gross income for casualty losses.

b. Basis of assets to compute depreciation is reduced by one-half of the amount of the investment tax credit, and the offset of the credit against tax liability is reduced from 90 to 85 percent.

c. Construction period interest and taxes must be capitalized and written off over ten years.

d. Tightening of rules for determining which costs are currently deductible and which must be allocated to long-term contracts and for defining completion of contracts.

e. Increase in taxation of incomes derived from foreign oil and gas activities and from corporations operating in U.S. possessions; restrictions on the issuance of tax-exempt bonds for private purposes; tightening of rules on taxation of income from bonds issued at a discount or characterized as having been issued at a discount; modification and extension of the targeted jobs tax credit; and limitation of tax benefits resulting from corporate mergers and acquisitions.

f. Additional reporting requirements by brokers and for payments of remuneration for services, tips, and state and local income tax refunds; changes in penalty provisions on tax deficiencies; modification of voluntary withholding on pensions; and revenues gained from additional IRS enforcement personnel.

g. Modification of the tax treatment of life insurance companies and annuities and reduction in the limits on contributions to, and benefits from, tax-qualified pension plans.

h. Federal employees are made subject to the hospital insurance trust fund payroll tax, the wage base for the federal unemployment tax is increased to $7,000, and the federal tax rate is increased to 3.5 percent.

i. Increases in cigarette and telephone excise taxes and reinstatement of aviation excise taxes.

the tax base by limiting medical deductions to expenses exceeding 5 percent of adjusted gross income and the casualty loss deduction to losses in excess of 10 percent of adjusted gross income. It also reduced the extent to which unemployment compensation benefits may be excluded from the tax base.

In addition, the minimum tax has been restructured to represent a broad-based alternative to the regular income tax. Under current law, the taxpayer pays the larger of (1) tax liability under the regular tax, determined by applying a graduated rate schedule to a base reduced by a large number of preferences or (2) tax liability under the alternative minimum tax, levied on a broader base but at a low 20 percent rate. Ideally, the preferences would be completely eliminated and subject to the full schedule of individual marginal tax rates, which could then be reduced as the base is broadened.

In fact, the 1982 act moved corporate taxation somewhat in this direction by including 15 percent of an enumerated list of special tax preferences in the base of the regular corporate income tax. As shown in table 7-3, the 1982 act also expanded the corporate tax base in a number of other respects, in large measure by cutting back on benefits enacted just one year earlier in the Economic Recovery Tax Act. In particular, the generous depreciation provisions of the 1981 act that were scheduled to have been further liberalized in the years 1985 and thereafter were held at their pre-1985 levels. The ability of corporations to transfer these tax benefits to other parties (safe-harbor leasing) was also restricted.

Administration Proposals

Two tax proposals in the administration's 1984 budget would move further in the direction of base broadening. They are: (1) to include in the individual income tax base 50 percent of social security benefits for higher-income taxpayers and (2) to include in both individual and social security tax bases employer contributions for health and medical insurance in excess of a monthly floor amount. The latter proposal not only would broaden the base of both payroll and income taxes but, perhaps even more significant, would break new ground by treating employer fringe benefits as a potentially major source of tax base expansion.[26]

Further proposals for broadening the tax base can be made in

26. Not all of the administration's tax proposals in the 1984 budget move in the direction of broadening the tax base. In particular, the proposals for a tuition tax credit for elementary and secondary education, special tax incentives for saving for dependent children's higher education expenses, tax incentives for redevelopment in designated enterprise zones, and the jobs tax credit for the long-term unemployed involve revenue losses of $1.7 billion in fiscal

Table 7-4. Revenue Gains from Proposals to Broaden the Tax Base, Fiscal Year 1986[a]
Billions of dollars

Proposal	Revenue gain
1. Eliminate tax-exempt bonds for private purposes	1.5
2. Repeal deduction for consumer interest	10.5
3. Repeal deduction for state sales taxes	6.4
4. Repeal charitable deduction for nonitemizers	2.3
5. Repeal net interest exclusion	3.4
6. Tax the accrued interest on life insurance reserves	6.6
7. Tax employee on employer contributions to health plans[b]	6.0
8. Tax workers' compensation income replacement benefits	2.8
9. Full taxation of unemployment benefits	2.5
10. Tax veterans' compensation benefits	1.8
11. Tax 50 percent of social security benefits[b]	4.7
12. Tax nonstatutory fringe benefits	1.3
13. Repeal tax credit for employee stock ownership plans	2.1
14. Tax employee on employer-paid group life insurance	2.7
15. 5 percent tax on pension fund earnings[c]	5.5
16. Cut by 50 percent business deductions for entertainment	1.2
17. Require full basis adjustment for investment tax credit	3.0
18. Repeal percentage depletion for oil and gas	1.9
19. Repeal expensing of intangible drilling costs for oil and gas	4.2
20. Cut back corporate tax preferences by additional 15 percent[d]	0.7
21. Repeal tax preferences for DISC (export-oriented) corporations[e]	1.1
22. Repeal windfall profit tax provisions of 1981 tax act	1.0
23. Freeze credit for estate and gift tax at 1983 level	1.1
Total[f]	74.3

Sources: Congressional Budget Office, *Reducing the Deficit: Spending and Revenue Options* (CBO, 1983), pp. 269–319; and Department of the Treasury, Office of Tax Analysis.

a. Proposals would take effect January 1, 1984, except for item 5, which would be effective January 1, 1985.

b. As proposed in 1984 budget.

c. Includes Keogh and individual retirement accounts.

d. An additional 15 percent cutback from current law but excluding energy preferences.

e. Department of the Treasury, *The Operation and Effect of the Domestic International Sales Corporation Legislation* (GPO, 1982), p. 19.

f. The effect of interactions among the proposals may cause the total revenue gain to differ slightly from the sum of the individual changes shown here.

almost limitless variety. The usual approach is to review the various tax expenditures (see appendix C) and to compile a list of those considered most objectionable as well as most politically ripe for repeal.[27] To illustrate the revenue-raising potential of this type of base broadening, table 7-4 presents a list of changes that could be

1986 and are a decided step backward from the advances enacted in the Tax Equity and Fiscal Responsibility Act.

27. Several recent compilations of base-broadening tax options illustrate this approach. One set of options was prepared for the tax-writing committees during consideration of the

made to increase revenues by about $74 billion in fiscal 1986. Each of these methods of broadening the tax base could be justified as improving the equity or efficiency of the tax structure.

Taxation of Consumption or Income?

In evaluating the potentialities of broadening the tax base, one must also address the question of exactly what kind of broad-based tax should be the goal. The two alternatives usually considered are an income tax and a consumption tax. The latter is not a sales tax but rather a tax paid by individual households, presumably at graduated rates, on a base calculated by subtracting saving from income. With a comprehensive accounting of financial flows into and out of various forms of saving and borrowing, it is possible to determine the value of consumption for each individual household.

In 1977 the Treasury Department published models of both a comprehensive income tax and a comprehensive consumption tax.[28] The choice between them involves fundamental issues of equity, efficiency, and simplicity of the tax system. Although these issues cannot be dealt with in detail here,[29] the major points of difference can be explained by thinking of income in any period as the sum of consumption plus saving, the latter being equal to the change in the taxpayer's net wealth (positive or negative) over the period.[30]

The debate between advocates of the two kinds of tax focuses on

---

1982 tax legislation. See *Description of Possible Options to Increase Revenues*, prepared for the Senate Finance Committee (GPO, 1982), and for the House Ways and Means Committee (GPO, 1982). See also Congressional Budget Office, *Reducing the Deficit: Spending and Revenue Options* (CBO, 1983), pp. 250–51, 269–319; and Emil M. Sunley, "Tax Policy Options," in Center for National Policy, *Budget and Policy Choices 1983: Taxes, Defense, Entitlements* (Washington, D.C.: Center for National Policy, 1983). In addition, Congressman Dan Rostenkowski, chairman of the House Ways and Means Committee, has proposed a revenue-raising package that would freeze all tax cuts currently scheduled to take effect after 1983. Many of the options presented in these sources appear in table 7-4.

28. Department of the Treasury, *Blueprints for Basic Tax Reform* (GPO, 1977).

29. See, however, Joseph A. Pechman, ed., *Comprehensive Income Taxation* (Brookings Institution, 1977); and Pechman, ed., *What Should Be Taxed: Income or Expenditure?* (Brookings Institution, 1980). For further writings supporting the consumption tax, see David Bradford, "The Economics of Tax Policy toward Savings," in George M. von Furstenberg, ed., *The Government and Capital Formation* (Ballinger, 1980), pp. 11–71; and Bradford, "The Choice Between Income and Consumption Taxes," *Tax Notes*, vol. 16 (August 23, 1982), pp. 715–23.

30. This is the well-known Haig-Simons definition of income. See Robert Murray Haig, "The Concept of Income—Economic and Legal Aspects," in Haig, ed., *The Federal Income Tax* (Columbia University Press, 1921), p. 7; and Henry C. Simons, *Personal Income Taxation* (University of Chicago Press, 1938), p. 50. See also Richard Goode, "The Economic Definition of Income," in Pechman, *Comprehensive Income Taxation*, pp. 1–30.

the appropriate tax treatment of saving or the change in net wealth. Supporters of the income tax argue largely on equity grounds that income from all sources, whether used for current consumption or accumulated for future use, should be subject to tax. Many supporters of the consumption tax want to exempt from tax the accumulation of wealth in order to favor investment and economic growth.

More precisely, a tax on consumption does not distort the choice between current consumption and future consumption. Furthermore, since future consumption made possible by drawing down past saving includes the interest earned on saving, the future consumption base is greater than the present consumption forgone. As a result, the present value of a household's tax liability is independent of its consumption pattern over time. An income tax, in contrast, bears more heavily on households that choose to save and undertake their consumption in later years. This is because current saving, not just the future consumption generated by that saving, is subject to tax.

Consumption tax advocates implicitly assume that the accumulation of wealth has no separate value to individuals beyond its power to support future consumption. If this were true, it would be of little importance how long wealth is held, how much is accumulated, or indeed whether large amounts of wealth could be transmitted to future generations; whenever the wealth is ultimately consumed, that consumption, including all interest earnings, would be taxed.

However, many believe that wealth provides benefits to a household other than the support of future consumption. Wealth can confer power, influence, security, and access to opportunities that simply are not available to those of lesser means, and those advantages are not adequately reflected in future consumption.[31] Because wealth as such does confer substantial benefits, proponents of an income tax are understandably reluctant to abandon a tax on wealth accumulation, even if the cost may be a somewhat diminished rate of accumulation.[32]

31. This view is expressed, for example, in the Meade report, pp. 372–73.

32. For an expression of this view, see Richard Goode, "The Superiority of the Income Tax," in Pechman, *What Should Be Taxed*, p. 71. Also see Eugene Steuerle, "Equity and the Taxation of Wealth Transfers," *Tax Notes*, vol. 11 (September 8, 1980), pp. 459–64. It should also be noted that the empirical question of the extent to which saving and investment have been discouraged by the income tax is unsettled. For two views on this issue, see Michael J. Boskin, "Taxation, Saving, and the Rate of Interest," *Journal of Political Economy*, vol. 86 (April 1978), pt. 2, pp. S3–S27; and E. Philip Howrey and Saul S. Hymans, "The Measure-

The choice, however, need not be between taxing the accumulation of wealth at the *same* rate as consumption (under a comprehensive income tax) and not taxing it at all. The consumption tax could be combined with separate wealth taxes of various kinds. In particular, estate and gift taxes could be restructured to tax consistently and at graduated rates the transfer of wealth to succeeding generations.[33]

A major difference between income and consumption taxes concerns the treatment of interest expenses. Under comprehensive income taxation, all capital income, whether realized or unrealized and whether in cash or in kind (as in the case of owner-occupied housing), would be taxed and all interest expenses would be deductible. Only net capital income would be included in the tax base.

Under a comprehensive consumption tax, capital income would be exempt from taxation and no deduction would be allowed for interest expenses.[34] The taxpayer would receive the full before-tax return on assets and pay the full before-tax cost of funds.

The two models for broadening the base, then, are a comprehensive income tax and a comprehensive consumption tax combined with a wealth-transfer tax. Either could satisfy reasonably well the efficiency and equity objectives of a well-functioning tax system. In fact, with respect to the taxation of labor income, the two tax bases

ment and Determination of Loanable-Funds Saving," in Pechman, *What Should Be Taxed*, pp. 1–31.

33. For a similar view, see Paul N. Courant and Edward M. Gramlich, "Tax Reform: There Must Be a Better Way" (Washington, D.C.: National Policy Exchange, 1981), pp. 47–48. The Meade report also proposed a similar program for the United Kingdom, recommending "a progressive expenditure tax regime (to combine encouragement to enterprise with the taxation of high levels of personal consumption), and . . . a system of progressive taxation on wealth with some discrimination against inherited wealth." See the Meade report, p. 518.

Such a tax structure need not necessarily work at cross-purposes to the idea behind consumption taxation. Statutory tax rates under a wealth-transfer tax could be set so that the implicit rate on capital income would be lower than the rate that would apply directly under a comprehensive income tax, thereby allowing a trade-off between equity and efficiency objectives. Also, if individuals behave as if the only motive for saving were future consumption within their own lifetimes, as many advocates of the consumption tax suggest, even a steep estate tax would not penalize wealth accumulation, for current owners of wealth would never expect to pay the tax. With an explicit bequest motive for saving, some estate tax would be expected to be paid, but it is precisely the transmission of inherited wealth that is of most concern to those who might otherwise favor the consumption tax.

34. Consumption tax rules can be implemented in two different ways. Either saving and investment can be deducted from the tax base—the conventional calculation of the consumption tax base as income minus saving; or alternatively, saving is not deducted but the return to capital is not included in the tax base. For a discussion of these two approaches, see Department of the Treasury, *Blueprints for Basic Tax Reform*, chap. 4, "A Model Cash Flow Tax," pp. 113–43.

are identical. In the case of capital income, however, it is critically important to make an explicit choice between a consumption base and an income base in the design of future tax policy.

The basic structural deficiencies of current tax law derive from a confused mixture of consumption tax and income tax elements. Income tax rules apply to the full deductibility of interest and to the taxation of some forms of capital income. Consumption tax rules apply to a wide range of other forms of capital income. A consistent structural view of the tax system would ensure that changes in the tax law proposed and enacted under the pressures of the moment do not conflict with other provisions of the law. Tax provisions designed to stimulate saving and investment would have to pay heed to the treatment of the interest cost of borrowed funds. Tax incentives for capital formation would be more uniform by industry and activity. Only a consistent structural framework could avoid the present outcome, which dissipates potential gains from a low average tax rate on capital income by encouraging firms and households to undertake fundamentally uneconomic transactions.

Base Broadening to Achieve Structural Tax Reform

The earlier discussion indicates that desirable as base broadening may be as a general approach to increasing revenues, it is also necessary to broaden the base in a way that is structurally consistent. The income tax and consumption tax models provide alternative frameworks to ensure this consistency. With either framework as a guide, it is possible to both increase revenues and at the same time move toward eliminating the structural deficiencies of current law.

Broadening the Base of the Income Tax

Many people believe that the income tax should remain the nation's primary revenue source but should be strengthened where it has been eroded. Moreover, since much of the erosion of the tax base (and not coincidentally dissatisfaction with the income tax itself) reflects the problem of taxing nominal values that increase with inflation, a consistent application of this view would hold that the income tax should be indexed both for rate brackets and, where possible, for proper measurement of the tax base. The income tax would then represent as comprehensive a tax on real income as is practicable.

The longer-term goal under this view would be to bring about the following changes in the tax system.

1. Repeal all savings incentives and exclusions of capital income in the tax base, deductions for individual retirement accounts, the 15 percent net interest exclusion, the exclusion of accrued interest on life insurance reserves, the 60 percent exclusion of realized capital gains, and the complete exclusion of unrealized gains at death.

2. Repeal depreciation deductions that are more generous than actual or economic depreciation and eliminate the investment tax credit.

3. Tax in full all compensation in the form of employee fringe benefits, including health insurance, life insurance, disability insurance, employer contributions and earnings on pension plans, child care facilities, recreation facilities, employee discounts, and other benefits.

4. Tax in full transfer benefits (above amounts contributed) for social security, railroad retirement benefits, unemployment compensation, and workers' compensation.

5. Reduce or eliminate personal deductions not needed to measure income, such as state and local sales taxes.

6. Provide inflation adjustments for the nominal dollar amounts in the tax code, such as the rate brackets, as well as for the proper measurement of the real tax base.

7. Use the revenues produced by broadening the tax base to reduce marginal tax rates.

All these items, with the exception of item 6, are traditional base-broadening measures that have long been on the agenda of those promoting a comprehensive income tax.[35] In contrast, full indexing of both the rate brackets and the measurement of the tax base has not been emphasized by all proponents of the comprehensive income tax despite the widespread recognition that the failure to index distorts greatly the efficiency of the tax structure and arbitrarily shifts real tax burdens.[36]

35. See, for example, Pechman, *Comprehensive Income Taxation*, especially the appendix by Joseph J. Minarik, "The Yield of a Comprehensive Income Tax," pp. 277–98; and Pechman and Scholz, "Comprehensive Income Taxation and Rate Reduction."

36. These efficiency and equity effects have been pointed out by numerous researchers. For a sampling of views, see Martin J. Bailey, "Inflationary Distortions and Taxes," in Aaron, *Inflation and the Income Tax*, pp. 291–319; Martin Feldstein, Jerry Green, and Eytan Sheshinski, "Inflation and Taxes in a Growing Economy with Debt and Equity Finance," *Journal of Political Economy*, vol. 86 (April 1978), pt. 2, pp. S53–S70; and Lawrence H.

Complete indexing for inflation would require adjustments to depreciation allowances, capital gains, and interest in order to measure the real tax base. The failure to index interest does not seriously affect the total tax paid on capital income because the effects on borrowers and lenders tend to be offsetting.[37] Moreover, indexing for interest would involve enormous complexity. A practical indexing scheme, therefore, would probably have to be restricted to depreciation allowances and capital gains. Indexing only these items is an admittedly imperfect arrangement, but it may represent a practical compromise between the complexities of full indexing and the gross distortions of not indexing at all.

The argument has been made that with inflation trending downward both bracket creep and income mismeasurement will become less important in the future. It may be premature, however, to claim that the nation's long-term inflation problem has been solved. More important, it makes good policy sense to implement structural tax changes that can serve well under a range of unpredictable circumstances. Many of the provisions of current law that have the most serious distorting effects when inflation is fairly low—such as the exclusion of 60 percent of capital gains and greatly accelerated depreciation allowances—have been introduced or justified as an appropriate response to high rates of inflation. If the objective of policy is to establish a truly comprehensive income tax, the best insurance against such ad hoc changes in the future may well be to put indexing in place as part of the overall scheme.[38]

In this connection, it seems particularly ill advised to raise revenues by repealing the indexing of individual income tax brackets

Summers, "The Non-Adjustment of Nominal Interest Rates: A Study of the Fisher Effect," in James Tobin, ed., *Macroeconomics, Prices, and Quantities* (Brookings Institution, 1983), pp. 201–41.

37. In the case of unindexed interest payments, the borrower of funds is allowed a deduction for the nominal cost of borrowing (including both the real cost of funds after inflation and the inflation component of the interest payment), whereas the lender of funds takes into the tax base the entire nominal interest receipt. There may be a transfer of real income between the two parties in this transaction but no change in the aggregate real tax base. Of course, individual lenders who see themselves as paying tax on interest earnings that are nominally high but low in real terms are unlikely to be comforted by the greater deduction allowed to borrowers. There is a real equity problem, therefore, in not indexing interest payments. However, the difficulty of indexing the countless number of individual lending and borrowing transactions in the economy would render such indexing impractical.

38. At some point, where future inflation is expected to be quite low, the cost of indexing may outweigh the benefits. For a full discussion of these issues see Aaron, *Inflation and the Income Tax*.

Table 7-5. Revenue Gains from Repealing or Modifying Indexation of the Individual Income Tax, Fiscal Year 1986
Billions of dollars

Proposal[a]	Revenue gain
Repeal indexing	17.3
Postpone indexing for one year	10.2
Limit indexing to excess over 3 percent inflation	10.2
Limit indexing to excess over 2 percent inflation	6.8

Source: Department of the Treasury, Office of Tax Analysis.
a. Assuming inflation rates in the administration's 1984 budget.

scheduled to take effect in calendar 1985. As table 7-5 shows, large amounts of revenue could be raised by repealing or modifying indexing, from $7 billion to $17 billion in fiscal 1986 depending upon the specific proposal. By fiscal 1988 the repeal of indexing could raise more than $40 billion. However, as noted earlier, increasing tax revenues by imposing a higher structure of tax rates (either indirectly through bracket creep or directly) exacerbates the distortions in the current tax system and forgoes the opportunity for structural reform. Primary emphasis should continue to be placed on broadening the tax base.

Recently a number of proposals have been put forward in the name of comprehensive income taxation for some version of a comprehensive flat-rate tax.[39] The appeal of these proposals is that the tax base can be sufficiently expanded to increase revenues while at the same time reducing statutory tax rates. In one sense, these proposals are just another example of traditional base broadening. But the schedule of tax rates under many of these schemes would be very much flatter than under current law.[40] Under a pure flat-rate tax, the structure of tax liabilities—and even more significant, the increase in after-tax incomes—would greatly favor high-income individuals.[41] The pattern of tax rates, however, is independent of the appro-

39. Senator Bill Bradley and Congressman Richard A. Gephardt have proposed a flat-rate tax combined with a progressive surtax (see footnote 40). Senator Dan Quayle, Senator Dennis DeConcini, and others have introduced proposals with a single flat rate on all income.

40. The Bradley-Gephardt bill is a notable exception in that a flat tax rate of 14 percent of taxable income would apply to the majority of taxpayers, but taxpayers with adjusted gross income in excess of $40,000 for joint returns ($25,000 for single returns) would pay an additional surtax ranging from 6 percent to 14 percent. The top combined tax rate would thus be 28 percent.

41. For illustrations of this result see Pechman and Scholz, "Comprehensive Income Taxation and Rate Reduction."

priate definition of the tax base. There is no logical necessity for changing average tax burdens throughout the income scale as part of a base-broadening strategy.[42]

The role of the corporate income tax in the income tax approach to base broadening is admittedly not easy to define. In concept, income earned at the corporate level should be attributed to the shareholders having legal claim to it and taxed directly to them, although the corporation could continue to pay taxes as a withholding agent for its shareholders. Such integration of corporate and personal taxes requires the solution of numerous administrative and practical problems.[43] A number of these problems relate to the appropriate treatment at the shareholder level of the variety of tax preferences available to corporations.

Measuring corporate income on a comprehensive basis could serve two desirable purposes in an income tax system. First, it could eliminate a source of resource misallocation across firms and industries within the corporate sector. Second, it could facilitate the possibility of integration of corporate and personal taxes in the future. At the same time, the correct measurement of corporate income would allow the degree of effective taxation at the firm level to be determined directly by the corporate tax rate rather than by the extent to which corporate income escapes tax through various tax preference devices. The corporate tax base, no less than the individual base, should be a comprehensive one.

As indicated by this discussion, not all of the elements required for comprehensive income taxation are listed in table 7-4. Notably missing, for example, are indexing capital gains and depreciation allowances for inflation, taxing capital gains at full rates, and transforming the current arbitrary depreciation rules to rules based on economic depreciation. These changes are difficult to implement and controversial, but they could be packaged together for future reforms. For example, full taxation of capital gains together with indexing could represent a reasonable trade-off.

However, some of the items listed in table 7-4 would not necessarily be included in the tax base of a comprehensive income tax. For

42. The burdens on after-tax incomes of individuals within income classes could be changed substantially, of course, depending upon the losses from giving up their particular tax preferences compared to the gains from rate cuts.

43. For a discussion of these issues, see Charles E. McLure, Jr., *Must Corporate Income Be Taxed Twice?* (Brookings Institution, 1979).

example, the deductibility of interest for consumer loans (item 2) can conceptually be justified in an income tax framework, and an increase in estate and gift taxes (item 23) would be of lesser importance under a comprehensive income tax. Nonetheless, with just the items shown except for these two, $63 billion could be raised in fiscal 1986 by using the comprehensive income tax as a model for tax reform.

A Comprehensive Consumption Tax

The consumption tax model would also involve a comprehensive tax base in that ideally the only deduction from income would be for saving.[44] By definition, a comprehensive consumption tax could not have a broader base than a comprehensive income tax and therefore would require higher tax rates to raise the same revenue. But a comprehensive consumption tax base could easily be larger than the *current* tax base. This is because current law, as noted, is very far from a comprehensive income tax base.

A fully comprehensive consumption tax would expand the current tax base by disallowing the deductibility of all interest expenses, strengthening estate and gift taxes, and taxing all forms of compensation. It would narrow the current tax base by allowing full deductions for all forms of saving, not just contributions to individual retirement accounts or to employer-provided pension plans.

A significant advantage of the comprehensive consumption tax approach is that no inflation adjustment needs to be made to the tax base. Since capital income would not be subject to tax, problems of the erosion of depreciation deductions or the taxation of inflated capital gains are not at issue. However, as long as graduated tax rates were applied to personal consumption, tax brackets would still have to be indexed for inflation.

If the comprehensive consumption tax were adopted as the model for structural tax reform, it would not be necessary to implement this model immediately and in full. It is only necessary to adopt tax changes that are consistent with a consumption tax base. The confused tax base under current law affords the opportunity for both broadening the base to raise revenues and doing so in a way that moves in the direction of a comprehensive consumption tax. The

---

44. Equivalently, the return to capital could be exempt, as discussed in footnote 34.

base-broadening items in table 7-4 dealing with untaxed compensation, the deductibility of interest, other deductions not needed to
calculate consumption, and the recently narrowed estate and gift tax
are fully consistent with a consumption tax approach to structural
tax reform. These include items 2, 3, 4, 7, 8, 9, 10, 11, 12, 14, 16, and
23, which taken together would produce $43 billion in revenue in
fiscal 1986.

If further revenues are needed, two alternatives may be considered short of increasing tax rates on the new base. The first, most
consistent structurally with the personal consumption tax, is to deal
more broadly with the interest deduction issue than just to disallow
the deduction for consumer interest. For both households and business firms, it would be possible to disallow the deductibility of interest to the extent that capital income is not subject to tax. If the tax
structure did evolve into a truly comprehensive consumption tax,
interest expenses would not be deductible at all. Under current law,
an approach to such a comprehensive treatment of interest expenses
at the household level could be to disallow interest expenses—including mortgage, consumer, and investment interest—in excess of
taxable capital income receipts. This would raise revenues of $18.5
billion in fiscal 1986, compared with $10.5 billion from repealing the
deduction for consumer interest only. However, the possible adoption of phase-in rules and less comprehensive restrictions on the
interest deduction would bring in less than $18.5 billion.

At the firm level, deductibility of interest expenses on borrowing
to purchase capital equipment could also be restricted. For depreciable property the restriction in principle should relate to the degree of
accelerated depreciation on assets purchased with the borrowed
funds. Interest expenses should be totally disallowed in the case of
assets that could be completely written off in the year acquired. One
possibility under current law would be to adopt some restriction of
the interest deduction that would depend upon the benefits available
from accelerated depreciation.

The second approach to raising additional revenues would be to
increase excise taxes on particular items of consumption. Examples
of excise taxes that could be raised are those on alcohol, tobacco, and
uses of energy (see table 7-6). This approach would not deal with the
inconsistencies in the taxation of capital income under current law.

However, higher energy taxes, such as the excise tax on imported

Table 7-6. Revenue Gains from Alternative Consumption-Based Taxes, Fiscal Year 1986
Billions of dollars

Item	Revenue gain[a]
Excise taxes	
Continue tax of 16 cents per pack on cigarettes[b]	1.9
Continue 3 percent tax on telephone services[c]	1.1
Double alcohol taxes	3.8
Value-added tax of 1 percent[d]	10.5
Energy-based taxes	
Oil import fee of $2 per barrel	4.3
Tax on domestic and imported oil of $2 per barrel	8.5
Increase gasoline tax by 5 cents per gallon	4.1

Sources: CBO, *Reducing the Deficit*, pp. 253, 258; and Department of the Treasury, Office of Tax Analysis.
a. Revenue gain is net of lower income tax receipts.
b. Tax is scheduled to fall to eight cents per pack after September 30, 1985.
c. Tax is scheduled to terminate after December 31, 1985.
d. Author's estimate; assumes that a reasonable tax base for the value-added tax would be approximately 50 percent of consumption expenditures.

and domestic oil proposed by the president, may have considerable merit in their own right. Any external costs imposed on the nation as a result of uncertain foreign supplies of oil should be reflected in higher energy prices paid by consumers. Excise taxes on all oil consumption would do this. It may also be desirable to offset currently declining energy prices with higher energy taxes in order to maintain incentives for both domestic production and energy conservation. Furthermore, reductions in the demand for imported oil caused by higher energy taxes would tend to weaken the oil cartel maintained by the producing countries and would be likely to lower world energy prices, thereby shifting part of the tax burden abroad. To accomplish these objectives, oil excise taxes should be put into effect as soon as possible and should be viewed as permanent, in contrast to the president's temporary standby tax on oil to take effect on October 1, 1985.

A national sales or value-added tax (VAT) has also been suggested as a possible new revenue source. The VAT could conceivably be incorporated into the tax structure of this country, as it is in Europe,[45] and would generate about $10.5 billion in revenue for each percentage point of the tax rate at 1986 levels.[46] However, the tax

45. See Henry Aaron, ed., *The Value-Added Tax: Lessons from Europe* (Brookings Institution, 1981).
46. These estimates assume that a reasonable tax base for the value-added tax would be about one-half of consumption expenditures. This degree of slippage from a comprehensive

could not be tailored effectively to individual circumstances and would not improve the equity or efficiency of the overall tax structure, as would general base-broadening strategies.

Summary and Conclusions

Both a comprehensive consumption tax combined with meaningful taxation of wealth transfers and a comprehensive income tax provide reasonable models for structural tax reform. Although their relative merits will continue to be debated, it is clear that a tax system based consistently on either model would represent a vast improvement over current law.

The deficiencies in the present tax system are serious. Much income escapes taxation altogether. The taxation of capital income is a mixture of income tax and consumption tax elements. The particular mixture in current law gives rise to serious resource misallocations and provides numerous opportunities for taxpayers to obtain arbitrage profits at little or no social gain. Structural tax change based on either income tax or consumption tax rules would contribute substantially to equity and efficiency. Efficiency would be improved by a tax system that did not discriminate among firms or industries and that treated consistently the interest costs of borrowed funds. Equity would be improved by taxing individuals in the same circumstances at more nearly the same levels.

Using either model as a standard, many possibilities exist for broadening the tax base, rather than increasing tax rates, to expand the revenue yield of the tax system. Base broadening under the income tax could generate approximately $63 billion in fiscal 1986. In the case of the consumption tax, substantial revenues could also be raised through base broadening, although supplementary revenue measures might also be required.

An increase in tax rates—whether a hidden increase such as the repeal of indexing or an explicit increase such as the president's standby surcharge—should be avoided if at all possible. It would merely raise the tax liabilities of those whose income is already in

value-added tax base has been assumed by most analysts of this tax. See, for example, Charles E. McLure, Jr., "Value Added Tax: Has the Time Come?" presented at a conference sponsored by the Center for Policy Research of the American Council for Capital Formation, Washington, D.C., January 19–21, 1983.

the tax base and would forgo the opportunity to improve the structure of the tax system.

The need to deal with large-scale deficits has forced upon the nation an opportunity for significant structural tax reform. It is not an opportunity that should be thrown away lightly.

CHAPTER EIGHT

The Choices Ahead

HENRY J. AARON

THE GRIM budgetary forecast for 1984 and beyond contrasts strikingly with the future described in President Reagan's first budget message. In March 1981 the president foresaw rapid and sustained economic growth and a balanced budget by 1984 if Congress accepted his tax and spending proposals and if the Federal Reserve followed his prescriptions for restricted growth of the money supply. Congress granted virtually all the president's fiscal requests, and the policies of the Federal Reserve closely resembled those he sought.

Rather than growing steadily, however, the economy has sagged, with unemployment rising from 7.5 percent in January 1981 to 10.8 percent in December 1982. Only in the effort to reduce inflation has progress exceeded the president's plan, in large part because a slack economy has worked as always to weaken wage demands and retard price increases. This year the president foresees slow economic recovery and ever-widening deficits unless policy is changed.

This chapter examines why the prospect of a balanced budget has turned into a vista of unending deficits. It indicates how much of this deterioration is attributable to policies supported by the administration and adopted by Congress, how much to the decline in economic activity, and how much to revisions of the projected growth of economic capacity. The chapter then examines why steps to reduce

THE AUTHOR thanks Barry P. Bosworth, Harvey Galper, Robert W. Hartman, Darwin G. Johnson, Robert D. Reischauer, and Frank S. Russek, Jr., for reading earlier versions of this chapter and making helpful comments. Karen Hanovice provided research assistance.

Table 8-1. Alternative Deficit or Surplus Projections, Selected Fiscal Years, 1981–88
Billions of current dollars

Deficit or surplus projection	1981	1983	1984	1986	1988
Carter projections, 1981[a]	−55	−4	35	142	[b]
Reagan projections, 1981[a]	−55	−19	3	32	[b]
Current services projections, 1983	−58[c]	−208	−232	−271	−300
Proposed 1984 budget, 1983	−58[c]	−208	−189	−148[d]	−117[d]

Sources: Office of Management and Budget, "Federal Government Finances, March 1981 Edition," table 1; OMB, "Federal Government Finances, 1984 Budget Data, February 1983," table 1; and OMB, unpublished data. Figures are rounded.

a. Beginning in 1982, Public Law 97-35 classified purchases of petroleum for the strategic petroleum reserve as off-budget; this reduced outlays and the deficit in 1982 and later years. These figures reflect this reclassification.

b. Forecasts for this year not made in 1981.

c. Actual.

d. Assumes adoption of standby tax increases.

deficits early in the economic recovery would do more harm than good, but why reductions in the long-term deficits are essential if the economy is to achieve a sustained and balanced economic recovery. Finally, it presents the choices Congress faces as it sets national priorities for 1984 and beyond.

The Reagan Program to Date

When President Reagan took office in 1981, official forecasts projected that federal expenditures would rise less rapidly than gross national product; hence the share of GNP claimed by federal outlays was projected to fall. Taxes, in contrast, were projected to rise steadily as a proportion of GNP, as inflation and rising real incomes drove people into successively higher personal income tax brackets.[1] As a result, the $4 billion deficit projected for fiscal 1983, based on legislation in effect when Reagan took office, was expected to become a surplus in fiscal 1984 and beyond (see table 8-1).

Four factors—growth of defense spending, tax cuts, growth of the public debt and interest payments, and sluggish economic performance—combined to transform these optimistic forecasts of fiscal surplus into today's gloomy projections of limitless deficits. A fifth factor, cuts in nondefense spending, has partially offset the deficit-increasing effects of the other four.

1. Taken as a group, taxes other than the personal income tax rise at about the same rate as gross national product.

Nondefense Spending

In 1981 and again in 1982 President Reagan requested large cuts in nondefense spending, and Congress granted most of them. These cuts took place swiftly; as a result, spending is projected to be $57 billion lower in 1984 and $61 billion lower by 1986 than it would have been without the cuts.

The budget divides nondefense spending into "social contract entitlements," "other entitlements," and "other nondefense spending."[2] The budgetary trend for social contract entitlements differs sharply from that for other entitlements and other nondefense spending. Outlays for social contract programs are expected to rise $34 billion between 1981 and 1984 (after adjustment for inflation) despite legislative cuts (see table 8-2). They are growing because case loads have expanded (mostly because of increased unemployment and despite a narrowing of coverage under unemployment insurance),[3] costs have risen (notably for health benefits), and wage histories of newly eligible retirees and disabled persons have exceeded those of previous beneficiaries.

In contrast, real nondefense spending other than on social contract programs will fall $37 billion between 1981 and 1984 and another $27 billion by 1988 under the president's proposed budget (see table 8-2). The sharpest reduction in nondefense spending has been in the miscellaneous category of "other nondefense" programs. This category includes such diverse activities as health care for American Indians, energy research, and congressional staff salaries. Between 1981 and 1988 the share of federal spending devoted to these programs is projected to fall by nearly one-half, and real spending for them will drop by over one-third. Real outlays on other entitlements have declined slightly as legislated cuts in such programs as food stamps, aid to families with dependent children, and

2. Social contract entitlements include old-age, survivors, and disability insurance; medicare; medicaid; and unemployment insurance. The Office of Management and Budget does not classify unemployment insurance as a "social contract entitlement," but puts it in the miscellaneous category "all other nondefense." This chapter classifies unemployment insurance as a social contract program; it was enacted in 1935 in the same bill that created old-age insurance, the largest of the social contract programs. "Other entitlements" include guaranteed student loans; general retirement and disability insurance other than social security; federal employee retirement and disability; subsidized housing; food and nutrition assistance; supplemental security income, aid to families with dependent children, and the earned income tax credit; income security for veterans; veterans' education, training, and rehabilitation; and general revenue sharing.

3. See chapter 6.

Table 8-2. Federal Outlays, by Category, Selected Fiscal Years, 1981–88

Category	1981	1983	1984	1986	1988
Billions of 1983 dollars[a]					
Total outlays	740	805	809	856	890
National defense	185	215	236	281	306
Social contract[b]	239	278	273	286	303
Other entitlements	95	94	88	85	84
Other nondefense	144	130	114	98	91
Interest	77	89	98	106	106
Percent of GNP[c]					
Total outlays	22.9	25.2	24.3	23.4	22.6
National defense	5.6	6.7	7.0	7.6	7.7
Social contract[b]	7.4	8.7	8.2	7.8	7.7
Other entitlements	3.0	3.0	2.7	2.3	2.1
Other nondefense	4.5	4.1	3.4	2.7	2.4
Interest	2.4	2.8	3.0	2.9	2.7
Deficit	2.0	6.5	5.4	3.5[d]	2.3[d]
Percent of total outlays[c]					
Total outlays	100	100	100	100	100
National defense	24	27	29	33	34
Social contract[b]	33	34	34	33	34
Other entitlements	13	12	11	10	9
Other nondefense	20	16	14	12	11
Interest	10	11	12	12	12

Sources: OMB, "Federal Government Finances, 1984 Budget Data, February 1983," table 7; OMB, unpublished data; and *Budget of the United States Government, Fiscal Year 1984*, p. 2-10.

a. Outlays in 1983 dollars calculated with deflators used by the Office of Management and Budget for various categories.

b. Social contract programs include old-age, survivors, and disability insurance, medicare, medicaid, and unemployment insurance.

c. Percentages based on current dollars.

d. Includes effects of standby tax increases. Without the standby tax increase, deficits would be 1.0 percent higher in 1986 and 1988.

student loans have somewhat more than offset growth in case loads and average benefits in these and other programs. As a proportion of the budget they are projected to drop between 1981 and 1988.

Defense Spending

Presidents Ford and Carter initiated increases in defense spending that President Reagan and the last Congress have sharply accelerated. Real outlays for defense rose an average of 4.7 percent per year between 1978 and 1982, and Carter called for a 4.8 percent annual increase from 1982 to 1986.

During his campaign and since his election, Reagan has consistently supported even higher defense outlays. Under the president's proposals, real budget outlays on defense are projected to rise $38

Table 8-3. National Defense Outlays, Actual and Budget Requests, Fiscal Years 1976–88
Billions of constant 1983 dollars

Year	Actual	Outlays			
		1982 Carter budget	1982 Reagan budget amendments	1983 budget	1984 budget
1976	162	...	...	...	...
1977	164	...	...	...	...
1978	165	...	...	...	...
1979	171	...	...	...	...
1980	176	...	...	...	...
1981	185	192	190	...	...
1982	198	200	203	200	...
1983	...	210	226	221	215
1984	...	220	240	238	236
1985	...	230	270	261	261
1986	...	242	290	281	281
1987	...	...	...	294	294
1988	...	...	...	...	306

Sources: Author's calculations based on OMB, "Federal Government Finances, 1984 Budget Data, March 1983," tables 11, 12; OMB, "Federal Government Finances, 1983 Budget Data, February 1982," tables 10, 11; and OMB, "Federal Government Finances, March 1981 Edition," tables 9, 10. Figures are rounded.

billion, or 9.4 percent annually from 1982 to 1984 (see table 8-3). Budget authority of $246 billion already enacted for 1983 promises outlay increases in the near future even if none of the additional increases in budget authority that Reagan seeks are granted.

Taxes

In 1981 Reagan called on Congress to cut personal income tax rates by 30 percent and to accelerate depreciation deductions. These measures were hailed as a supply side tax cut that, according to the president, would boost saving and investment. Personal income taxes had claimed 10 to 12 percent of personal income from 1960 to 1978 (excluding the Vietnam War surcharge). Bracket creep—the tendency of inflation to move people into higher tax brackets— raised effective rates after 1978; by 1983 income taxes were projected to exceed 15 percent of personal income and to continue rising if no action were taken. Businesses were demanding that something be done to prevent inflation from eroding the value of depreciation deductions based on historical costs. Nearly all politicians agreed that some form of tax cut was needed. The debate, therefore, was not over whether taxes should be cut, but by how much, in what form, and when.

In the Economic Recovery Tax Act of 1981, Congress responded by cutting personal income taxes by 23 percent over three years and accelerating the rate at which businesses could take deductions for depreciation. These reductions did not go as far as the president wanted in some ways; for example, he had sought larger general reductions in tax rates than Congress enacted. In other ways Congress cut taxes more than Reagan had requested; for example, the maximum tax rate on capital income was reduced from 70 to 50 percent, the same maximum that had applied to earned income since 1972.[4]

By 1982 congressional resolve to cut taxes was overwhelmed by dismay about looming deficits, attributable in good measure to tax-cutting actions taken the year before. As a result, Congress repealed or modified some of its 1981 actions in the Tax Equity and Fiscal Responsibility Act of 1982. However, even with the 1982 increases (most of which affected business taxes) and other changes enacted by the Ninety-seventh Congress, revenues were cut massively—by $93 billion in 1984, rising to an estimated $211 billion in 1988, or 19 percent of the revenues that would have been collected had no action been taken in 1981 or 1982 (see table 7-2). Increases in payroll tax rates offset less than 2 percent of that reduction.

Net Interest

Though often ignored, interest outlays constitute the third largest spending activity of the federal government, firmly ensconced behind defense and social security cash benefits and well ahead of hospital insurance for the elderly and disabled.

Interest outlays have exceeded Reagan's 1981 forecasts and will continue to do so for two reasons. First, interest rates have been higher than the president projected in 1981. Second, the size of the debt has risen sharply, reflecting deficits of unanticipated size. The national debt held by the public fell from 96 percent of GNP in 1947

4. For a discussion of changes in tax laws enacted during 1981 and 1982, see chapter 7. Also see John Karl Scholz, "Individual Income Tax Provisions of the 1981 Tax Act," in Joseph A. Pechman, ed., *Setting National Priorities: The 1983 Budget* (Brookings Institution, 1982), pp. 251–62.

to 24 percent in 1974, because debt increased less rapidly than the value of total output. Between 1974 and 1981 debt rose to 27 percent of GNP. Between 1981 and 1988 debt is projected to rise to 49 percent of GNP if policies are not changed. Because the budget projects declining interest rates, however, interest outlays in constant dollars are expected to grow only about 9 percent annually and to decline from 3.0 to 2.7 percent of GNP.[5]

Economic Activity

The principal reason why deficits in 1983 and 1984 will exceed Reagan's initial forecasts is the failure of the economy to perform as well as the president had hoped. In 1981 he expected unemployment in calendar year 1983 to average 6.6 percent; in the 1984 budget it is projected to average 10.7 percent. The 1984 budget estimates that the 1984 GNP will be $532 billion (in current dollars) less than the administration forecast two years ago. The failure of real output to live up to projections explains about three-quarters of this difference; reduced inflation explains the rest.

Both these factors translate into enlarged deficits. In general, decreases in GNP reduce revenues from most sources, and increases in unemployment boost public spending through such programs as unemployment insurance and food stamps. On the expenditure side, decreases in inflation translate directly into lower outlays under programs that are indexed, such as social security, civil service pensions, and military retirement. But most programs are not indexed. So even the good economic news, the unexpectedly rapid drop in inflation, has contributed to increased deficits by slowing growth of revenues more and faster than it has reduced spending.

In combination, slowed real growth, reduced inflation, and increased unemployment have increased expenditures and reduced revenues.

5. There is considerable dispute about whether the portion of interest rates that compensates people for the loss they suffer in lending to the government during inflation represents a real expenditure. If the federal government engaged in real-income accounting, the portion of interest payments that just compensates lenders for these losses would be exactly offset in government accounts by the gain the government enjoys in being able to repay debt in dollars worth less than the ones it borrowed. Under real-income accounting, this gain would offset a large part of interest payments, and government spending would be reduced by about 2 percent of GNP.

**Table 8-4. Effect of Reagan Administration Policy Changes on the Budget Deficit,
Fiscal Years 1983, 1984, and 1986**

Billions of dollars

Policy change	1983	1984	1986
Projected deficit			
Baseline before Reagan[a]	155	123	45
Policy changes during 1981–82	39	83	205
Baseline, January 1983	194	206	250
Sources of changes in deficit			
Net tax reductions	68	93	154
Expenditure changes	−29	−10	51
Sources of changes in expenditures			
Additions			
Defense[b]	15	37	84
Net interest	3	10	28
Reductions			
Entitlements	−21	−31	−35
Other nondefense	−26	−26	−26

Source: Congressional Budget Office, *Baseline Budget Projections for Fiscal Years 1984–1988*, pp. 35, 57. Figures are rounded.

a. To facilitate examination of the effects of policy changes undertaken in the last two years, the estimated baseline deficit in this table is presented on the basis of present and projected economic conditions as of January 1983, rather than on the basis of economic conditions expected in 1981. In the 1981 economic assumptions, the Congressional Budget Office projected surpluses in 1983 ($18 billion), 1984 ($77 billion), and 1986 ($209 billion). These estimates differ from those shown as the baseline before Reagan because of changed economic assumptions and estimating methods that caused a downward swing in the estimates of $173 billion in 1983, $200 billion in 1984, and $254 billion in 1986.

b. Defense policy change increased by difference between CBO baseline defense outlays and CBO estimates of defense outlays in the 1984 budget (CBO, *An Analysis of the President's Budgetary Proposals for Fiscal Year 1984*, p. 82) and by OMB's estimate of the reduction in planned on-budget defense outlays in the 1984 budget from prior policy.

Sources of Current and Projected Deficits

Table 8-4 displays the effects on the deficit of changes in budget policy undertaken since President Reagan took office. The timing of the impact on the budget of policies adopted in the past two years differs greatly. The nondefense cuts affected outlays promptly, but the size of these cuts will grow slowly. In contrast, tax cuts had large immediate effects on the deficit, and their effects will grow rapidly. Commitments to increase defense spending add little to outlays until two or three years after they are made.

Little of the increase over baseline in the 1983 deficit is attributable to policies adopted in the past two years. Most is attributable to the weakness of the economy. In fiscal 1983 spending cuts (the excess of reductions in nondefense spending over increases in defense spending) offset somewhat less than half the tax cuts.

The imbalance between measures that reduce the deficit and

those that add to it, perceptible in 1983, becomes plain in 1984 and glaringly apparent in 1986. Reductions in nondefense expenditures in 1986 do not fully offset even the increase in defense spending that the administration seeks; tax cuts and the increase in interest outlays caused by enlarged deficits have no budgetary counterweight. Table 8-4 makes clear that during its first two years in office the administration successfully pushed tax and spending policies that promised a large deficit in 1983 and growing deficits in later years.[6] Anticipation of these deficits is widely believed to have contributed to high interest rates. By slowing growth in the money supply to reduce final demand and thereby to slow inflation, the Federal Reserve also contributed to high interest rates. The combination of large expected deficits and slow growth in the money supply helped push real interest rates (the excess of interest rates over the rate of inflation) to historic highs.

Reagan's Proposals for 1984 and Beyond

Reagan's 1984 budget affirms unwavering commitment to the outlay priorities he enunciated during the first half of his administration. The 1984 budget calls for virtually the same real defense outlays in 1984 as did the 1983 budget (see table 8-3).[7] Real defense outlays for the period from 1984 through 1987 are also unchanged.[8] The budget continues the administration's commitment to lower nondefense outlays, although the cuts requested this year are not so large as those requested and enacted in 1981 and 1982.

In brief, the 1984 budget, like the two previous budgets of this administration, calls for continued increases in defense spending that would more than offset proposed cuts in nondefense spending. In the absence of tax increases other than those connected with social security, the president's program would leave a deficit of $197 billion in 1986 and similar deficits in later years.[9] The continuation

6. Also see appendix tables A-2 and A-3.

7. This statement is based on the assumption that the pay freeze reduces defense outlays but has no effect on the capability of the armed forces.

8. The president's 1984 budget message is misleading in stating "I will adjust our program . . . by proposing $55 billion in defense savings over the next 5 years." *Budget of the United States Government, Fiscal Year 1984*, p. M-10. The budget later states that defense outlays will maintain the defense buildup while achieving savings due to lower inflation.

9. The $197 billion deficit is based on the projected actual deficit of $148 billion (see table 8-1), plus $46 billion in standby tax increases (assumed not to be passed), plus additional estimated interest outlays of $3.4 billion.

of large deficits during economic expansion, particularly as the economy is projected to be nearing full employment in 1988, is a disturbing prospect. The 1984 budget proposes a standby individual and corporation income tax increase and an oil excise tax. But this proposal is contingent on a number of conditions—that Congress enacts all of the president's recommendations for the 1984 budget, that the economy is growing in 1985, and possibly other conditions as yet unspecified. Congressional leaders from both parties have declared the standby tax increase proposal dead.

In 1981 Congress followed presidential leadership in passing a three-year tax cut only to find that the spending reductions necessary to keep total revenues and expenditures in balance were not proposed, and some that were proposed were found unacceptable. Whether or not Congress relies on the deficit-reducing powers of a standby tax, deficits will not vanish. Congress cannot responsibly escape the onerous chore of dealing more convincingly than the president has with the nasty task of raising taxes.

Broad Trends

President Reagan has repeatedly called for reduced federal spending and for a shift away from spending on social programs, many of which he regards as ineffective, to national defense, which he believes must be increased sharply. The budget policy of the administration not only has failed to reduce federal spending, but has substantially increased it. Nearly all of the increase is attributable to increases in defense and interest payments (see table 8-2). Federal spending as a percentage of GNP rose sharply during President Reagan's first two years in office, from 22.9 percent in 1981 to 25.2 percent in 1983; even if the 1984 budget is approved in full, until 1988 the federal share will remain higher than it was in 1981, because of increased defense outlays and the recession.[10]

In redirecting federal expenditures, however, Reagan has enjoyed marked success (see table 8-2). He has secured sharply accelerated growth in defense spending. By 1988 real defense spending under his proposals would be 65 percent above outlays in 1981 (see table 8-3).

10. Budget statistics do not accurately indicate the ways the Reagan administration has reduced the federal presence in the American economy. For example, by relaxing federal environmental, safety, and other regulations the administration has removed or lowered federal barriers to actions that private industry or state and local governments perceive to be in their economic interest.

By 1988 real outlays for social contract entitlement programs are projected to have risen 27 percent over 1981 levels. This increase occurs despite program cuts legislated in the last two years and additional cuts requested in the 1984 budget. Other entitlements and other nondefense spending, however, will have dropped 27 percent between 1981 and 1988 if all of the changes proposed in the 1984 budget are enacted.

One can view these trends from various points of reference. The administration has stressed the inadequacy of defense spending by emphasizing the fact that the proportion of GNP devoted to defense, projected to reach 7.7 percent in 1988, will remain below the share in 1970 (8.1 percent) or in 1960 (9.1 percent). It has also emphasized that outlays on all entitlements will reach 9.8 percent of GNP in 1988, more than the corresponding levels in 1970 (6.1 percent) and 1960 (4.6 percent). On the other hand, proponents of education, training, pollution control, or other discretionary programs might point to the fact that nondefense spending other than on entitlements will constitute only 3.4 percent of GNP in 1984, down from 4.5 percent in 1970, and that by 1988 the share will be only 2.4 percent of GNP, the lowest level since before World War II.

Such comparisons do little to clarify the budgetary choices that need to be made. First, they can obscure large increases in outlays, particularly if GNP is growing. GNP in constant dollars is forecast to be 23 percent greater in 1988 than it was in 1980, 68 percent greater than in 1970, and 147 percent greater than in 1960. More important, much depends on the year one selects for comparison with the present one. Defense claimed 1.6 percent of GNP in 1940 and 4.7 percent in 1950. Most would agree that the proportions for 1940 or 1950 mean little today. The world and this nation are different today from what they were then. The proportions in 1960 and 1970 are not so musty as those from 1940 and 1950, but they also come from an era when not only the nation's income but also its international responsibilities and domestic commitments and other social and economic conditions were very different from today's.[11]

11. The silliness of the practice of comparing current expenditures with those from the past was satirized three decades ago by David Riesman. Describing a fictional U.S. campaign to disrupt the Soviet economy and political system by parachuting surplus U.S. consumer goods into Russian population centers in order to precipitate riots, he reported also on the debate inside the United States. "Addressing the Stanford Alumni Club of Los Angeles, Herbert Hoover spoke for millions in observing that the monthly cost of the airlift has already

Second, large aggregates contain programs designed to achieve quite different purposes. It is more helpful to look at specific programs or groups of programs designed to achieve similar objectives and to compare real outlays in different years. By grouping unlike programs, one conceals what has been happening, as the growth in one program can obscure reductions in other programs intended for quite different purposes.

The 1984 budget, for example, classifies unemployment insurance among "all other nondefense" outlays, rather than as an entitlement. With unemployment insurance in the former category, discretionary and other nondefense spending in current dollars declines by a seemingly small amount, from $146 billion in 1981 to $142 billion in 1984.

If one considers unemployment insurance as an entitlement, however, "all other nondefense" spending falls from $126 billion in 1981 to $113 billion in 1984. And if one adjusts for inflation, real spending in this category drops 24 percent in those three years. From 1981 to 1988, proposed cuts will reduce this category of spending 39 percent. This category of discretionary nondefense spending includes such diverse programs as pollution control and abatement (down 53 percent between 1981 and 1988 in real dollars), farm income stabilization programs (up 47 percent),[12] community and regional development (down 50 percent), air transportation (up 9 percent), and training and employment programs (down 64 percent).

Given the major changes in the allocation of government spending that have occurred during the first two years of the Reagan administration and the sharp deterioration in economic conditions, the American people and Congress learn little about the choices they face from references to the shares of GNP flowing to broad and diverse categories of programs. The real questions concern what programs are essential and how much should be spent on them. Once these decisions are made, enough taxes should be levied to cover total outlays when the economy is operating at high employment.

---

exceeded the entire Federal budget for the year 1839." David Riesman, "The Nylon War," in *Individualism Reconsidered and Other Essays* (Free Press, 1954), p. 432.

12. This increase excludes the value of commodities returned to farmers under the payment-in-kind program; counting the value of these goods would add roughly another 50 percent.

The Structural Deficit or Surplus

The preceding fiscal prognosis shows an unending hemorrhage of red ink, even if the president's budget proposals are adopted. Indeed one justification for many of the proposed cuts is precisely that intolerable deficits lie ahead and that heroic measures are necessary to reduce, if not to eliminate, them. But in order to understand what measures are necessary it is important to recognize how big the problem really is and what harm deficits do.

The Actual Deficit and the Structural Deficit

Actual deficits are a poor guide to fiscal policy because they do not distinguish between two sources of change in revenues and expenditures that have very different implications for long-run balance. First, the deficit can change because Congress amends tax or expenditure laws to cut taxes, reduce nondefense spending, or increase defense outlays, for example. Second, revenues and expenditures can fluctuate because reversible changes in economic conditions temporarily boost expenditures or cut revenues.

Changing the law alters the structural deficit or surplus, the measure of how much the government would have to borrow or be able to lend at a fixed rate of unemployment. It is customary to calculate the structural deficit at the lowest unemployment rate the economy can sustain. The question of precisely what rate of unemployment should stand as the full-employment goal today arouses considerable controversy, although official estimates vary little.[13]

Reversible cyclical fluctuations in economic activity, such as a rise or fall in unemployment, may have powerful effects on the actual surplus or deficit. Reversible fluctuations affect the structural deficit or surplus only by increasing the national debt and future interest obligations; otherwise their influence on the budget vanishes when the economy returns to a given level of economic activity.[14]

13. See appendix A for a discussion of the full-employment rate of unemployment.

14. The neat distinction suggested in the text between changes in law and reversible economic events oversimplifies reality. Changes in the price level are reversible in principle; but the changes in tax collections that arise because inflation pushes people into higher personal income tax brackets are regarded as permanent, just as if Congress legislated changes in tax rates. Hence inflation changes the structural deficit or surplus. In a similar sense, some changes in law may not affect the structural deficit. For example, a law that called for an increase in, say, unemployment benefits only if the unemployment rate exceeded 9 percent would have no effect on the structural deficit or surplus defined at a 6 percent unemployment rate.

To see how changes in policy affect the economy, one must calculate what the surplus or deficit would be if the economy were operating at a constant proportion of its potential. The calculation based on full potential output is usually called the structural or high-employment deficit or surplus. Changes in the actual deficit jumble together the consequences of policy changes with the effects of reversible movements in economic activity. It is possible for the budget to show a structural surplus at the same time that it is in actual deficit because the economy is operating well below capacity. Although the federal sector has shown an actual surplus in only fourteen of the eighty-eight quarters from 1960 through 1981, there was a structural surplus in thirty-one of those quarters.[15]

Effects of Deficits

When it comes to the economic effects of federal deficits, most economists agree that there is some good news and some bad news. The good news, when the economy is operating below full employment, is that increased federal spending and reduced federal tax collections add directly to demand for goods and services and tend to reduce unemployment. The addition to demand—directly from federal spending or indirectly from the higher private demand encouraged by lowered taxes—increases total demand for goods and services. This increase in demand is not beneficial if the economy is operating near capacity, however. In that event it is likely to cause excess demand and to increase inflation.

The bad news, even when the economy is operating below capacity, but especially when it is near capacity, is that an increase in the deficit raises federal borrowing, thereby increasing competition for credit with private borrowers and state and local governments. Because of this competition, interest rates—the price of credit—tend to rise and some private and state and local government borrowing is cut off. As a result, demand for goods and services by private investors and consumers or by state and local governments is reduced.

Most economists hold that when the economy is operating below capacity, the beneficial effects from an increased federal deficit out-

15. Frank de Leeuw and Thomas M. Holloway, "The High Employment Budget: Revised Estimates and Automatic Inflation Effects," *Survey of Current Business*, vol. 62 (April 1982), pp. 26–27. The unemployment rate at which the high-employment surplus and deficit were calculated rose over this period as the characteristics of the labor force changed.

weigh the harmful ones, at least for a year or two. Some argue that these beneficial effects occur only if monetary policy accommodates the extra borrowing associated with enlarged deficits. Otherwise, it is argued, the stimulative effects of these deficits would be fully offset in the private sector. But almost all agree that at a time of substantial economic slack strenuous efforts to reduce the federal deficit through legislation would not help, and might retard, economic recovery during its early stages. Conversely, economists also agree that when the economy returns to high employment a large federal deficit will discourage domestically financed investment. Indeed, one can go further and argue that private economic activity will be retarded by the high real interest rates to which large structural deficits will contribute, and that recovery will be stopped well before full employment.

Government deficits and private investment are alternative uses of private saving. Gross private saving in the United States has averaged just under 17 percent of GNP in recent years.[16] The structural deficit projected for 1988, if policy is unchanged, will equal 4.2 percent of GNP (see chapter 2). Unless gross private saving were to increase—and given the historical record, a significant increase does not seem likely—a 4.2 percent deficit would absorb about one-fourth of all private domestic saving. The predictable result would be increased real interest rates that would depress private investment and keep the international value of the dollar artificially high, thus discouraging U.S. exports and encouraging imports.

While gross investment has averaged 17 percent of GNP, net investment—gross investment less depreciation—has averaged only 8 percent. Thus, a 4.2 percent government deficit would absorb half of the domestic saving available for net capital formation.[17] Additions to domestic real capital formation could continue if there were an influx of foreign capital or if the government increased the fraction of outlays used for capital formation. There is little justification, however, for a country as rich as the United States to borrow from other nations in order to sustain its investment. Nor is there much prospect that government-sponsored capital formation will increase.

16. Edward F. Denison, "Another Note on Private Saving," Washington, D.C., April 27, 1981.

17. According to administration estimates, the structural deficit will be 6 percent of GNP in 1988, three-quarters of domestic saving.

Table 8-5. The Structural Surplus or Deficit under Alternative Policies, Selected Fiscal Years, 1981–88

Billions of dollars

Policy	1981	1983	1984	1986	1988
1981 law[a]	−16	−38	−9	50	...
Current law	−16	−77	−102	−155	−218
Proposed 1984 budget with standby tax revenue	n.a.	−76	−59	−32	−34
Proposed 1984 budget without standby tax revenue	n.a.	−76	−59	−82	−89

Sources: Author's calculations based on estimated structural deficit as reported in appendix A, and *Budget of the United States Government, Fiscal Year 1984.* These estimates are based on assumptions regarding expenditures and revenues made by the Congressional Budget Office, except that real potential output at which the structural deficit is computed is assumed to rise at 2.9 percent per year. I use the administration's estimate of revenues that would be generated by the standby tax.

n.a. Not applicable.

a. A hypothetical projection of surplus or deficit if none of Reagan initiatives had been undertaken.

For these reasons the case is compelling for reducing the structural deficit as the economy returns to high employment. There is disagreement, however, about how strenuous the efforts should be to reduce the budget deficits for 1984 and 1985 while unemployment is expected to remain high and existing capital is underused.

As the economy returns to high employment, the actual deficit will automatically tend to decline, unless changes in policy offset this cyclical improvement. Unfortunately, as table 8-4 indicates, that is precisely the problem that the United States faces after 1984. Each year anticipated economic recovery tends to reduce the actual deficit, because tax collections rise as economic activity increases. But the structural deficit grows, because defense increases and tax cuts —even with reductions in domestic spending—more than offset the gains from an expanding economy (see table 8-5).

Forecasts

If current policies, including the administration's defense budget, are not changed, the structural deficit will be $102 billion in 1984 and will rise to $218 billion in 1988 (see table 8-5). The administration proposes a combination of domestic expenditure cuts and tax increases that will reduce structural deficits after 1984. This program includes the standby tax, passage of which is unlikely. However, even without the standby tax, the deficits would be much lower than those that would result from current law.

For purposes of comparison, table 8-5 also shows the structural surplus or deficit that would have resulted in 1983, 1984, and 1986 if none of the initiatives of Reagan's first two years had been undertaken. In that event the structural deficit would have been small in 1984 and there would have been a substantial surplus in 1986. Table 8-5 demonstrates that the deficit has been created during the past two years by policies that were inconsistent with a structurally balanced budget. Had no action been taken, however, personal tax rates would have far exceeded any in the previous two decades.

The president's program when he took office included four elements: a defense buildup, tax reductions, nondefense spending cuts, and slow growth of the money supply. Given the state of the budget, he could have achieved some, but not all, of his goals while preserving the prospect of a balanced budget in 1986. Given the reductions in domestic spending, he could have supported most of the defense buildup; but he would have had to forgo any reduction in tax rates. Alternatively, without a defense buildup he could have supported tax cuts about two-thirds as large as those enacted in 1981 and 1982.

In practice, the administration program ignored the budgetary reality that tax cuts greater than spending cuts create structural deficits or reduce surpluses. The administration predicted that increases in labor supply, saving, and investment would result from the tax cut of 1981. Their failure to materialize means that extra economic growth from the tax cut will not help to reduce structural deficits; indeed, the 1984 budget reports a reduction in the predicted growth of economic capacity below rates previously expected (see appendix A). As a result, the United States now faces future deficits so large that they will contribute to high real interest rates and promise to reduce seriously the flow of savings to private domestic and foreign investment.

How to Reduce the Structural Deficit

The structural deficit facing the nation is so large that as a practical matter spending cuts alone cannot and should not reduce it to tolerable levels. A sizable increase in taxes will be necessary to bring the structural deficit by 1988 down to levels customarily associated with high employment—1 percent or less of GNP. Given the GNP of $5 trillion projected for 1988, that goal would require a deficit of $50 billion or less.

The amount of the tax increase that is necessary depends on the resolution of three central questions. Will nondefense spending be cut and, if so, by how much? By how much will defense spending be increased? How much should the structural deficit be reduced?

Nondefense Spending

Even if Congress reduces nondefense spending by as much as the administration requests (which seems unlikely as well as undesirable), structural balance cannot be achieved by 1988 without a tax increase. This statement holds even if Congress settles on defense outlays well below those the president seeks. In addition to the changes in social security, the president proposes many reductions and a few increases in nondefense programs. In combination, they would reduce nondefense spending by $22 billion in 1984 and $58 billion in 1988.[18]

The largest of these cuts would result from a proposal to make support payments to farmers in kind, rather than in cash; reductions in expenditures under medicaid and medicare and limits on favorable tax treatment accorded health insurance premiums paid by employers; curtailment of education, training, employment, and social services; a freeze on pay of federal employees and a cut in their retirement benefits; and reductions in income security programs other than social security.

Congress is likely to accept some but not all of the administration's proposed cuts and may enact some increases. The proposal to assist farmers by giving them commodities rather than cash lets Congress cut future spending and the deficit without reducing agricultural aid, because the surplus commodities have been paid for already and giving them away does not count a second time as an expenditure. The administration estimates the budget saving at $2.6 billion in 1984 and $3.5 billion in 1986 if the payment-in-kind plan is enacted.[19] Congress may take some steps in addition to those already enacted in the 1983 social security legislation to reduce growth in expenditures under medicare and medicaid. It is also likely to exam-

18. The expenditure estimate includes an estimated reduction in interest payments of $2 billion, part of which is attributable to reductions below current services in defense and social security spending and to increases in taxes contained in the social security amendments.

19. These savings may be regarded by some as deceptive. The donated commodities come from reserves of the Commodity Credit Corporation, which has authorized reserves of $25 billion. When these reserves are exhausted, Congress must increase the capitalization of the CCC, or it will go out of business. Any increase in the capitalization of the CCC will appear as a federal outlay in the future.

ine seriously proposals to change tax rules to discourage costly employee health benefits.[20]

For three reasons, however, the congressional response to most nondefense cuts proposed for 1984 is likely to be cooler than during the first two years of the Reagan administration. First, the 1982 elections increased Democratic party strength in the House of Representatives and are said to have weakened the expenditure-cutting resolve of some Republicans who previously followed presidential leadership only reluctantly. Second, many of the programs that Reagan seeks to cut this year were cut deeply in both 1981 and 1982. Third, the deterioration of the economy and the sharp rise in unemployment have reduced the willingness of many in Congress to cut further programs that buffer people against the consequences of joblessness and declining incomes.

Real outlays for education, training, employment, and social services, for example, were reduced by 25 percent between 1981 and 1983. The 1984 budget would reduce them by an additional 7 percent in 1984 and 26 percent by 1988. The outlook for congressional acceptance of these proposals is dim.

Other real cuts requested in 1984 spending that Congress is likely to view skeptically include reductions in conservation and land management (15 percent); recreational resources (14 percent); mass transit assistance (12 percent); small business assistance (35 percent, already down 27 percent from 1982 to 1983); food and nutrition assistance (6 percent); benefits for disabled coal miners (5 percent); and aid to families with dependent children (9 percent). The opposition to cuts in these programs will hinge less on their inherent popularity than on the facts that most have been cut already and that many serve populations commonly regarded as worthy of some assistance.

On balance, it seems likely that Congress will approve only a fraction of the requests for reductions in nondefense spending that the president has included in the 1984 budget, and it may enact offsetting increases in some programs. For these reasons, the sum of the reductions sought by the administration is clearly the maximum in nondefense cuts that Congress might enact; the possibility of no net reductions represents a reasonable lower bound.

20. See chapter 5 for an examination of these issues.

Defense Spending

Few now advocate larger outlays for defense than does President Reagan. The administration budget calls for defense outlays in 1988 that are $91 billion higher (in 1983 dollars) than those in 1983. Chapter 3 examines two alternative defense budgets, both of which entail less rapid growth than the president seeks, but that still would increase defense spending more rapidly than in any other peacetime year since World War II. These budgets would result in real defense outlays in 1988 that are $51 billion to $56 billion higher than those in 1983. Leading Democrats have called for increases in defense outlays of 4 percent per year, a rate of growth that would produce real defense outlays in 1988 that are $45 billion higher than those in 1983. The debate about what the United States should spend on defense will take place within the range of these four options—from a low of a $45 billion increase to a high of $91 billion.

Taxes

How much taxes must be raised depends on what the nation decides to do about nondefense spending, defense spending, and the structural deficit. Table 8-6 indicates the size of these tax increases given alternative goals regarding the structural deficit (no deficit or $50 billion deficit), defense spending (the four alternative options), and nondefense spending (cuts proposed by the administration or no net reductions). (Table 8-6 incorporates the assumption that the short-run social security financing problem is resolved with changes that reduce the deficit as much as would those recommended by the National Commission on Social Security Reform and incorporated in the 1984 budget.)

To eliminate the structural deficit by 1988, a tax increase ranging from $29 billion to $153 billion would be necessary, depending on defense and nondefense spending. For example, if nondefense spending is not cut, a tax increase ranging from $95 billion to $153 billion by 1988 would be necessary to eliminate the structural deficit, depending on the level of defense spending (table 8-6, rows 1 through 4, column b). If the full defense budget proposed by the administration and all nondefense cuts are enacted, a tax increase of $86 billion would be necessary (row 4, column d). If all of the nondefense cuts proposed by the administration were approved and defense outlays

Table 8-6. Tax Increases in Fiscal 1986 and 1988 Required to Achieve Alternative Goals by 1988

Billions of dollars

	No nondefense cuts[a]		Administration nondefense cuts[b]	
Defense spending level	1986 (a)	1988 (b)	1986 (c)	1988 (d)
Structural deficit zero in 1988				
1. 4 percent annual growth	42	95	14	29
2. Modified program[c]	47	103	18	36
3. Modified program with insurance[c]	52	110	20	42
4. Administration proposals[d]	76	153	42	86
Structural deficit $50 billion in 1988				
5. 4 percent growth	27	50	−17	−12
6. Modified program[c]	33	58	−8	−6
7. Modified program with insurance[c]	37	64	0	−1
8. Administration proposals[d]	52	109	18	42

Sources: Author's calculations of a baseline deficit estimated from the high-employment deficit of table A-2 (assuming 2.9 percent productivity growth) less the OMB's defense cuts and the social security package. I subtracted alternatively the four defense cut options and the administration's nondefense cuts to yield the remaining deficit paths. The tax increases necessary to achieve structural deficits of zero and $50 billion were calculated under the assumption that the majority of the increases would occur later in the five-year period, so as not to hamper an economic recovery. At each step interest savings on the public debt were estimated.

a. No nondefense cuts means that no net change from current services for domestic spending or taxes occurs, other than the social security proposals.

b. Administration nondefense cuts means that the sum of net nondefense spending cuts and tax increases (other than the standby tax proposal) exactly equals the administration request.

c. For a description of these defense programs, see chapter 3.

d. "Administration proposals" is the 1984 budget request for defense.

set at the levels proposed in chapter 3, tax increases of $36 billion to $42 billion would be necessary (rows 2 and 3, column d). If growth of real defense spending is held to 4 percent per year, a tax increase of $29 billion to $95 billion would be necessary, depending on how much nondefense spending is reduced (row 1, columns a through d).

(The tax increases for 1986 in table 8-6 are estimated on the basis that little attempt will be made to raise taxes in 1984 or 1985 because of continued high unemployment, but that major increases will be made in 1986, 1987, and 1988 as needed to achieve the 1988 goal.)

If a structural deficit of $50 billion in 1988 is regarded as acceptable, much smaller tax increases suffice under all assumptions regarding defense and nondefense spending (lower half of table 8-6). For example, if the options for defense spending examined in chapter 3 were adopted and nondefense spending were not cut at all, tax increases of $58 billion to $64 billion would be necessary (rows 6 and

7, column b); and if all of the administration's proposed nondefense cuts were enacted, no tax increase at all would be required (rows 6 and 7, column d).

Alternative Tax Packages

President Reagan has proposed tax increases, most of which take effect in fiscal 1986.[21] The standby tax increase would raise revenues by $50 billion in 1986 and $55 billion in 1988.[22] Tax increases of this magnitude, together with the rest of the administration's program for defense increases and nondefense cuts, would produce a structural deficit of under 1 percent of GNP in 1988. Smaller defense increases and nondefense cuts are consistent with the same goal.

Although the president's standby tax proposals seem to have been stillborn, Congress cannot escape a fundamental problem. Unless real defense spending is increased much less than any option now under discussion *and* nondefense spending is cut as deeply as the administration wants, large tax increases will be necessary to prevent structural deficits from absorbing private saving and thereby reducing investment, growth, and the chances for sustained economic recovery. The magnitude of the task is illustrated by comparison with the tax increase enacted in 1982 when Congress, facing the prospect of deficits similar to those now forecast, managed to raise taxes by $64 billion for 1987 and $68 billion for 1988 (see table 7-2).

The tax increases examined in chapter 7 fall into two broad categories: those based on the model of a comprehensive income tax and those based on the model of a consumption tax (income less saving). Within each category there is a choice between broadening the tax base and raising nominal rates (see chapter 7). Table 8-7 lists the various tax changes that could be implemented to yield additional revenues and the amounts of revenues that could be generated in 1986 and 1988. These approaches can be used alone or in combination.[23] For example, one could combine income tax base broadening or consumption tax base broadening with, say, energy-based taxes or modifications of indexing. Table 8-7 makes clear that conventional

21. Taxes in the social security package and the cap on excludable health insurance premiums take effect before 1986.

22. These estimates assume high employment. The revenue increases would be $46 billion in 1986 and $51 billion in 1988 on the administration's economic assumptions.

23. Indeed, such measures as the inclusion of fringe benefits in the personal income tax base improve the coverage of both income and consumption.

Table 8-7. Revenue from Alternative Tax Changes, Fiscal Years 1986 and 1988
Billions of dollars

Tax change	1986	1988
Income tax, base broadening	47–66	58–80
Income tax, 10 percent surcharge	36	42
Consumption tax, base broadening	29–44	32–52
Excise tax increases	3–8	4–9
4 percent value-added tax	42	50
Energy-based taxes	5–25	5–25
Modify or repeal indexing	7–17	12–44

Source: Based on 1986 estimates in chapter 7, tables 7-4, 7-5, and 7-6, projected to 1988.

and well-understood revenue measures are available that can be used to close any remaining structural deficit. They can be packaged to yield $50 billion, $75 billion, or even more in additional revenues by 1988.

The president has proposed one approach involving sharply increased defense outlays, sharply reduced nondefense outlays, and a particular set of tax increases. If the members of Congress find the president's program unacceptable, fiscal prudence requires that they develop one of their own that will accomplish the same fiscal result.

Conclusion

Whatever one may think of the pace of the increases in expenditures on national defense; however one regards the significant reductions in nondefense spending; and whatever one's judgment on the size and form of the tax reductions fashioned by Congress in response to presidential leadership, these policies taken individually represent legitimate initiatives by a president who saw himself as fulfilling the wishes of the people who elected him.

Taken together, however, they are fiscally inconsistent. They have placed undue responsibility on monetary restraint as a means of lowering inflation. They have resulted in structural deficits that may abet recovery during its early stages but will place federal borrowing athwart the path to full economic recovery. While efforts to reduce these deficits immediately would be more likely to retard than to advance the early stages of economic recovery, the continued demands for credit by the federal government as the economy approaches high employment will absorb private saving, tend to keep real interest rates high, and suppress domestic investment. If these deficits are not removed, growth will be slowed and the chances for sustained recovery will diminish steadily.

In its 1984 budget the administration explicitly recognizes this problem, but claims that responsibility for its creation lies with previous administrations. President Reagan does not deviate in any significant degree from the policy of building up defense and cutting nondefense spending. In calling for a standby tax, the administration implicitly recognizes that previously enacted tax reductions were larger than is consistent with its expenditure program. The package it proposes would reduce the structural deficit to less than 1 percent of GNP in 1988. Without the standby tax increase, however, the structural deficit would be over twice as large.

To the extent that Congress does not approve nondefense spending cuts proposed by the administration, the need to raise taxes becomes correspondingly greater. To the extent that Congress elects to increase national defense less than the president requests, the need for additional revenues diminishes. But all politically plausible and fiscally responsible options imply that there is no way for Congress and the president to avoid the always-painful task of increasing taxes.

APPENDIX A

Estimates of the Structural Deficit

JOSEPH A. PECHMAN

THE SURPLUS or deficit in the federal budget in any year depends on the level of business activity as well as on the spending and tax decisions made by Congress. During a recession, tax receipts automatically decline in response to the fall in incomes and employment, and outlays for unemployment benefits and other entitlement programs increase. As the economy recovers, the process is reversed: receipts automatically rise and spending declines. These automatic cyclical movements in the surplus or deficit make changes in fiscal policy difficult to identify.

To measure changes in the government's fiscal program, it is necessary to remove from the actual surpluses or deficits the effect of changes in economic activity. This is ordinarily done by calculating the surplus or deficit at a constant level of unemployment—usually near "full" employment, but not a level associated with accelerating inflation. The surplus or deficit that remains after the cyclical component has been removed is called the "structural" or "high-employment" surplus or deficit. This is the appropriate surplus or deficit to use as a measure of past changes in fiscal policy and as a basis for setting future policy.

The purpose of this appendix is to explain the methods of estimating the high-employment budgets used in chapters 2 and 8 and to

THE AUTHOR thanks Elisabeth H. Rhyne and Frank S. Russek, Jr., for their assistance in the preparation of the estimates and Henry J. Aaron and Barry P. Bosworth for their comments and suggestions. Evelyn M. E. Taylor typed the manuscript.

compare them with alternative projections by the Office of Management and Budget and the Congressional Budget Office.

Methods of Calculation

The high-employment budget is now officially calculated by the Bureau of Economic Analysis of the Department of Commerce.[1] The method of calculation is as follows. (1) The high-employment rate of unemployment is specified. (2) Estimates are made of the potential gross national product, the output that could be produced at high employment with the existing working-age population and technology. (3) The receipts and outlays that would occur at potential GNP under policies currently in place are recalculated. Since receipts would be larger with a higher level of GNP, the difference between actual and potential GNP is used to make the correction for receipts. Outlays are affected by the unemployment rate; therefore the difference between actual unemployment and the specified high-employment unemployment rate is used to adjust outlays.

In principle, estimates of the structural deficit or surplus can differ for a number of reasons. In practice, estimates of the response of receipts and outlays to changes in GNP differ only slightly. The major differences concern the estimates of potential GNP and the unemployment rate at high employment. These differences have become significant as output growth has declined and the rates of unemployment and inflation have increased. Those who regard these recent shifts as permanent estimate potential GNP to be lower and the high-employment unemployment rate to be higher than in the past. Those who believe that the decline in growth and increase in unemployment and inflation are mostly cyclical in nature have not reduced their estimates of potential GNP or raised their estimates of sustainable unemployment.

The Bureau of Economic Analysis assumes that the growth of potential GNP has been 2.9 percent a year since 1978. This year, however, the Office of Management and Budget assumed a lower potential growth rate of 2.2 percent a year between the fourth quarter of 1978 and the fourth quarter of 1982 and 2.4 percent a year

---

1. See Frank de Leeuw and others, "The High-Employment Budget: New Estimates, 1955–80," *Survey of Current Business*, vol. 60 (November 1980), pp. 13–43; and de Leeuw and Thomas M. Holloway, "The High-Employment Budget: Revised Estimates and Automatic Inflation Effects," *Survey of Current Business*, vol. 62 (April 1982), pp. 21–33.

thereafter.[2] The Congressional Budget Office retained the assumption of a 2.9 percent potential growth rate through the fourth quarter of 1982, but reduced it to 2.6 percent for 1983–88.[3]

In the Bureau of Economic Analysis estimates potential GNP has been the output level associated with a 5.1 percent unemployment rate since 1975. However, the sustainable unemployment rate has been increasing because of the changing characteristics of the labor force and worsening inflation. The CBO now uses 6 percent as the midpoint of a set of "standard-employment" unemployment rates ranging from 5 to 7 percent. The OMB uses an unemployment rate of 6.25 percent in its estimates of the structural deficit.

Implications of Reduced Potential Growth

If high employment is associated with more unemployment than in the past, the gap between actual and high employment is reduced. This change lowers the proportion of the projected actual deficit that is cyclical in nature and raises the structural deficit. Reducing the projection of potential GNP growth has the same effect.

Whether the federal budget should run a small surplus or small deficit at high employment depends on the strength of private demand. If private demand is high enough, a federal surplus would be desirable to avoid crowding out private investment. It is quite possible, however, that a modest federal deficit would be required to achieve the high-employment target. Whatever target is chosen, the structural deficit adds to the legislative action needed to meet the target.

However, recent experience provides no evidence to suggest that the potential growth rate has declined significantly from 2.9 percent a year. Unemployment in fiscal 1982 averaged 8.9 percent of the labor force, or 2.9 percentage points higher than the CBO's high-employment unemployment rate. If it is assumed that potential GNP continued to grow at 2.9 percent in recent years, the gap between potential and actual GNP in 1982 was 7.8 percent. This GNP gap is 2.7 times the unemployment gap, which is roughly consistent with the historical relationship observed between the two measures.[4]

2. *Budget of the United States Government, Fiscal Year 1984*, pp. 2-17, 2-18.
3. Congressional Budget Office, *The Outlook for Economic Recovery* (Government Printing Office, 1983), pp. 62–71.
4. The relationship between the GNP gap and the unemployment gap was discovered by Arthur M. Okun. His calculations suggested that the GNP gap was about three times the

Table A-1. Potential Gross National Product under Various Growth Assumptions, Fiscal Years 1979–88

Billions of current dollars

	Potential gross national product		
Fiscal year	OMB estimate[a]	CBO estimate[b]	Estimate using higher growth rate[c]
1979	n.a.	2,360	2,360
1980	n.a.	2,644	2,644
1981	n.a.	2,986	2,986
1982	n.a.	3,289	3,289
1983	3,478	3,632	3,551
1984	3,751	3,792	3,850
1985	4,030	4,129	4,159
1986	4,320	4,417	4,476
1987	4,623	4,675	4,817
1988	4,945	5,000	5,176

Sources: Author's calculations based on data in *Budget of the United States Government, Fiscal Year 1984*, pp. 2-17, 2-18; and Congressional Budget Office, *The Outlook for Economic Recovery* (Government Printing Office, 1983), pp. 63–71.

n.a. Not available.

a. Assumes 2.2 percent potential growth rate for 1979–82 and 2.4 percent for 1983–88.

b. Assumes 2.9 percent potential growth rate for 1979–82 and 2.6 percent for 1983–88 and a 2.5 percent lower GNP deflator in 1988 (1972 = 100) than in the OMB projections.

c. Assumes 2.9 percent potential growth rate and changes in the GNP deflator as projected by the OMB.

It is also difficult to justify a potential growth rate lower than 2.9 percent for the next five years. The labor force is expected to rise by 1.5 to 2.0 percent a year. Even if hours of work decline somewhat, the lower growth rates used by the CBO and the OMB would leave little room for annual productivity growth.

For these reasons, the high-employment budget estimates used in chapters 2 and 8 of this volume are based on a continuing growth of potential output of 2.9 percent a year for 1979–88. The unemployment rate at high employment is assumed to be 6 percent for the period.

Table A-1 compares potential GNP in current dollars under the three sets of assumptions. The first two are the estimates by the OMB and the CBO. The third assumes that potential GNP will continue to grow 2.9 percent a year.[5] The differences are substantial.

---

unemployment gap, but more recent experience suggests that the ratio has declined somewhat. See Arthur M. Okun, "Potential GNP: Its Measurement and Significance," in American Statistical Association, *Proceedings of the Business and Economics Statistics Section* (Washington, D.C.: ASA, 1962), pp. 98–104.

5. The estimates of potential GNP are in current dollars and are based on different inflation rates (see table A-1, footnote b).

Table A-2. High-Employment Deficits in the Current Services and Proposed Reagan Budgets under Various Growth Assumptions, Fiscal Years 1979–88

Billions of dollars

Fiscal year	Current services budget			Reagan budget		
	OMB estimate[a]	CBO estimate[b]	Estimate using higher growth rate[c]	OMB estimate	CBO estimate	Estimate using higher growth rate[c]
1979	n.a.	27.7	27.7	n.a.	27.7	27.7
1980	n.a.	38.8	38.8	n.a.	38.8	38.8
1981	n.a.	16.5	16.5	n.a.	16.5	16.5
1982	n.a.	23.0	24.3	n.a.	24.3	24.3
1983	137.6	69.0	77.0	136.8	68.9	76.1
1984	163.5	91.0	101.8	120.8	64.1	59.1
1985	196.1	128.0	130.6	137.2	78.9	71.7
1986	229.4	159.0	155.0	106.2[d]	54.8[d]	31.9[d]
1987	267.9	187.0	190.1	118.3[d]	74.3[d]	40.5[d]
1988	290.5	215.0	218.0	106.8[d]	79.7[d]	34.3[d]

Sources: Author's calculations based on data in *Budget of the United States Government, Fiscal Year 1984*, pp. 2-17, 2-18; *Special Analyses, Budget of the United States Government, Fiscal Year 1984*, p. A-13; and Congressional Budget Office, *The Outlook for Economic Recovery*, pp. 63–71.

n.a. Not available.

a. These figures differ from the published estimates in *Budget of the United States Government, Fiscal Year 1984* (p. 2-18) because they exclude the off-budget deficit.

b. Includes projected outlays under the defense program authorized by the congressional budget resolution for fiscal 1983.

c. Assumes 2.9 percent potential growth rate and includes projected outlays under the president's defense program.

d. Includes standby tax increases proposed by the president.

Potential GNP in fiscal 1988 under the 2.9 percent assumption is $231 billion higher than the OMB estimate and $176 billion higher than the CBO estimate.

Alternative Estimates of the Structural Deficit

Table A-2 translates the current services and proposed Reagan budgets to a high-employment basis, using the 2.9 percent potential growth rate. The corresponding estimates under the OMB and CBO growth assumptions are also given in the table. The CBO estimate of current services includes projected outlays under the defense program authorized by the congressional budget resolution for fiscal 1983, while the other two current services estimates include projected outlays under the president's planned defense program. All the estimates in table A-2 for the proposed budget assume that the deficit reductions recommended by President Reagan will be fully

Table A-3. Actual and High-Employment Deficits in the Current Services and Proposed Reagan Budgets Assuming Potential Growth Rate of 2.9 Percent, Fiscal Years 1979–88[a]

Billions of dollars

				Reagan budget			
				Actual		At high employment	
	Current services[b]			Without standby taxes	With standby taxes	Without standby taxes	With standby taxes
Fiscal year	Actual[c]	Cyclical component	At high employment				
1979	27.7	. . .	27.7	27.7	27.7	27.7	27.7
1980	59.6	20.8	38.8	59.6	59.6	38.8	38.8
1981	57.9	41.4	16.5	57.9	57.9	16.5	16.5
1982	110.6	86.3	24.3	110.6	110.6	24.3	24.3
1983	208.5	131.5	77.0	207.7	207.7	76.1	76.1
1984	231.5	129.7	101.8	188.8	188.8	59.1	59.1
1985	253.1	122.5	130.6	194.2	194.2	71.7	71.7
1986	270.8	115.8	155.0	193.7	147.7	81.5	31.9
1987	291.7	101.6	190.1	191.1	142.1	93.0	40.5
1988	300.4	82.4	218.0	168.1	116.7	89.0	34.3

Sources: *Budget of the United States Government, Fiscal Year 1984*, pp. 2-18, 9-53; *Special Analyses, Fiscal 1984*, p. A-13; and author's estimates.

a. High-employment deficits are calculated at a constant 6 percent unemployment rate and a trend rate of growth of real GNP of 2.9 percent a year beginning in fiscal 1979.

b. Includes projected outlays under the president's defense program.

c. These figures differ from the published estimates in *Budget of the United States Government, Fiscal Year 1984* (p. 2-18) because they exclude the off-budget deficit.

implemented; they differ primarily because of the differing growth rate assumptions.[6]

As would be expected, the structural deficit is lower under the 2.9 percent potential growth rate assumption than under the growth assumptions made by the OMB and the CBO. However, the structural deficit in the current services budget remains high even under the higher growth assumption: it rises from $77 billion in fiscal 1983 to $218 billion in 1988. But if the deficit reductions proposed by the president were implemented, the structural deficit in 1988 would be reduced to $89 billion without the standby tax increase and to $34 billion with the standby tax increase (see table A-3).

6. A small part of the difference is the result of the different GNP deflator used by the CBO (see table A-1, footnote b).

The higher growth rates assumed in calculating the high-employment deficits imply that unemployment will be higher than the outlay estimates assumed in the budget beginning in fiscal 1986. The amounts involved are: $6 billion for 1986, $11 billion for 1987, and $16 billion for 1988. These amounts are *not* added to the proposed budget deficits shown in tables A-2 and A-3 in order to maintain consistency with the published figures.

APPENDIX B

Federal Credit Activities

ELISABETH H. RHYNE

THE FEDERAL government conducts a number of programs that combine elements of financial intermediation with the standard fiscal function of subsidizing favored activities and individuals. Under the label of federal credit activities, these programs either select borrowers directly or seek to influence the types of activities that will receive financing and the terms. In fiscal 1982 more than a fifth of all funds advanced in U.S. credit markets flowed through one of these federal credit programs—a total of $88 billion.

Just as scientists argued for years about whether bacteria should be classified as plants or animals, managers of the budget process have been arguing for years about whether federal credit activities belong in the official unified budget. The participants in this debate have not reached a consensus, though there is general agreement that the new credit budget, which supplements the budget with information on direct and guaranteed loans, is a step forward. The budget controversies arise in part because loans and loan guarantees are not quite the same as direct expenditures of federal funds and in part because the activities among the credit programs are themselves so heterogeneous. The proper classification of federal credit is not of purely academic concern. How credit enters the budget process may influence the propensity of decisionmakers to expand or reduce federal credit activities.

THE AUTHOR is grateful to Barry P. Bosworth, Andrew S. Carron, and Richard Emery for their advice and comments. Kathleen Elliott Yinug typed the manuscript.

Table B-1. Federal and Federally Assisted Loans and Federal Government Outlays, Selected Fiscal Years, 1970–82

Billions of dollars

Type of loan or outlay	1970	1975	1980	1981	1982
Direct loans					
On-budget	3.0	5.8	9.5	5.2	9.1
Off-budget	...	7.0	14.7	20.9	14.3
Guaranteed loans	8.0	8.6	31.6	28.0	20.9
Government-sponsored					
enterprise loans	5.2	5.6	24.1	32.4	43.4
Total loans[a]	16.1	27.0	79.9	86.5	87.6
Outlays					
On-budget	195.7	324.2	576.7	657.2	728.4
Off-budget	...	8.1	14.2	21.0	17.3
Total outlays	195.7	332.3	590.9	678.2	745.7

Sources: *Special Analyses, Budget of the United States Government, Fiscal Year 1984*, p. F-4; *Special Analyses, Budget of the United States Government, Fiscal Year 1981*, p. 144; and *Budget of the United States Government, Fiscal Year 1984*, p. 9-55. Figures are rounded.
a. Net lending.

Types of Federal Credit

The federal government intervenes in credit markets in many ways, but only three are considered to constitute federal credit: direct loans, guaranteed loans, and lending by government-sponsored enterprises (table B-1).

Direct loans are extensions of appropriated funds from the Treasury to the borrower, who then repays the government with interest over the lifetime of the loan. Most direct loan programs operate as revolving funds; they relend the monies recovered through interest income and principal repayment. Only the annual net use of federal funds is defined as a federal outlay, $23.4 billion in fiscal 1982.

Not all federal outlays resulting from direct loans are included in the budget, however. The largest share of loans, $14.3 billion, was financed "off-budget," primarily by the Federal Financing Bank, an arm of the Treasury, at the request of other federal agencies. The exclusion of these direct loans by law from the budget, and of outlays by several smaller loan and expenditure programs, creates an artificial distinction between outlays included in the budget and those that are not. The Federal Financing Bank has been successful at achieving its original debt-management goal, which is to consolidate federal agency borrowing under the Treasury, but the off-budget status of this institution gives an unintended advantage to the agencies that can use it to finance their lending programs. Because there are no receipts to offset these outlays, off-budget spending adds dollar for dollar to an off-budget deficit. Since the practice of excluding the outlays of certain federal entities from the budget began in 1973, the off-budget deficit has added $103 billion to outstanding federal debt, $97 billion of it attributed to loans of the Federal Financing Bank.

Guaranteed loans are made when the government pledges to repay all or part of the principal and interest of a private loan in the event of default by the borrower. For example, in the single largest credit program, the Federal Housing Administration (FHA) insures mortgage lenders to prevent losses from home buyer default. Guaranteed loans involve no federal funds except when default occurs, and therefore appear in the budget only when default claims are paid.

There is little difference in principle between on-budget direct loans, off-budget loans, and guaranteed loans. Disparate budget treatment is hard to justify. Each is intended to provide credit on favorable terms to selected borrowers. If direct loans are assumed to be financed by Treasury borrowing, each creates a government security in credit markets. All can be used to provide interest subsidies, though in fact, direct loan programs typically offer lower interest rates than guaranteed loan programs.

Government-sponsored enterprise loans, unlike direct loans and loan guarantees, are not extended by federal government agencies, but by private institutions with unique links to the government. These are the Federal National Mortgage Association (known colloquially as Fannie Mae); the Federal Home Loan Bank System; its derivative, the Federal Home Loan Mortgage Corporation (Freddie Mac); the three parts of the Farm Credit System; and the Student Loan Marketing Association. These enterprises aim to make their respective markets function more efficiently, and thus to reduce the cost of credit. They operate by converting small individual loans such as mortgages into larger standardized securities that are attractive to a broader range of investors. The government-sponsored enterprises began as federal agencies, but all government capital has since been retired. Nevertheless, the securities of these enterprises continue to enjoy advantages in credit markets over private corporate debt because it is widely believed that they have moral and political government backing, if not legal guarantees, and because special provisions of law provide them with benefits such as exemption from the registration requirements of the Securities and Exchange Commission.

The lending activities of government-sponsored enterprises are considered part of federal credit because their entry into credit markets is intended to serve national public goals. Yet they are not controllable through the same budget mechanisms as are federal agency activities. Their expenses do not appear in the budget, nor does Congress set their yearly activities. Government control takes the form of informal consultation with Congress and the administration, or legislation amending their congressional charters.

The government influences borrower selection in credit markets in a variety of other ways, such as regulation of financial institutions and special tax provisions. A case in point is the federal tax exemption for income from debt securities of state and local governments. This exemption allows state and local governments and private enterprises or individuals to whom they contribute their tax-exempt status to borrow at rates substantially lower than private borrowers receive. Tax and regulatory mechanisms are not part of the annual budget process, and are not considered in this appendix.

Federal Credit and the Budget

One goal of the budget process is to set aggregate federal activity in keeping with an assessment of its effect on future economic conditions. Another goal is to foster an efficient decisionmaking process that leads from choices on major governmental priorities to control of individual programs. The budget accounting framework should support each of these goals. Accounting based on federal expenditures—cash outlays—provides adequate information on direct spending. For federal credit, on the other hand, no single measure suffices, in theory or in practice.

The budget process now uses two measures for credit program activity, the budget itself and the credit budget. The budget records the consumption of federal cash, and hence shows only net lending (loan disbursements less repayments) for direct loans and guaranteed-loan default claims. It deviates from its own principle, however, because of the exclusion of off-budget loans. The credit budget mea-

Table B-2. Effects on the Credit Budget of Policy Changes and Changes in Economic Conditions, Fiscal Years 1981–85

Billions of dollars

Type of loan and effect of change	1981	1982	1983, estimate	1984, estimate	1985, estimate
Direct loans	53.5	47.6	49.1	38.8	37.4
Effect of policy change	n.a.	−2.0	0.3	−6.2	1.3
Effect of changes in economic conditions[a]	n.a.	−3.9	1.2	−4.1	−2.7
Guaranteed loans	76.5	53.7	102.7	98.7	101.0
Effect of policy change	n.a.	−2.6	4.9	0.8	0.0
Effect of changes in economic conditions	n.a.	−20.2	44.1	−4.8	2.3
Total credit budget	130.0	101.3	151.8	137.6	138.4

Source: Author's calculations based on figures in *Budget of the United States Government, Fiscal Year 1984*, pp. 5-25–152. Figures are rounded.
n.a. Not available.
a. Includes changes in disaster-relief loan programs.

sures the gross amount of authorized direct and guaranteed loan principal (table B-2). It includes all federal programs, and its units are those the congressional appropriations process uses. Yet even with both systems, confusion remains.

Assessment of Economic Impact

Any federal credit program can be described as having a financial component (an exchange of assets) and a subsidy component (the extent to which credit is extended below its market price). These two components of federal credit affect the economy in different ways. The pure financial component changes the characteristics of outstanding debt, for example, by packaging mortgages into an easily tradable security. The effects of government-sponsored enterprise lending and the FHA mortgage insurance program are almost wholly of this type. Change in the nature of financial instruments may affect the demand for and hence the price of credit. This in turn may alter real savings and investment decisions. Very little research is available to measure the size and direction of such an effect.

The subsidy component is more easily analyzed. A credit subsidy is defined as the equivalent cash grant value of a federal loan or loan guarantee. Subsidies in credit programs may take a variety of forms, from the obvious one of low interest rates to the less identifiable forms of longer maturities or smaller security requirements. In theory, the combined subsidy value of all federal credit programs should be estimated and entered as their contributions to gross national product, that is, their fiscal effects. In fact, reliable subsidy estimates are not available. The value of the subsidy cannot be read simply from a glance at loan terms. There must be a comparison with the terms the same borrower would have faced in the absence of federal assistance. This is often unknown, especially for programs with no direct market equivalent, such as the guaranteed student loan program. Finally, many federally assisted borrowers could not have received credit privately under any terms. For them, the cash value of the subsidy would seem to cover virtually the entire loan amount. The only published estimate of credit subsidies is the Office of Management and Budget's estimate of the present value of interest subsidies in direct loans, which was $12.1 billion in fiscal 1982, but this estimate does not include allowance for the above-market risk of federal borrowers, for subsidies in forms other than interest rate reduction, or for guaranteed loans.

In the absence of a better measure of economic impact, the new credit budget has become the vehicle for setting aggregate targets for federal credit activity. The first congressional budget resolution for fiscal 1983 contained language to make these totals officially binding for the first time. Some supporters of the credit budget as a control device hope that the macroeconomics of federal credit will soon become well enough understood that the "right" aggregate level can be chosen. This hope assumes that just as the size of budget outlays and receipts can be set to have a specific effect on economic growth, a particular volume of federal lending can be associated with a fiscal effect. However, because subsidies differ, the fiscal impact of a credit budget made up largely of near-market FHA-insured mortgages would differ sharply from one containing the same volume of mortgages made under the Farmers Home Administration's low-interest Rural Housing Insurance Fund. The credit budget framework is useful, but it cannot yet offer much assistance in setting macroeconomic policy.

Program Oversight and Control

Another purpose of the budget is to foster the smooth flow of decisions from broad priority choices to individual programs. The credit budget is making a significant contribution here by controlling discretionary credit programs. Congress makes annual deci-

Table B-3. Loans Generated in Demand-Determined Credit Programs, Fiscal Year 1982
Millions of dollars unless otherwise specified

Type of loan	Obligations or commitments		
	January 1982 estimate	Actual	Error (percent)
Direct loans			
Farmers Home Administration disaster-relief loans	1,600	2,100	31
Commodity Credit Corporation price supports	8,600	11,500	34
Small Business Administration disaster-relief loans	640	237	−63
Guaranteed loans			
Student loans	9,500	6,895	−27
FHA-insured mortgages	28,609	18,576	−35
VA-guaranteed mortgages	19,542	5,983	−69
Export-Import Bank loans	8,000	5,832	−27
Small Business Administration business loans	3,000	2,019	−33
Total	79,491	53,142	−33
Addendum:			
Government National Mortgage Association securities	48,000	36,382	−24

Source: Author's calculations based on figures in *Budget of the United States Government, Fiscal Year 1983, Special Analysis F: Federal Credit Programs;* and *Special Analyses, Fiscal 1984*, pp. F-1-63. Figures are rounded.

sions on loan programs by using outlays, a measure that is a by-product of past and current decisions. A direct loan program, lending at a steady level from its repayments and interest income, would show no budget effect; Congress could easily neglect its new activity. The credit budget sets controls on the annual volume of new loans at the point at which the government becomes legally bound to lend or guarantee a loan. Moreover, the credit budget includes all government credit, which brings greater focus on off-budget loans and guaranteed loans. Its system of limitations on the gross volume of obligations works best for credit activities that are fully discretionary, such as energy or economic development loans, in which the volume chosen by the government generally is the binding constraint.

The credit budget does not work as well for a large classification of credit programs, particularly guaranteed loan programs, which are demand-determined or whose size is intended to vary with certain conditions (table B-3). These programs function like entitlements, although most are not strictly entitlements because eligible recipients have no legal claim to benefits. A restriction on volume may contravene a fundamental design feature of the program. The limited amount of loans may go to borrowers that the private sector would already serve, instead of the marginal borrowers that the program is intended to help. To date there have been few tests of volume restrictions on these programs, for Congress has always placed limitations far above expected need. The best control mechanisms may be similar to those used for true entitlements: revisions in the basic program features, such as eligibility rules or amount of subsidy. These features may be the prime means of controlling both the volume and the economic effect of such a credit program. For example, an administration proposal to simplify the commitments of the FHA for mortgage insurance may have a greater effect on the program's ultimate size than its proposed limitation. Through the reconciliation process the credit budget could be a vehicle to encourage such changes, but it is hampered by the lack of detailed knowledge of the connections leading from changed program rules through market conditions to final loan volume.

The Level of Activity in Fiscal 1982

The activity of federal credit programs in fiscal 1982 demonstrates how sensitive many of the programs are to economic conditions. Between 1981 and 1982 the amount of new direct loans obligated fell from $53.5 billion to $47.6 billion, an 11 percent decline, and guaranteed loans fell from $76.5 billion to $53.7 billion, a decrease of 28 percent (table B-2). This is an enormous decline and, as table B-3 shows, was not anticipated in the fiscal 1983 budget estimates.

That the drop in federal credit support was so large is surprising because several of the large programs were designed to operate in a countercyclical manner, increasing their support when private markets faced severe restraints. A decline in federal credit during a period of tight private credit and high interest rates shows the demand sensitivity of credit but does not provide information on cyclical impact. For if the drop in federal credit were proportionally smaller than that in private markets, some stimulative effect could be posited.

Decreases in direct loans are spread across a range of programs, some resulting from the lack of demand for the loans and some because of cuts brought about by legislative and administrative pol-

Table B-4. Net Lending by Government-Sponsored Enterprises, Fiscal Years 1981 and 1982

Billions of dollars

Item	1981	1982	Change
Student Loan Marketing Association	2,052	1,689	−363
Federal National Mortgage Association			
Corporation loans	4,050	9,159	5,109
Mortgage-backed securities	. . .	8,100	8,100
Farm Credit System	9,984	5,602	−4,382
Federal Home Loan Bank System	20,516	2,411	−18,105
Federal Home Loan Mortgage Corporation	339	16,983	16,644
Adjustment to eliminate double counting[a]	−4,501	−1,496	3,005
Total	32,440	42,448	10,008

Source: *Special Analyses, Fiscal 1984*, pp. F-46–47; and *Special Analysis F, Fiscal 1983*, pp. F-41–43. Figures are rounded.

a. Lending between enterprises and loans guaranteed by federal budget agencies.

icy. The reduction in guaranteed loans is greater primarily because more of the large guaranteed loan programs depend on loan demand. With very high interest rates and poor prospects for economic growth, demand shriveled during fiscal 1982, and especially hard hit were housing programs. The two largest programs, FHA mortgage insurance and Veterans Administration (VA) mortgage guarantees, fell $10.7 billion. Even programs that normally turn away borrowers because they exhaust their guarantee authority, such as the Export-Import Bank and the Small Business Administration, fell far short of their allowed maximums. Default rates in many programs showed substantial increases. The Small Business Administration, for example, paid $845 million in claims on guaranteed loans, compared with $472 million in fiscal 1981.

The government-sponsored enterprises showed large swings in their net lending, resulting both from major changes in demand and from change in the financial system itself (table B-4). Farm credit was predictably very low; the Farm Credit System was operating at $5.6 billion, a little over half its 1981 level. All other changes reflect shifts in the housing finance system. Fannie Mae and Freddie Mac cycled large amounts of old, low-interest mortgages through their swap programs to improve the balance sheets of the thrift institutions. They also began offering mortgage-backed securities modeled on the Government National Mortgage Association (Ginnie Mae) program to enable them to process a greater number of mortgages quickly and improve the secondary mortgage market (allowing for a permanent shift by thrift institutions away from holding the mortgages they originate). The Federal Home Loan Bank system reduced net new lending to savings and loan institutions because normal sources of funds have begun to reappear.

The Administration's Fiscal 1983 and 1984 Credit Proposals

For 1983 the administration is estimating a 50 percent increase in the credit budget above that for 1982, largely predicated on a strong recovery in mortgage markets (table B-2). The volume of FHA-insured and VA-guaranteed mortgages is estimated to rise by more than $40 billion in 1983. Although an increase over the depressed 1982 levels is likely, these estimates may be optimistic.

The 1984 credit budget shows a moderate reduction from 1983, reflecting the continuing efforts of the administration to restrict federal credit activity. In the budgets for fiscal 1982 and 1983 the administration proposed more serious reductions in direct and guaranteed loans than those proposed for the budget as a whole, taking advantage of the discretionary status of most programs. Some efforts have succeeded fully or partially: Economic Development Administration loans, energy development credit, and some Small Business Administration and Farmers Home Administration loan programs, among others, have been curtailed or ended. Subsidies have been reduced in several programs, notably the guaranteed student loan program. Several of the largest proposed reductions, however, have faced repeated resistance from Congress, particularly those affecting the Rural Electrification Administration (REA), FHA mortgage insurance, and Ginnie Mae mortgage-backed securities. The administration has yielded on these proposals in the past, in part because there would have been no on-budget savings from the reductions. For 1984 it is once again proposing reductions in the activities of the Rural Electrification Administration, FHA, and Ginnie Mae, though the discussion of the proposals emphasizes changes in demand rather than reductions as a result of policy changes. The largest credit budget proposal suggests converting the Farmers Home Administration's low-income housing loan program, the most heavily subsidized program, into a block grant. The only major increases proposed are for export promotion through the Export-Import Bank and the Department of Agriculture. Beyond

1984, the credit budget, projected in future fiscal years (1985–88) for the first time, remains stable.

Next Steps in Credit Budgeting

The credit budget has helped educate a range of people, especially in Congress and the executive branch, about federal credit activities, and it has resulted in control of the volume of loans of some programs for the first time. Efforts to improve understanding of and control over direct loans and guaranteed loans should not stop, however. First, the budget treatment of federal credit remains less than satisfactory, and should be resolved. Second, work on the important task of reviewing the operating policies of individual programs has hardly begun.

Budgeting for credit now operates under a confusing dual system. The credit budget supplements the unified budget, without correcting the problems of the unified budget. Incentives remain to escape budget discipline by using off-budget loans, primarily through the Federal Financing Bank, and guaranteed loans. However, as described above, the present credit budget is not well suited to reflect the economic effects of credit or to control demand-based programs. Greater attention to subsidies is needed. Creating a satisfactory accounting framework would require a decisive step in one of two directions: either the budget could be made more inclusive, so that off-budget lending would be abolished, or the budget could be divided into separate spending and credit portions. A completely separate credit budget could be designed to fit the nature of credit programs, including all the important measures: new lending and guaranteeing, net changes in the outstanding portfolio, subsidies, and losses. The President's Commission on Budget Concepts suggested such a division in 1967. The proposal included the key provision that each time a loan or guarantee is extended, the estimated subsidy value of that loan must be requested as a regular budget expenditure. This would cover expected losses due to below-cost interest rates and defaults. Thus only to the extent that the program was not self-sufficient would it enter the budget, and there would be no intrusion of loan principal to cloud the spending budget picture. Credit would then be controlled by volume in the credit portion and by subsidy appropriations in the spending portion.

Separate spending and lending sections in the budget would

neatly distinguish between the pure financial component and the subsidy components of credit programs.[1] Transition to such a system would, however, require a cooperative effort between Congress and the administration, including development of new budget definitions and a major educational campaign. If this cannot be done immediately, a simple interim improvement would be to repeal the legal provisions that give off-budget federal entities their favored status. Inclusion of all federal outlays in budget totals would merely be the consistent application of current budget definitions to all agencies. It would raise the reported (but not the actual) deficit by the amount of off-budget outlays.

Changes in budgeting for credit programs will be of little avail if not accompanied by improvement in program management. Little is known about whether programs are actually expanding credit in their target areas and about long-run program costs. Program-specific terminology keeps information in the hands of a few program experts, and the systems themselves are often designed to hide rather than identify problems in the loan portfolio. The Export-Import Bank, for example, may label nonperforming loans "delinquent" indefinitely to avoid acknowledging losses.[2] Thus it is very difficult to determine the financial soundness of its portfolio. The Small Business Administration follows similar practices, resulting in a long lag between borrower default and final recognition of losses. Full and consistent reporting on defaults and delinquencies is a crucial prerequisite to evaluating the success of a program. Past program experience can provide information about the true subsidy value of programs that cannot be assessed directly. Better tracking of interest rates and maturities in federal programs and their private market counterparts would also allow subsidy estimates to be refined. With improved information on current programs, overall federal credit policy can be based on a better understanding of how the federal government can affect credit markets and on a more conscious choice about the appropriate role of the government as a lender.

1. The national income accounts, upon which the assessment of the economic impact of the federal budget is based, already adjust the published budget total to remove all on-budget lending.

2. Richard Feinberg, *Subsidizing Success: The Export-Import Bank in the U.S. Economy* (Cambridge University Press, 1982), p. 98.

APPENDIX C

Tax Expenditures

JOHN KARL SCHOLZ

TAX EXPENDITURES are departures from a normal tax structure that are designed to favor a particular activity or group of taxpayers. The term *tax expenditures* emphasizes the similarity between subsidies delivered through the tax system and direct governmental expenditures for the same purposes; however, direct expenditures enter the budget as outlays, while tax expenditures reduce receipts. Recognizing the need to analyze tax expenditures as part of the budget process, the Treasury Department compiled the first list of tax expenditures in 1968. Six years later, the Congressional Budget Act of 1974 formally established the concept in law by requiring an annual listing of tax expenditures to appear in the budget. The act also directs all congressional committees to identify legislative changes that affect tax expenditures related to their activities and to provide estimates of the effect of such changes on tax receipts.

The 1974 act defines tax expenditures as "revenue losses attributable to provisions of the federal tax laws which allow a special exclusion, exemption, or deduction from gross income or which provide a special credit, a preferential rate of tax, or a deferral of tax liability." The legislative history of the 1974 act indicates that income is to be defined as closely to economic income as measurement permits. Thus, realized capital gains are included in full, whereas imputed income, such as imputed rent on owner-occupied houses, is omitted

THE AUTHOR thanks Harvey Galper for his constructive advice.

because it is difficult to measure. The rate schedules, exemptions, and usual accounting conventions are part of the normal tax structure and are not considered tax expenditures.

Under this definition a tax expenditure occurs when two conditions are fulfilled: the provision must be special in that it applies to a narrow class of transactions or transactors; and there must be a general provision to which the special provision is a clear exception. A special provision implies a reference standard against which the exemption can be compared. As in the past, this year's concept of tax expenditures uses the general provisions of the Internal Revenue Code as the reference standard. In the last two years thirteen modifications of the reference standard have been made by the Reagan administration. The chief modifications are to omit from the tax expenditure budget the accelerated cost recovery system (ACRS) enacted under the Economic Recovery Tax Act of 1981, the graduated rates of the corporation income tax, and the deduction for two-earner married couples. None of the modifications have been accepted by the Congressional Budget Office and the Joint Committee on Taxation. The tables in this appendix follow the reference standard used in previous years. Hence the tables include the excess of ACRS depreciation over straight-line depreciation, the cost of the graduated corporate income tax rates, and the deduction granted to two-earner married couples.

In the 1983 and 1984 budgets, tax expenditures have been estimated as outlay equivalents rather than revenue reductions, as in previous budgets. These estimates measure tax expenditures as the outlays that would be required to provide an equal after-tax income to the taxpayer. Since taxpayers would have to pay taxes on the higher income derived from the annual budget outlays, the outlay equivalents for many tax expenditures are higher than the revenue losses as traditionally estimated. The federal deficit is not changed by the methodology, because both outlays and receipts are raised by the amount of the outlay equivalent.

Tax expenditures in fiscal 1984 are estimated at $388.4 billion.[1] If they were replaced by direct expenditures of the same value to tax-

1. Total tax expenditures are the sum of the revenue effects of the individual items, each computed separately with the assumption that there are no other changes in the tax laws. This sum probably underestimates the total revenue effect, because people are pushed into higher brackets if all or a group of tax expenditures are repealed simultaneously.

Table C-1. Effect of Tax Expenditures on the Federal Current Services Budget, Fiscal Year 1984[a]

Billions of dollars

Item	Outlays	Receipts	Deficit
Current services budget	880.3	648.8	231.5
Tax expenditures	388.4	388.4	...
Revised total	1,268.7	1,037.2	231.5

Sources: *Special Analyses, Budget of the United States Government, Fiscal Year 1984,* pp. A-13, G-26–28; and *Tax Expenditures: Budget Control Options and Five-Year Budget Projections for Fiscal Years 1983–1987* (Congressional Budget Office, 1982), p. 20.

a. Current services outlays and receipts are the amount the government would spend and collect if all programs were continued at the 1983 level with no policy changes, except for defense outlays, which are included at the level planned by the Reagan administration.

payers, both outlays and receipts would be raised by $388.4 billion; thus current services outlays in 1984 would be $1,268.7 billion instead of the $880.3 billion reported in the budget, and receipts would be $1,037.2 billion, but the deficit would remain at $231.5 billion (table C-1).[2]

The major tax expenditures are (1) personal deductions under the individual income tax (for state and local income taxes, sales and property taxes, charitable contributions, medical expenses, and interest paid); (2) exclusions from taxable income (state and local government bond interest, employee benefits, and transfer payments such as social security, unemployment compensation, and welfare); (3) preferential treatment of long-term capital gains; and (4) tax credits and accelerated depreciation for investment. A list of the major tax expenditures is given in table C-2.

Tax expenditures have grown much faster than direct outlays over the past several years. Inflation has pushed taxpayers into higher marginal tax-rate brackets; hence the exclusions and deductions that tax expenditures provide are more valuable. The large marginal rate reductions granted in the 1981 tax act reversed this effect somewhat. Some tax expenditures are becoming more widely used. During 1974–81 the percentage increase in tax expenditures directed toward natural resources and the environment was seven times as large as the percentage increase in direct outlays; and the

2. Current services outlays and receipts are the amounts the government would spend and collect if all programs were continued at the January 1, 1983, level with no policy changes. In a departure from previous practice, the current services outlays for 1984–88 include the estimated cost of the buildup of President Reagan's defense program.

Table C-2. Outlay Equivalents for Major Tax Expenditures, Fiscal Year 1984

Millions of dollars

Tax expenditure	Amount
Deductibility of state and local nonbusiness taxes	31,400
Deductibility of charitable contributions	9,160
Deductibility of mortgage interest and interest on consumer debt	38,865
Deductibility of medical expenses	2,635
Deductibility of casualty losses	520
Deduction for two-earner married couples	10,040
Exemptions for elderly and blind and tax credits for elderly	2,590
Exemptions for parents of students aged 19 and over	945
Exclusion of employer contributions to pensions, health, and welfare plans[a]	118,345
Exclusion and deferral of interest payments[b]	24,595
Exclusion of benefits and allowances to armed forces personnel	2,980
Exclusion of transfer payments	31,120
Dividend exclusion	1,680
Earned income credit[c]	340
Residential, conservation, and new technology energy credits	1,525
Job credits	710
Credits for child and dependent care expenses	2,430
Tax credits or exclusions for income from abroad	3,995
Preferential treatment of capital gains[d]	32,520
Investment tax credit[e]	21,615
Accelerated depreciation[f]	20,495
Safe harbor leasing rules	3,035
Excess of percentage over cost depletion and expensing of exploration and development costs	5,635
Credit for, and expensing of, research and development expenditures	220
Deferral of income of domestic international sales corporations and controlled foreign corporations	2,605
Excess bad debt reserves of financial institutions	1,090
Reduced rates on first $100,000 of corporate income	14,935
Reinvestment of dividends in public utility stock	670
Other	1,675
Total	388,370

Sources: *Special Analyses, Fiscal 1984*, pp. G-26–28; and *Tax Expenditures*, p. 20.

a. Includes contributions to individual retirement accounts and prepaid legal services and plans for the self-employed.

b. Includes exclusion of interest on state and local government debt and life insurance savings and deferral of interest on federal savings bonds.

c. Estimated tax subsidy provided by the earned income credit. The credit also increases budget outlays by $1.1 billion.

d. Includes treatment of capital gains for rehabilitation of structures.

e. Includes credit for the preservation of historic structures.

f. Includes expensing of certain capital outlays.

percentage increase in tax expenditures supporting commerce and housing credit was eighty times as large.

The inclusion of estimates of tax expenditures in the budget encourages the administration and Congress to consider these subsi-

Table C-3. Federal Current Services Outlays and Tax Expenditures, by Function, Fiscal Year 1984[a]

Billions of dollars unless otherwise indicated

		Tax expenditures	
Budget function	Current services outlays	Amount[b]	Percent of outlays
National defense	253.7	3.0	1.2
International affairs	12.8	4.8	37.5
General science, space, and technology	8.1	0.2	2.5
Energy	4.1	6.7	163.4
Natural resources and the environment	11.2	3.4	30.4
Agriculture	15.3	2.5	16.3
Commerce and housing credit	2.1	149.5	7,119.0
Transportation	26.1	0.1	0.4
Community and regional development	7.2	0.5	6.9
Education, training, employment, and social services	27.1	26.0	95.9
Health	92.9	33.9	36.5
Income security	289.7	121.7	42.0
Veterans' benefits and services	26.1	2.3	8.8
Administration of justice	5.5	. . .	. . .
Net interest	105.2	0.5	0.5
General government	5.9	0.3	5.1
General purpose fiscal assistance to state and local government	7.2	33.0	458.3
Subtotal	900.2	388.4	43.1
Allowance for civilian agency pay raises	1.9	. . .	. . .
Undistributed offsetting receipts	−21.6	. . .	. . .
Total	880.3	388.4	44.1

Sources: *Special Analyses, Fiscal 1984*, pp. A-7, G-26–28; and *Tax Expenditures*, pp. 20, 51–60. Figures are rounded.

a. Current services outlays and receipts are the amounts the government would spend and collect if all programs were continued at the 1983 level with no policy changes, except for defense outlays, which are included at the level planned by the Reagan administration.

b. Amount obtained by addition of individual items in each category.

dies in budget decisions. The total of tax expenditures is 43 percent as large as that of budget outlays before allowances for civilian agency pay changes and offsetting receipts (table C-3). For some budget functions, tax expenditures exceed direct outlays (for example, aid for commerce and housing and aid to state and local governments). The distributional effects of tax expenditures are often quite different from those of direct expenditures; for example, the deductibility of mortgage interest is of little benefit to the poor, whereas rent subsidies help them.

There is a continual tug-of-war between those who advocate greater use of tax expenditures and budget and tax experts who resist the proliferation of special tax provisions because they complicate the tax laws and are frequently less efficient than direct expenditures. Congressional appropriations committees prefer direct outlays, and the tax committees prefer tax expenditures. The budget committees, recognizing both the similarities of and the differences between the two approaches, are trying to focus the attention of Congress on the merits of individual proposals rather than letting the choice of the legislative committee determine how the subsidy is to be delivered. Budget decisions can truly be effective only when it is recognized that tax expenditures are similar to direct expenditures.

There is some evidence that this similarity is now being acknowledged. The House Committee on Rules held hearings in 1981 on a provision that would include tax expenditures among the aggregates specified as targets or limitations in budget resolutions. These hearings were one of several ways in which Congress attempted to involve spending committees in the evaluation and control of tax expenditures.

Tax expenditures were significantly reduced by the Tax Equity and Fiscal Responsibility Act of 1982. The act reduced the revenue losses from tax expenditures by $11 billion in 1983 by modifying fifteen provisions (two were liberalized). The principal revenue gains came from requiring firms to deduct half the investment tax credit before calculating depreciation for tax purposes, tightening safe harbor and other leasing provisions, and restricting the medical expense deduction.

Because of the urgent need for revenue, the government can be expected to give close attention to the possibility of curbing wasteful and inefficient tax expenditures. In the 1984 budget the Reagan administration has introduced two proposals that would reduce existing tax expenditures: one would place a cap on the exclusion for employer-provided health insurance premiums, and the other would restrict the exclusion of social security benefits. Four proposals would establish new tax expenditures or increase existing ones: tuition tax credits, tax preferences for firms locating in enterprise zones, jobs tax credit for the long-term unemployed, and savings accounts for higher education. The net effect of these proposals is to reduce the outlay equivalent of tax expenditures by $3.6 billion in 1984.